The Axioms of Religion

MERCER
UNIVERSITY PRESS

Endowed by
TOM WATSON BROWN
and
THE WATSON-BROWN FOUNDATION, INC.

The Axioms of Religion

A New Interpretation of the Baptist Faith

E. Y. Mullins

Edited with an introduction and notes by

C. Douglas Weaver

Mercer University Press

Macon, Georgia

MUP/P392

E. Y. Mullins's *The Axioms of Religion* was first published in 1908.

Books published by Mercer University Press are printed on acid free paper
that meets the requirements of American National Standard for
Information Sciences—Permanence of Paper for Printed Library
Materials.

Mercer University Press is a member of Green Press initiative
(greenpressinitiative.org), a nonprofit organization working to help
publishers and printers increase their use of recycled paper and decrease
their use of fiber derived from endangered forests. This book is printed on
recycled paper.

Cataloging-in-Publication Data is available at the Library of Congress.

Contents

Preface to This Edition

Most observers consider E. Y. Mullins to be the most influential Southern Baptist theologian and denominational leader of the twentieth century. Mullins was president of Southern Baptist Theological Seminary from 1899 to 1928. He served as president of the Southern Baptist Convention (1921–1924) and also served the worldwide Baptist community as president of the Baptist World Alliance (1923–1928). His book *The Christian Religion in its Doctrinal Expression* (1917) was an influential textbook of theology in Southern Baptist life. However, his *The Axioms of Religion* (1908) was his most creative and most enduring work. At the time it was written, the book was hailed as virtual Baptist orthodoxy, not simply by Southern Baptists but among American and international Baptists as well.

Some contemporary scholars have continued to praise Mullins, and find his "axioms" adaptable and thus useful to twenty-first century Baptist life. Some believe that Mullins's ideas, despite some theological deficiencies and expressions of time-conditioned Baptist triumphalism, can still make distinctive contributions. Other scholars in recent years have severely criticized what is called the excessive individualistic Baptist path of Mullins and his legacy.

This volume is being published to acknowledge the historical impact of E. Y. Mullins upon Baptist life. *The Axioms of Religion* is a Baptist, and even an American, "classic." Whether Mullins's thought is commended, modified or abandoned, understanding his voice is a key to grasping the distinctive contours of Baptist identity. I will argue in my critical introduction that Mullins, when read in light of his historical and cultural context, can and should be read. Some of his views are easily criticized as time-conditioned, but others have been distorted and misrepresented. Reading Mullins himself, rather than just his supporters and critics, will contribute to the contemporary dialogue about the relationship between individual faith and the community of faith.

It is a good time to assess fully Mullins and *The Axioms of Religion* as a part of the larger focus on identity that is occurring in Baptist circles. The book reached the magical number of one hundred years old in 2008. And Baptists worldwide celebrate their four hundredth birthday in 2009.

I have included an introduction that hopefully will provide readers context in order to maximize their understanding of the text of *The Axioms of Religion*. In my introduction I have given a biographical overview of Mullins, a survey of the extensive literature (pro and con) about Mullins's theology and impact upon Baptist life, as well as an overview of his theology, particularly his ecclesiology and his understanding of soul competency—what Mullins considered *the* distinctive in Baptist identity. I argue that Mullins's *The Axioms of Religion* was his attempt to maintain the Baptist focus upon embodying the New Testament Church, without resorting to the faulty historical claims that Landmarkism had helped popularize in Baptist life. To read Mullins is to read an apologist.

The text of *The Axioms of Religion* has been reproduced verbatim from Mullins's 1908 version. In his work, Mullins did not provide full bibliographical data when he included a footnote. I have added this information. Because he was writing for a popular audience, Mullins also did not footnote many of the references he used in the text. To the extent possible, I have included full bibliographical data for these multiple occurrences. I have also annotated the text with explanatory comments in footnotes when extra information seemed advantageous to the reading of a one-hundred-year-old text. It is my goal that these additions will enhance significantly the reading and the understanding of Mullins's work.

I am grateful to Marc Jolley and Mercer University Press for recognizing the value of publishing a new critical edition of the full text, with annotations, of *The Axioms of Religion*. Several people provided important assistance in this project. Brock Ratcliff did a summer mentorship with me (2007) while a student at G. W. Truett Theological Seminary. His research assistance was invaluable. Paul Hood-Patterson, administrative associate in the Department of Religion at Baylor University, helped with numerous tasks. Brandon Frick, graduate student at Baylor University, did the book's index. I am grateful to Bill Bellinger, Chair of the Department of Religion at Baylor University, for his encouragement and support of my research efforts. I am grateful to theologian Fisher Humphreys of Beeson Divinity School and to Bill Pitts, church historian at Baylor University, for reading my critical introduction and providing helpful comments. Thanks are also due to the Baptist History and Heritage Society for highlighting Mullins in the winter 2008 issue of their journal, *Baptist History and Heritage*. Some of the material in my introduction (see footnote 32) has been adapted from an article that I wrote for that issue, "The Baptist Ecclesiology of E. Y. Mullins: Individualism and the New Testament Church."

As always, I am grateful to my family—Pat, Aaron, Andrea, and Camden—for their support and love. To my mother, Elsie Mae Weaver, who was raised in an era in which E. Y. Mullins was read and reread, I dedicate this volume.

C. Douglas Weaver
Associate Professor of Religion
Director of Undergraduate Studies
Department of Religion
Baylor University
2008

Preface

The motives which led to the preparation of this volume are set forth in the first chapter. For a number of years the author has felt that a fresh statement of the Baptist position was possible which would enable the world to understand us better. A series of addresses, including one before the American Baptist Publication Society in St. Louis, Mo., in 1905, another the same year at The Baptist World Congress in London, England, two addresses in Richmond, Va., in 1906, before Richmond College and The Baptist General Association, and another at the Baptist Convention of North America, at Jamestown, in 1907, set forth in one form or another the principles which are elaborated in the following pages. Upon the occasion of each of the above addresses the writer was urged by many to expand the views expressed into a book. This he has here attempted to do, and submits the result to the judgment of his brethren.

The aim has been constructive and irenic in the highest sense. Of course the author has frankly taken issue with those of other faiths in the exposition of his own views where occasion required. But the chief object in view has been to expound New Testament Christianity in some of the more fundamental and important aspects. God has given to the Baptists of the world a great and sublime task in the promulgation of principles on the preservation of which the spiritual and political hopes of the world depend. In America the Baptists have had a marvelous growth in influence, in numbers, in wealth, and all other forms of power. We are, in spite of our vast territory, our great numbers, and our emphasis upon individualism, a remarkably homogeneous people. The author hopes that in the pages which follow will be found some contribution toward the higher thinking, the deepening spirituality, and the increasing unity and practical efficiency of our people.

It should be remarked that the sixteenth chapter is almost an exact reproduction of the address at Jamestown in May, 1907, on the "Contribution of Baptists to American Civilization." Chapters three and four are, in part, the address delivered for the Baptist Historical Society of Virginia in November, 1906, at Richmond College. There are some slight differences of style as between these chapters and the remainder of the book which are to be accounted for by the fact that they were first given as addresses.

Louisville, Kentucky
E. Y. M.

Introduction

Biographical Overview of E. Y. Mullins

Edgar Young Mullins was born in Franklin County, Mississippi, on January 5, 1860. The Mullins family—E. Y. was one of nine siblings—moved to rural Corsicana, Texas, when he was eight years old. After completing high school, Mullins was a member of the first class of what is now Texas A&M University (1876–1879). He then worked as a telegraph operator in order to save money for law school.

Mullins's vocational direction changed after his conversion to the Christian faith. Although he was raised in church—both his father and grandfather were Baptist ministers—Mullins had never become a Christian. However, on November 7, 1880, his father baptized him. Mullins had attended a revival meeting which was sponsored by First Baptist Church in Dallas, and had experienced a profound conversion. The experience led Mullins to accept a call to vocational ministry and enroll in Southern Baptists' only seminary, Southern Baptist Theological Seminary in Louisville, Kentucky, in 1881.[1] Mullins graduated from seminary in 1885. Having excelled as a student, Mullins was chosen to be a graduation speaker. His topic, "Manliness in the Ministry," reflected the era's emphasis on the "strengths" found in masculinity. Mullins wanted to be a missionary to Brazil, but funds were not available through the Foreign Mission Board of the Southern Baptist Convention. Consequently, upon graduation he became pastor of Harrodsburg Baptist Church in Kentucky. A year later—June 2, 1886, to be precise— Mullins married Isla May Hawley. Subsequently, the couple had two sons but both died at an early age. In the spring of 1888,

---

[1] William E. Ellis, *A Man of Books and a Man of the People* (Macon GA: Mercer University Press, 1985) 7; Timothy D. F. Maddox, "E. Y. Mullins: Mr. Baptist for the 20th and 21st Century," *Review and Expositor* 96/1 (Winter 1999): 88. The oldest biographical treatment of Mullins is by his wife, Isla May Mullins, *Edgar Young Mullins: An Intimate Biography* (Nashville: Sunday School Board of the SBC, 1929).

Mullins declined an opportunity to move to San Antonio in his home state of Texas when his wife's health would not permit relocation.[2]

In July 1888, Mullins did accept the pastorate of Lee Street Baptist Church in Baltimore, Maryland. During his seven-year tenure, Mullins, a typical "southern evangelical," made evangelism the priority of his ministry. Mullins also attempted to embody a "man of books and a man of the people" philosophy of ministry. He took a course in logic at Johns Hopkins University and served as one of the editors of the *Maryland Baptist*, contributing a weekly piece named "The Signal Station." His first book, a series of sermons entitled *Christ's Coming and His Kingdom*, was also published (1894). At the time, Southern Baptists and other Protestants considered Baltimore the hub of an increasingly dangerous presence of American Catholicism. Not surprisingly, Mullins called Roman Catholicism an "apostate church." However, he refrained from calling the Pope the "antichrist" as many Protestant conservatives were wont to do.[3]

Mullins left the pastorate to become an associate secretary at the Foreign Mission Board of the Southern Baptist Convention in 1895, but he stayed only six months (September 1895–March 1896). Evidently his popularity as a lecturer across the South created tension with R. H. Willingham, director of the mission agency. Consequently, Mullins returned to the pastorate at Newton Centre Baptist Church in Newton, Massachusetts. In contrast to his previous congregations, the church had a more educated membership. Numerous faculty members of Newton Theological Institution were members, including the school's president, Alvah Hovey. Observers have speculated about the influence of scholars from the larger Harvard community upon Mullins's later writings.[4] While in Massachusetts, Mullins continued to develop a rapport with Northern Baptists. The call of Southern ministers to Northern Baptist churches was not a rarity in the late nineteenth century.

---

[2] Scott Bryant, "The Unifying Leadership of Edgar Young Mullins, 1899–1928" (Th.M. thesis, Boston University, 2002) 6–8. For studies of "muscular Christianity," see Donald Hall, ed., *Muscular Christianity: Embodying the Victorian Age* (Cambridge: Cambridge University Press, 2006).

[3] Maddox, "Mr. Baptist," 90; Bryant, "Unifying Leadership," 9; Ellis, *Man of Books*, 25–29.

[4] William D. M. Carrell, "Edgar Young Mullins and the Competency of the Soul in Religion" (Ph.D. diss., Baylor University, 1993) 70–76.

With the tightening of denominational identities in the early decades of the twentieth century, Mullins's extensive work across regions would soon be a relic of the past.[5]

Mullins became the fourth president of his alma mater, the Southern Baptist Theological Seminary, in 1899. The seminary was engulfed in a life-threatening conflict now called the Whitsitt Controversy. President William H. Whitsitt had created a firestorm with his work as a church historian. From his reading of primary-source historical records, Whitsitt concluded that Baptist origins dated to 1641 and the recovery of believer's baptism by *immersion* in England. The popular belief in church successionism—associated with an influential nineteenth-century Baptist movement called Landmarkism but with precedents throughout Baptist history—was that Baptists could trace their lineage directly back to the New Testament. In other words, Baptists were the New Testament Church, instituted when John the Baptist baptized Jesus in the Jordan River. When Southern Baptists threatened to withhold financial support and thus endanger the life of the seminary, Whitsitt resigned.[6]

During the Whitsitt Controversy, Mullins wrote articles for the *Religious Herald* of Virginia that voiced support for Whitsitt and criticized the Landmarkers for their "pitiless," "unreasonable and reckless" "attack."[7] Nevertheless, when Mullins was mentioned as a candidate for the seminary presidency he was not well known among school trustees and was considered an outsider to the Whitsitt Controversy. Mullins was nominated for the presidency by W. E. Hatcher of Grace Street Baptist Church in Richmond, Virginia, an acquaintance from his days at the Richmond-based Foreign

---

[5] Ellis, *Man of Books*, 67, 72. Ellis noted that the increasing influence of the SBC Sunday School Board restricted cooperation with the North.

[6] See William H. Whitsitt, *A Question in Baptist History: Whether the Anabaptists in England Practiced Immersion before the Year 1641?* (Louisville: Chas. T. Dearing, 1896); Rosalie Beck, "The Whitsitt Controversy: A Denomination in Crisis" (Ph.D. diss., Baylor University, 1984).

[7] E. Y. Mullins, "Notes and Comments from Newton Centre," *Religious Herald* 16/39 (October 8, 1896): 1. See also E. Y. Mullins, "The News from New England—Tremont Temple and Newton Centre," *Religious Herald* 16/21 (May 21, 1896): 1; E. Y. Mullins, "Our New England Budget," *Religious Herald* 16/25 (June 18, 1896): 1; E. Y. Mullins, "A Roman Catholic Party among the Baptists," *Religious Herald* 16/29 (July 16, 1896): 1.

Mission Board. Mullins was surprised when he heard that he had been nominated, but he accepted and began a twenty-eight-year tenure (1899–1928). In addition to his presidential duties, Mullins was professor of theology.[8]

The Louisville seminary accomplished several firsts during Mullins's initial decade. In 1902 the seminary opened classes to women, although they were not registered as students. In 1907, with the strong support of Professor W. O. Carver, the Woman's Missionary Union Training School was opened. Mullins also established Founders Day and ventured to invite former president Whitsitt to return to speak at the anniversary of the seminary's origins.[9] A year earlier, a new chair in Sunday school pedagogy was initiated which was financially underwritten by both the seminary and the Sunday School Board of the Southern Baptist Convention.[10]

Mullins provided a forum for seminary scholarship with the creation of the journal the *Review and Expositor* (1904). In his position as editor in chief, he wanted the journal to help unify Baptists by providing a safe setting for scholarly Baptist voices whether they came from the North, the South, or outside the United States. According to a seminary history, ecumenical cooperation was implied when Mullins declared, "It will neither be possible nor desired to maintain a rigid doctrinal uniformity...for considerable diversity of opinion will appear."[11] For his first decade, the seminary faculty contributed to the interdenominational International Sunday School Association before the Sunday School Board of Southern Baptists began to assert a more restrictive influence.[12]

During his tenure as president, the seminary claimed numerous accomplishments. The student population increased from 256 to 501; the faculty grew from six to twelve members. Mullins conducted a building

---

[8] Bryant, "Unifying Leadership," 31–34.

[9] H. Clark Maddux, "Edgar Young Mullins and Evangelical Developments in the SBC," *Baptist History and Heritage* 33/2 (Spring 1998): 69; William A. Mueller, *A History of Southern Baptist Theological Seminary* (Nashville: Broadman Press, 1959) 189.

[10] Mueller, *Southern Baptist Theological Seminary*, 183–84, 187.

[11] Ibid., 186.

[12] Ellis, *Man of Books*, 72.

campaign to fund the campus's move from downtown to its present location, called The Beeches.[13]

As the dominant scholarly voice among Southern Baptists in the first half of the twentieth century, Mullins wrote prolifically in popular and scholarly journals. He was at heart an apologist for the Christian faith.[14] He penned seven books while president: *Why is Christianity True* (1905), *The Axioms of Religion* (1908), *Baptist Beliefs* (1912), *Freedom and Authority in Religion* (1913), *Commentary on Ephesians and Colossians* (1913), *The Christian Religion in its Doctrinal Expression* (1917), and *Christianity at the Crossroads* (1924). Besides *The Axioms of Religion*, the book that received the widest attention was *The Christian Religion in Its Doctrinal Expression*. The Southern Baptist Theological Seminary used the book as its standard textbook in theology until 1947.[15]

Mullins was active at all levels of denominational life. He was involved in the Baptist World Alliance from its inception in 1905 and served as its president from 1923 to 1928. He served as president of the Southern Baptist Convention from 1921 to 1924. Mullins was also active at the state and associational levels in Kentucky. He preached, lectured, and even served on ordination councils. Faculty colleagues like Harold Tribble considered him to be a great preacher. For much of his seminary career Mullins was a member of Broadway Baptist Church in Louisville (1919–1928).[16]

In the 1920s, Mullins was involved in the Southern Baptist version of the fundamentalist/modernist conflict that wreaked havoc in Northern denominations. The Southern conflict bore similarities to the Northern story: the dominant issue was evolution and teachers at denominational schools were accused of heresy. Mullins contributed to the fundamentalist manifesto, *The Fundamentals* (1910–1915), but his participation revealed the somewhat

---

[13]Gaines S. Dobbins, "Edgar Young Mullins," in Clifton J. Allen, ed., *Encyclopedia of Southern Baptists*, 4 vols. (Nashville: Broadman Press, 1958) 2:930.

[14] Ibid., 300; E. Glenn Hinson, "E. Y. Mullins as Interpreter of the Baptist Tradition," *Review and Expositor* 96/1 (Winter 1999): 115.

[15] Timothy George, "Systematic Theology at Southern Seminary," *Review and Expositor* 82/1(1985): 36.

[16] Bill Clark Thomas, "Edgar Young Mullins, A Baptist Exponent of Theological Restatement" (Ph.D. diss., Southern Baptist Theological Seminary, 1963) 60, 80.

moderate phase of the developing fundamentalist movement.[17] His article on "The Testimony of Christian Experience" touted personal experience as the cornerstone of a proper theological method.[18]

However, Mullins was no fundamentalist. In the clash with Southern Baptist fundamentalists who insisted that the Southern Baptist Convention adhere to a creed with an explicit anti-evolution statement, Mullins steered a more moderate or "progressive conservative" path.[19] He called fundamentalists "Radicals and Extremists" "who want to put the thumb screws on everybody who does not agree in every detail with their statements of doctrine." These "hyper-orthodox" leaders were "lacking in common sense," desired to control the Southern Baptist Convention and in so doing "harass and muzzle teachers in our schools."[20]

Mullins believed that science and religion were separate fields of study; they were not enemies but "co-workers on the temple of life."[21] The Bible was a book of religion, not a scientific text.[22] Mullins attempted to mollify the discontent of anti-evolutionists. He told the 1922 annual meeting of the Southern Baptist Convention that denominational schools should teach the

---

[17] George M. Marsden, *Fundamentalism and American Culture: The Shaping of Twentieth Century Evangelicalism, 1870–1925* (New York: Oxford University Press, 1980) 122.

[18] E. Y. Mullins, "The Testimony of Christian Experience," in A.C. Dixon, Louis Meyers, and R. A. Torrey, eds., *The Fundamentals: A Testimony to the Truth*, 12 vols. (Chicago: Testimony Publishing Company, 1919–1915) 3:76–85.

[19] The overarching theme of William Ellis's *A Man of Books and a Man of the People* was that Mullins embodied a moderate Southern Baptist leadership identity. Others called Mullins a "progressive conservative." See Thomas, "Baptist Exponent," 404.

[20] Russell H. Dilday, Jr., "E. Y. Mullins: The Bible's Authority Is a Living, Transforming Reality," in *The Unfettered Word: Southern Baptists Confront the Authority-Inerrancy Question*, ed. Robison B. James (Waco TX: Word Books, 1987) 114.

[21] E. Y. Mullins, *Christianity at the Crossroads* (Nashville: Sunday School Board of the SBC, 1924) 230.

[22] E. Y. Mullins, *Christian Religion in its Doctrinal Expression* (Philadelphia: Roger Williams Press, 1917) 153; E. Y. Mullins, *Baptist Beliefs* (Philadelphia: American Baptist Historical Society, 1912) 13; E. Y. Mullins, "Christianity in the Modern World (Opening Address Session 1925–1926, Southern Baptist Theological Seminary)" *Review and Expositor* 22 (October 1925): 488.

historic beliefs of the Christian faith. Evolution should not be taught as fact; at the same time he argued for "firm faith and free research" in the realm of science. The real issue was the affirmation of supernaturalism in the face of naturalistic claims.

In an attempt to keep the convention united, Mullins and other denominational loyalists led in the adoption of a new confession of faith, the *Baptist Faith and Message* (1925). The confession, largely written by Mullins, was based on the New Hampshire Confession of Faith.[23] It included a preface that emphasized that confessions were not creeds, but voluntary formulations of faith. The confession affirmed the sole authority of the Bible for "all religious opinions" but avoided mentioning evolution specifically because the "confession committee," none of whom affirmed evolution, did not believe a theological confession needed a statement on science. The committee did not want to inject the precedent of using science as the arbiter of ultimate truth.[24] Mullins also resisted the call to impose a specific scientific stance upon teachers in Baptist schools: "Loyalty to the vital facts and truths of the Gospel? Yes. But not loyalty in realms which lie outside of the revealed truth as it is in Jesus."[25]

At least in the early years of his career, Mullins seemed to toy with the idea of Christian theistic evolution.[26] Species evolved or developed but were directly created by God. By 1925 Mullins had ceased using the word evolution, having decided that it had become synonymous with a naturalistic account of creation. At the famous Scopes trial in Dayton, Tennessee, where evolution and a literal reading of the biblical account of creation clashed, Mullins was sought by both sides as a supporter. To the modernist Northern Baptist, Shailer Mathews, Mullins denied that he was an evolutionist of any kind. At the same time, Mullins refused the efforts of William Jennings Bryan

[23] Topics for articles in the 1925 *Baptist Faith and Message* that don't have antecedents in the New Hampshire Confession seem to be derived from Mullins's *Baptist Beliefs* (1912).

[24] Phyllis Rodgerson Pleasants, *Myth: Baptists Are Scientific Creationists*, Baptist Myths Pamphlet Series (Hewitt TX: Whitsitt Baptist Heritage Society, 2003).

[25] Mullins, "Christianity in the Modern World," 488.

[26] E. Y. Mullins, *Why Is Christianity True?* (Philadelphia: American Baptist Publication Society, 1905) 65; Russell Dilday, Jr., "The Apologetic Method of E. Y. Mullins," (Th.D. diss., Southwestern Baptist Theological Seminary, 1960) 100–101; Albert Mohler, Jr., "Baptist Theology at the Crossroads: The Legacy of E. Y. Mullins," *The Southern Baptist Journal of Theology* 6/4 (Winter 1999): 10.

to legislate against evolution. According to Mullins, "Baptists are playing with fire, and turning over the ark of God to the Philistines when they call in legislatures to enforce their interpretation of creation as taught in Scripture."[27]

Mullins did not refrain from a public stance during the 1928 national presidential election that involved the candidacy of Al Smith, a Roman Catholic and "soft" on Prohibition in the minds of Southern Baptists. In 1919, Mullins had written that ministerial leadership in the civic arena should be seen in the gift of mediation rather than partisanship. Ministers should not champion from the pulpit a "radical" or a "conservative" program, but should help people to "understand each other."[28] Mullins's change of heart revealed the pervasiveness of the Baptist disdain toward Smith. Mullins argued that preachers, while avoiding "mere Partyism," should be involved in politics when a significant moral issue was being attacked by a political party. Prohibition, Mullins declared, was such an issue. In late 1927, Mullins told the national convention of the Anti-Saloon League that the "solid (Democratic) South" would break if Smith were nominated. In an anti-saloon tract, Mullins sarcastically noted that the Democrats had nominated a "bone-dry running mate from Arkansas for the sopping wet head of the ticket from the sidewalks of NY." Unlike Baptist fundamentalists, Mullins focused only on Smith's views of Prohibition in his criticisms and he insisted that his opposition had nothing to do with religion.[29]

In 1928, Mullins became ill and died. One popular Southern Baptist pulpiteer eulogized that Mullins was "one among a 1000;" he demonstrated that the "old faith could live with the new knowledge" of the modern era.[30] Some scholars believe that Mullins became more conservative in his last years. Others added that the conflicting requirements of being a diplomatic seminary

---

[27] Phyllis Rodgerson Pleasants, "E. Y. Mullins: Diplomatic Theological Leader," *Review and Expositor* 96/1 (Winter 1999): 47; Thomas, "Baptist Exponent," 314–15; Ellis, *Man of Books*, 195.

[28] E. Y. Mullins, "Training the Ministry for Civic Leadership," *Religious Education* 9/6 (December 1919): 559.

[29] E. Y. Mullins, "Preacher and Politics," *Western Recorder* 102/34 (August 23, 1928): 7; Ellis, *Man of Books*, 212; E. Y. Mullins, "President Mullins on the Sad Plight of the Democrats," Western Recorder, 102/28 (July 12, 1928): 8.

[30] Henry Alford Porter, "An Interpretation, One among a Thousand," *Review and Expositor* 22/3 (July 1925): 20.

president responsible for fund raising eventually made Mullins generally more cautious.[31]

E. Y. Mullins: A Theologian of Religious Experience

Scholars[32] call Mullins a "theologian of religious experience."[33] He considered religious experience to be the starting point for theological reflection. Experience was the "the holy of holies of theology."[34] Mullins unequivocally touted the authority of the scriptures and opposed modernist attempts to redefine elements of traditional historic orthodoxy such as the deity of Christ. Mullins also argued that the truths of scripture were verified, not by an ecclesiastical authority or by church tradition, but by "discovery" through the "experience of His Grace working in us."[35]

From this experiential base, Mullins created and popularized the term "soul competency"—the term most associated with his legacy. Mullins defined soul competency as the right of each individual (soul) to relate directly to God. Baptists, of course, had highlighted the idea of "soul liberty" and the sacredness of the individual conscience since their origins in the seventeenth century.[36] Mullins continued and intensified the tradition. He highlighted

---

[31] Ellis, *Man of Books*, 148, 201–204. Pleasants, "Diplomatic Theological Leader," 56.

[32] Much of this section is an adaptation (with some subtraction, some addition, some revision) of my earlier article C. Douglas Weaver, "The Baptist Ecclesiology of E. Y. Mullins: Individualism and the New Testament Church," *Baptist History and Heritage* 43/1 (Winter 2008): 18–34. Used by permission of the Baptist History and Heritage Society, 3001 Mercer University Drive, Atlanta, Georgia 30341.

[33] Leroy Moore, "Crazy Quilt: Southern Baptist Patterns of the Church," *Foundations* 20 (1977): 20.

[34] E. Y. Mullins, "The Theological Trend: Address Delivered by President Mullins, July 14, 1905," *Review and Expositor* 2/4 (October 1905): 254. For example, Mullins said, "You can test the reality and power of Christ practically...The man born blind did not have to accept any theory of Christ...His faith worked." See Mullins, "Testimony of Christian Experience," 85.

[35] E. Y. Mullins, "Why I Am a Baptist (1926)" *The Whitsitt Journal* 15/1 (Spring 2007): 3.

[36] Baptists like Thomas Helwys said that each person must be free to follow (or not) God according to the dictates of conscience because each individual will stand before the judgment seat of God. References to Helwys and others who followed suit

soul competency as the "peculiar teaching" and the "historical significance" of Baptists and the foundation of the "axioms of religion," a set of six principles that he considered to be the essence of New Testament Christianity. Other Christian traditions that denied the voluntary nature of faith through the practice of infant baptism practiced "incompetent" religion. Furthermore, soul competency, according to Mullins, was not simply individualism, because humanity "is more than an individual. He is a social being. He has relations to his fellows in the Church, and in the industrial order, and in the State." Mullins actually used "individualism" freely in *The Axioms of Religion* and other writings—often as an interchangeable synonym of soul competency—but he made a concerted effort to insist that soul competency was not excessively individualistic.[37]

Much has been written about how much Mullins was indebted to Friedrich Schleiermacher, the father of modern liberal theology, who articulated an experiential-based methodology.[38] Some scholars readily acknowledge that Mullins drank deeply from the well of Schleiermacher's methodology; others note that Mullins was always quick to criticize the German theologian.[39] Mullins indisputably cited numerous nineteenth-century theologians frequently, especially Schleiermacher and pragmatist William James. Mullins insisted that his focus on the individual, however, was New Testament Christianity rather than the pantheistic subjectivism of

---

can be found in C. Douglas Weaver, *In Search of the New Testament Church: The Baptist Story* (Macon GA: Mercer University Press, 2008).

[37] See chapters 2 and 3 in *The Axioms of Religion*.

[38] Three dissertations have dealt with Mullins's theology. See Carrell, "Competency of the Soul;" Dilday, "Apologetic Method;" and Thomas, "Baptist Exponent." Carrell suggests that Mullins drew upon the writings of several American Baptists to coin the term soul competency. For a concise overview of Mullins's thought, see Fisher Humphreys, "E. Y. Mullins," in *Baptist Theologians*, ed. Timothy George and David Dockery (Nashville: Broadman, 1990).

[39] William Mueller says that Mullins was perhaps unduly influenced by Schleiermacher and William James. See Mueller, *Southern Baptist Theological Seminary*, 192. Russell Dilday said that Mullins was very cautious in his reading of Schleiermacher. See Dilday, "Apologetic Method," 44ff. Fisher Humphreys says Mullins's focus on experience was due more to the context of revivalism than Schleiermacher or William James. See Humphreys, "E. Y. Mullins," 34.

modern liberalism.[40] His focus was not a Schleiermacher-type experience of absolute dependence, without content or context.

According to Mullins, the "corrective" to excessive individualism was loyalty to the Bible and the lordship of Christ. The Bible's inspiration could be affirmed confidently via the inductive method which "goes directly to the Bible itself for the evidence of its own inspiration…It gathers the data from the Bible and on them builds up its view of the authority of the Bible."[41] The Bible was the record of God's "progressive revelation" and more of its truth was still to be discovered by faithful "competent" believers.[42]

Loyalty to the objective revelation in the scriptures avoided an anchorless subjectivism and was tied to the ultimate authority of the lordship of Christ.[43] A personal experience and morally transforming relationship with Jesus Christ—the heart of Christianity and the conversionist base of Baptist life—was guided by the Holy Spirit and was anchored to the objective revelation of "facts" about Jesus Christ recorded in the Bible.[44] Loyalty to Christ, who was the "seat of authority in religion and above and underneath and before the Bible"[45] and therefore the key to the scriptures, was the "center of liberty."[46]

Could soul competency be abused? Of course, but the freedom inherent in biblically based regenerate individualism—a voluntary personal relationship with Jesus Christ—was worth the risk. In vivid terms, Mullins said when a person was denied the right to think for him or herself, the

---

[40] E. Y. Mullins, *Freedom and Authority in Religion* (Philadelphia: Griffith and Rowland, 1913) 41–53.

[41] Ibid., 280.

[42] E. Y. Mullins, "Inaugurated President: Inaugural Address," *The Baptist Argus* 3/41 (October 12, 1899): 2. Dale Moody said that Mullins introduced the idea of progressive revelation to Southern Baptists. See Dale Moody, "Progressive Revelation," in *Encyclopedia of Southern Baptists*, 4 vols. (Nashville: Broadman Press, 1958) 2:1115.

[43] Mullins, *Christian Religion*, 77–78; Mullins, *Freedom and Authority*, 18–41.

[44] Mullins, "Why I Am a Baptist," 4–5; Mullins, *Freedom and Authority*, 31–32; Mullins, *Christianity at the Crossroads*, 259; Mullins, *Christian Religion*, 77–78.

[45] Mullins, *Freedom and Authority*, 393–94. For a good overview of Mullins's view of Scripture, see James Leo Garrett, "The Teachings of Recent Southern Baptist Theologians on the Bible," in *The Proceedings of the Conference on Biblical Inerrancy, 1987* (Nashville: Broadman Press, 1987) 289–95.

[46] E. Y. Mullins, "Baptist Life in the World's Life," *Review and Expositor* 25/3 (July 1928): 300–14; Mullins, *Christian Religion*, 154.

person would "remain intellectually and spiritually a moron under a system of compulsion and repression."[47] Mullins also acknowledged the risky but necessary freedom found in the corollary of soul competency: the right to the private interpretation of scripture that was central to the Protestant tradition.

> The right of private judgment is a dangerous word, but it is a winged and emancipating word. It is the sole guaranty that man will pass out of the childhood to the manhood stage of religion...It was the hammer with which Roger Williams broke the chain which united church and state...The right of private judgment; yes, a dangerous word, but a word which started man on a new voyage of spiritual discovery...It is true it produced the sects of Protestantism. But these, after all, are not comets or wandering stars without central control, plunging blindly through space...Loyalty to Christ balances their right of private judgment and is the guaranty that the faith of the New Testament shall not perish from the earth.[48]

Mullins clearly protected the experience of the individual believer. The expectation was, however, that a believer's experience would find unity in the collective experience of the church in response to Christ and the Bible: "The individual consciousness is not final. It is the collective consciousness which brings the true deliverance as to experience."[49]

Soul Competency the Basis for an Authentic New Testament Church

In 1917, E. Y. Mullins wrote his systematic theology, *The Christian Religion in its Doctrinal Expression.* Immediately upon its publication, questions arose as to why Mullins had not included a separate chapter on ecclesiology. Mullins responded that ecclesiology was taught in another department of the seminary outside the area of theology. In recent years, Mullins has been strongly attacked for this omission and, more broadly, for

---

[47] Mullins, "Baptist Life," 311.

[48] Ibid., 312. Baptists had followed the Protestant emphasis on private reading of Scripture since their infancy. William B. Johnson, the first president of the SBC, called it a Baptist distinctive.

[49] Mullins, "Outline of Lectures, 55–56." Quoted in Russell Dilday, "Mullins the Theologian: Between the Extremes," *Review and Expositor* 96 /1 (Winter 1999): 85.

emphasizing soul competency and individualism so that a proper doctrine of the church was essentially impossible.[50]

Mullins would, of course, disagree with the critics of today. He believed that voluntary individual faith did not lead away from the church, but led toward the creation of an authentic New Testament church—the only ecclesiology worth pursuing. While Mullins willingly employed an independent-minded definition of the church as "a voluntary association of believers united together for the purpose of worship and edification," he emphasized that the church was a spiritual community grounded in a common individual experience of grace, a common faith, and a common loyalty to Jesus Christ. It was the "spiritual home of the saved."[51] There could be no community of faith without converted individuals. In *The Axioms of Religion*, Mullins responded to criticisms of Northern Baptist holiness advocate A. J. Gordon, who said that traditional Baptist definitions of the church were too human-centered. Mullins concurred and affirmed that the Church was created by the "initiative of the Holy Spirit": "Individual believers were inevitably drawn together by spiritual affinity in fellowship; their renewed spiritual natures then impelled them to associate themselves together as a church."[52] Since the church was a spiritual community, its tasks were spiritual: missions, evangelism, and holy living.[53]

The focus on the regenerated individual not only led to the creation of the church, it led to a specific type of church polity: democratic congregationalism and local church autonomy. The right of each individual to go directly to God

---

[50] A book review also explained that Mullins sought to "bring the book within a compass which would make it useable as a text book." See the editorial, "A New Book of Great Importance," *The Baptist World* 21/52 (December 27, 1917): 5. Seminary professor E. C. Dargan had already written a textbook for ecclesiology. See E. C. Dargan, *Ecclesiology: A Study of the Churches*, 2nd ed. (Louisville: Charles T. Dearing, 1905). There was also precedent among nineteenth-century theologians—e.g., William Newton Clarke and James Boyce—for not having a separate chapter on ecclesiology in their systematic theologies. See below for specific criticisms of Mullins.

[51] Mullins, *Christian Religion*, 346; Mullins, *Why Is Christianity True?* 156; E. Y. Mullins, *Soul Freedom Applied to Church Life and Organization* (Nashville: Baptist 75 Million Campaign, n.d., ca. 1920) 4–5.

[52] Mullins, *Axioms of Religion*, 35, 132–33.

[53] Mullins, *Christian Religion*, 165, 430; Mullins, *Why is Christianity True*, 166, 349.

meant that all believers were spiritually equal and must therefore have equal privileges, including equal voice in church government.[54] According to Mullins, the decisions of the local congregation on ecclesiastical matters were the "consensus of the competent."[55] In these little "spiritual democracies" there existed a "priesthood of all believers" where "rich and poor, bond and freed, patrician and plebeian, Greek, Roman, Jew, Barbarian sat together equal before God."[56] Or in the words of Mullin's ecclesiastical axiom: All believers have a right to equal privileges in the church.[57]

Mullins contrasted the New Testament model of spiritual democracy with any and all hierarchical structures. A New Testament church had no use for hierarchies—Catholic or Protestant—that might "lord it over the conscience of the individual" or come between a local congregation and God. Affirming the priesthood of believers, Mullins exhorted, "No human priest may claim to be mediator between the soul and God because no possible reason can be assigned for any competency on his part not common to all believers."[58]

Congregational democracy was not freedom without boundaries, however. Mullins pictured the church as a paradox between the "absolute monarchy" of Christ and the "autonomy of the soul."

> Because the individual deals directly with his Lord and is immediately responsible to him, the spiritual society must needs be a democracy. That is, the church is a community of autonomous individuals under the immediate lordship of Christ held together by a social bond of common interest, due to a common faith and inspired by common tasks and ends, all of which are assigned to him by the common Lord. The church, therefore, is the expression of the paradoxical conception of the union of absolute monarchy and pure democracy. This we might say is the formula of the church. Every

---

[54] Mullins, *Soul Freedom*, 5–6; Mullins, *Axioms of Religion*, 127.

[55] Mullins, *Axioms of Religion*, 56.

[56] Mullins, *Why is Christianity True*, 351.

[57] Mullins, *Axioms of Religion*, 127.

[58] Mullins, *Axioms of Religion*, 56, 60.

form of polity other than democracy somewhere infringes upon the lordship of Christ.[59]

Spiritual democracy rooted in soul competency, however, meant disdain for the imposition of creeds. Mullins said that a denomination was not a "free lance" club; freedom was social, involved relationships with others, and did not equal "exaggerated individualism." Some creeds, the early ecumenical creeds for example, had served to defend and propagate the faith. However, Mullins warned that creeds led to a barren intellectualism and a dead orthodoxy. Whenever a church or individual was coerced, creeds were "death masks for defunct religion" and were barriers to a genuine spirituality in which "all believers are priests because of the free access of all to God by faith."[60]

Mullins's fear of creeds was consistent with the strong objections he had to anything that added hierarchy between equal believers and God. Private judgment in religious matters has created more than one church, he admitted, but only when individuals voluntarily came together in obedience to Christ was the New Testament church a possibility.[61]

Spiritual democracy also meant support for the traditional Baptist distinctive of religious liberty and the separation of church and state. According to Mullins, the state, like ecclesiastical hierarchies, was "incompetent" to judge spiritual matters.[62] Mullins at times joined forces with other Americans of his day who touted uncritically the worldwide triumph of political democracy. Because of their heritage of individualism and local

---

[59] Ibid., 129. Baptists before Mullins had emphasized this paradox of absolute monarchy and pure democracy. See Walter Shurden, "The Priesthood of All Believers and Pastoral Authority in Baptist Thought," *Faith and Mission* 7/1 (Fall 1989): 36–37.

[60] Mullins, *Baptist Beliefs*, 9; Mullins, *Freedom and Authority*, 301–302.

[61] Mullins, *Baptist Beliefs*, 7–8. Southern Baptist Theological Seminary, where Mullins was president, used the confessional statement the *Abstract of Principles*. For more on Mullins and creeds see C. Douglas Weaver, "The Baptist Ecclesiology of E. Y. Mullins: Individualism and the New Testament Church," *Baptist History and Heritage* 43/1 (Winter 2008): 18–34.

[62] Mullins, *Why is Christianity True*, 166; E. Y. Mullins, "The Vision of the Preacher Against the Background of the World War," *Baptist World* 22/24 (June 13, 1918): 4.

church independence, Mullins declared, Baptists were uniquely able to show the world "the efficiency of democracy in church life."[63]

Mullins, to the dismay of many Southern Baptists, willingly affirmed the idea of the universal church that referred to Christians of every era and every place.[64] He easily recognized that no denomination had a monopoly on biblical truth.[65] However, Mullins, in *The Axioms of Religion* and other writings, joined other Southern Baptists to adamantly oppose "church union" in this era that birthed ecumenical organizations. Mullins believed that the doctrinal compromise necessary to have such a group undercut the goal of restoring the authentic New Testament church. A Baptist simply could not unite with churches that practiced infant baptism, and thus failed to practice voluntary faith and maintain a converted church membership.[66] Ultimately, Mullins declared, genuine ecumenism would be Baptist in form: spiritual unity in the broader Church would be based on the New Testament church's

---

[63] E. Y. Mullins, "Baptists in the Modern World," *Review and Expositor* 8/3 (July 1911): 348; E. Y. Mullins, "Wanted: A Baptist Denomination," *Baptist Standard* 31/1 (January 1919): 1. For an analysis of Mullins's identification of political and religious democracy, see Christopher Canipe, "A Captive Church in the Land of the Free: E. Y. Mullins, Walter Rauschenbusch, George Truett, and the Rise of Baptist Democracy, 1900–1925," (Ph.D. diss., Baylor University, 2004). Mullins did tell ministers to beware of blindly following the government. He said that Christians, while patriotic, should not follow the adage, "My country, right or wrong." "My country always, of course, in the sense that I am for her, but not for her in her wrong." See E. Y. Mullins, "Leadership in the Ministry (Concluded)" *Record of Christian Work* 48/3 (March 1929): 161.

[64] Mullins, *Baptist Beliefs*, 64.

[65] E. Y. Mullins, "Baptist Theology in the New World Order," *Review and Expositor* 17/4 (October 1920): 402. See also Jerry M. Stubblefield, "The Ecumenical Impact of E. Y. Mullins," *Journal of Ecumenical Studies* 17 (Spring 1980): 96. Mullins affirmed that "all who truly are joined to Christ are our brethren in the common salvation, whether they be in the Catholic communion, or in a Protestant communion, or in any other communion, or in no communion." See E. Y. Mullins, "A Message of the Baptist World Alliance to the Baptist Brotherhood, to Other Christian Brethren, and to the World," in William T. Whitley and John Howard Shakespeare, *Third Baptist World Congress, Record of Proceedings* (London: Kingsgate Press, 1923) 224.

[66] Stubblefield, "The Ecumenical Impact of E. Y. Mullins," 96.

principles of voluntary participation and preservation of "soul competent" individualism.[67]

Mullins did not deal with the ministry in *The Axioms of Religion* or his other major works. The focus in the *Axioms* was clearly on the spiritual egalitarianism of the congregation. Nevertheless, Mullins wrote frequently in journals about pastoral ministry. He believed that the call to ministry—the call to pastor and preach—was a "higher calling" than other professional fields like medicine or teaching.[68] In a New Testament church, Mullins said, pastors as spiritual leaders deserved loyalty and support from the congregation. He contended, however, that there was no place for hierarchy and special clerical authority because these diminished the equality of "soul competent" believers. Biblical faith revolved around the congregation, not church officers who claimed apostolic succession.[69] Pastors were servant leaders, not to be elevated above the laity: "[Pastors] are not masters, but servants; they are not rulers, but guides; they are not officials clothed with authority, but teachers. They are simply first among equals, selected to perform certain duties because of their special fitness, and not because they exercise any authority. They are spiritual leaders."[70] For Mullins, soul competency, individual religious experience of God, and a doctrine of the church were inseparable. One led to the other. As one scholar summarized, "The believer's experience with God is continuous with believers from New Testament times to the present. Thus, Baptists can rightfully claim to embody the same principles as did the New Testament Church."[71]

Interpreting Mullins and The Axioms of Religion:
A Historical Overview of Supporters and Critics

The origins of *The Axioms of Religion*, as told by Mullins's wife, Isla May Mullins, is the stuff of legends. After listing six axioms on paper, Mullins

---

[67] Mullins, "Baptists in the Modern World," 350; E. Y. Mullins, "Recent Tendencies among Southern Baptists, No. 7, The Individual, The Church and the Convention in Cooperative Christian Work," *The Baptist World* 18/5 (January 29, 1914): 7.

[68] E. Y. Mullins, "A Dynamic Ministry," *Record of Christian Work* 47/1 (January 1928): 35; Mullins, *Christian Religion*, 363.

[69] Mullins, *Baptist Beliefs*, 67; Mullins, "Leadership in the Ministry," 93.

[70] Mullins, "Baptist Theology," 404.

[71] Carrell, "Competency of the Soul," 60.

showed them to his wife, who remarked that they were wonderful and then asked, "Where did you get them?" Mullins replied, "They just came to me—like a flash—the whole thing!" Isla May then responded, "Well, you will hear from them. I don't need to be a prophet to tell you that." While he clearly affirmed and built upon well-known Baptist principles, Baptists from around the world quickly lauded Mullins for the publication of *The Axioms of Religion* in 1908. Northern Baptist editor Curtis Lee Laws reflected that after the book's publication, "Baptists had turned to him as perhaps the best qualified man among us to express doctrinal views briefly, clearly and convincingly."[72] Seminary colleague W. O. Carver contended that the *Axioms* "became almost a charter of Baptist orthodoxy."[73] Texas preaching giant G. W. Truett asserted that Mullins's introduction of the "axioms" at the 1905 inaugural meeting of the Baptist World Alliance (BWA) gave him instant immortality in Baptist history. Townley Lord, historian of the BWA movement, confirmed the perspectives of Carver and Truett, declaring that the "axioms" became "normative for Baptists the world over."[74] It is no surprise that contemporary theologian Fisher Humphreys concluded that *The Axioms of Religion* "did more than any other single volume to define Baptist identity in the 20th century."[75]

The influence of *The Axioms of Religion* lived on through reprints and revisions by other sympathetic authors. In 1935, Mullins's seminary colleague and supporter Harold W. Tribble revised the book and it was published by the Sunday School Board of Southern Baptists with the telling title *The Baptist Faith*. The book, containing nine chapters in contrast to

---

[72] Isla May Mullins, *Edgar Young Mullins: An Intimate Biography*, 138–39; Curtis Lee Laws, "Dr. E. Y. Mullins Translated," *Watchman Examiner* 110/ 48 (November 29, 1928): 1513. William Wilkerson of the University of Chicago said that he preferred the older idea of soul liberty. See Hinson, "Interpreter," 117.

[73] W. O. Carver, "Edgar Young Mullins—Leader and Builder," *Review and Expositor* 26/2 (April 1929): 135. For the book's influence on Louie D. Newton, a prominent leader of the Southern Baptist Convention in the mid-twentieth century, see Louie D. Newton, *Why I Am a Baptist* (New York: Thomas Nelson & Sons, 1957) 63–70.

[74] George W. Truett, "A Quarter Century of World History," *Review and Expositor* 22/1 (January 1925): 59; F. Townley Lord, *Baptist World Fellowship* (Nashville: Broadman Press, 1955) 8, 69.

[75] Humphreys, "E. Y. Mullins," 335.

Mullins's seventeen, was intended as a training course for Sunday school workers.[76] The next year, Broadman Press, the publishing arm of the Southern Baptist Convention, republished Tribble's adaptation of the *Axioms* and it was combined with a work by seminary colleague W. O. Carver, entitled *The Furtherance of the Gospel.* The new book, *The Faith and Its Furtherance,* listed Mullins, Carver, and Tribble as authors.[77] In 1978, Herschel Hobbs, known as one of the most popular Southern Baptist statesmen of his era, revised Mullins's work under the original title, *The Axioms of Religion* (1978). Broadman Press published it with Mullins and Hobbs as authors. According to Hobbs, he sought to preserve Mullins's meaning without quoting him directly. Hobbs's edition included ten chapters in contrast to seventeen in the original.[78]

Each version of the *Axioms* was a promotion of Mullins's ideas until the most recent edition. In 1997, Southern Baptists again published a book entitled *The Axioms of Religion.* This time, the president of Southern Baptist Theological Seminary, Albert Mohler, chose to print twelve of the *Axiom's* seventeen chapters, along with other selected pieces by Mullins. Mohler did not include any of the original work's citations or content footnotes and his introduction was highly critical of Mullins's theology.[79]

In recent decades, a plethora of "moderate" Baptist analysts have voiced appreciation for the work of Mullins, even if they recognize the strong Baptist triumphalism of his era and some imbalance in his theological perspectives.[80] For example, E. Glenn Hinson said that Mullins's emphasis on soul competency captured the essence of the Baptist form of Christianity, i.e., voluntarism. Hinson applauded Mullins for his novel approach of not relying on biblical proof texts and for giving a strong apology for Baptist identity

---

[76] H. W. Tribble, *The Baptist Faith* (Nashville: Sunday School Board of the SBC, 1935).

[77] E. Y. Mullins, H. W. Tribble, and W. O. Carver, *The Faith and Its Furtherance* (Nashville: Broadman Press, 1936).

[78] Herschel Hobbs and E. Y. Mullins, *The Axioms of Religion*, rev. ed. (Nashville: Broadman Press, 1978) 11.

[79] E. Y. Mullins, *The Axioms of Religion*, comp. R. Albert Mohler (Nashville: Broadman/Holman, 1997).

[80] Humphreys, "E. Y. Mullins," 337. Mullins's Baptist boosterism was common among Baptists everywhere at this time, including prominent international leaders of the Baptist World Alliance.

without using the harsh rhetoric characteristic of Landmarkism.[81] William Hull said that Mullins desired to "build a rapprochement with the cutting edge of modern thought that was rapidly shaping the American landscape." According to Hull, Mullins coped well with the emerging Progressive era and successfully dialogued with the thought of more liberal thinkers to gauge the "temper of his times." For example, Mullins read the philosophy of pragmatists like William James but "pragmatism for Mullins was a way of avoiding a rush to judgment regarding debatable issues that were not ready to be either accepted or rejected." Russell Dilday, who wrote his dissertation on Mullins, has been one of Mullins's biggest supporters. He disagreed with anyone who argued that Mullins had a hyperindividualism. Rather, Mullins had a balance between biblical authority and the importance of individual religious experience.[82] Bill Leonard noted Mullins's commitment to freedom as the center of the Baptist heritage. Mullins was also called the embodiment of the "Grand Compromise" of the SBC in the early twentieth century. As such, he affirmed the seeming contradiction of relying on the objective authority of the Bible and the subjective experience of the individual.[83]

Other moderates found strengths and weaknesses in Mullins's writings. James Dunn affirmed that soul liberty/soul competency was the foundation for the historic Baptist commitment to religious liberty, although he acknowledged that Mullins's unbounded optimism for political democracy almost equated it with Christianity.[84] Walter Shurden's focus on soul freedom—"freedom for the individual"—is reminiscent of Mullins.[85] At the

---

[81] Hinson, "Interpreter," 113–15.

[82] Dilday, "The Bible's Authority," 104–24. William E. Hull, "Mullins and Mohler: A Study in Strategy," *Perspectives in Religious Studies*, 21 (2004), 315, 320.

[83] Bill J. Leonard, *God's Last & Only Hope: The Fragmentation of the Southern Baptist Convention* (Grand Rapids MI: Eerdmans, 1990) 76. William Carrell summed up what many current critics believe is a key problem with Mullins's perspective: "Repeatedly he (Mullins) argues that the consciousness verifies the final authority of Christ and the Bible while not realizing that this argument established the final authority of the human consciousness." See Carrell, "Competency of the Soul," 141.

[84] James Dunn, "Church, State, and Soul Competency," *Review and Expositor* 96/1 (Winter 1999): 70.

[85] Walter Shurden, *The Baptist Identity: Four Fragile Freedoms* (Macon GA: Smyth and Helwys, 1993); Walter Shurden, "The Coalition for Baptist Principles," *The Baptist Studies Bulletin* 6/6 (June 2007), www.centerforbaptiststudies.org/bulletin/

same time, Shurden noted a paucity of attention given to ministerial leadership in the *Axioms'* ecclesiological discussions.[86] Fisher Humphreys called Mullins a "great Baptist theologian" and *The Axioms of Religion* his most original book. Humphreys lauded Mullins for his "category of experience" with its emphasis on conversion followed by moral transformation. While Mullins successfully avoided slipping into subjectivism, Humphreys concluded, his "intoxification" with personal freedom served to diminish "social relationships for personal life."[87]

In recent years, Mullins and soul competency have attracted numerous severe critics. They can be loosely placed in three categories: American Baptists, Southern Baptist fundamentalists and/or conservatives, and the signers of the Baptist Manifesto who subsequently focused on a Baptist-Catholic identity.

American Baptists have voiced mixed responses to Mullins and the "axioms." In 1935, W. R. McNutt affirmed the ideas of Mullins, so much so that analysts suggested that McNutt pushed soul competency beyond a softening of Calvinism toward a free will centered Pelagian understanding of salvation. A more recent brief history of Baptists by Everett Goodwin cited Mullins with approval.[88] Theologian Bernard Ramm gave Mullins a mixed response regarding experience as an authority for religious truth. Mullins was correct to say that authentic religious experience does have "a remarkable and beneficial effect in the life of the believer." Yet, Mullins, under the "charm of pragmatism," made religious experience *the* authority when it can only be the

---

2007/june.htm (accessed February 1, 2008).

[86]Walter Shurden, "Priesthood of All Believers," 36–37.

[87] Humphreys, "E. Y. Mullins," 346.

[88] W. R. McNutt, *Polity and Practice in Baptist Churches* (Philadelphia: Judson Press, 1935); Carrell, "Competency of the Soul," 6; Everett Goodwin, *Down By the Riverside: A Brief History of Baptist Faith* (Valley Forge PA: Judson Press, 2002) 97–98. The current Web page of American Baptist Churches affirms that American Baptists hold that all who truly seek God are both competent and called to develop in that relationship. They have rejected creeds or other statements that might compromise each believer's obligation to interpret Scripture under the guidance of the Holy Spirit and within the community of faith. "Ten Facts You Should Know About American Baptists," http://www.abcusa.org/resources/10facts.pdf (accessed February 15, 2008).

"mediator of the authority or revelation."[89]

However, two of the harshest critics of Baptist individualism and Mullins have been Winthrop Hudson and Paul Harrison. At the beginning of the sixties, Hudson pushed Baptists to focus on ecumenism. He believed that the Baptist focus on individualism, manifested as local congregational autonomy, was based on an anarchical principle that breeds disunity, division, separation, fragmentation, and proliferation. Hudson charged Mullins with relying on the religious culture of the late nineteenth century rather than the Bible. Consequently, soul competency served to dissolve any real concept of the church for it interpreted the faith as a one-to-one relationship between God and the individual. The practical effect of the stress upon soul competency as the cardinal doctrine of Baptists, Hudson lamented, was to make "every man's hat his own church."[90]

Paul Harrison, in a study of power and authority in American Baptist churches, said that the earliest Baptists of the seventeenth century primarily focused on the freedom of God rather than the freedom of human beings. Because early Baptists never explicitly distinguished between this freedom of God and the means to emphasize it—congregational autonomy and individual freedom—later Baptists like Mullins placed almost exclusive emphasis on the sovereignty of man and the freedom of the local churches rather than concern for God's sovereignty.[91]

Southern Baptist conservatives, almost in unison, criticize the legacy of soul competency in contemporary Baptist life. Some want to claim Mullins for their own in some areas: they say that he was a functional biblical inerrantist, and they assert that Mullins approved of some confessional litmus tests for teachers at denominational schools. However, Southern Baptist analysts insist that Mullins's reliance on pragmatist William James and liberal theologian Freidrich Schleiermacher resulted in the exaltation of individual religious

---

[89] Bernard Ramm, "Baptists and Sources of Authority," *Foundations* 1/3 (July 1958): 10.

[90] Hudson especially disliked McNutt's appropriation of Mullins. Winthrop Hudson, "Shifting Patterns of Church Order in the 20th Century," in *Baptist Concepts of the Church*, ed. Winthrop Hudson (Philadelphia: Judson Press, 1959) 215–16.

[91] Paul M. Harrison, *Authority and Power in the Free Church Tradition: A Social Case Study of the American Baptist Convention* (Princeton NJ: Princeton University Press, 1959) 11–12, 18–21.

experience over the objective truth of the Bible. Soul competency thus led to a subjective relativized faith which produced a Southern Baptist liberalism characterized by doctrinal minimalism.

Reformed Southern Baptist theologians have been especially critical of Mullins. Albert Mohler, president of the Southern Baptist Theological Seminary, said that soul competency can be "good for the personal experience of repentance but it is an acid dissolving religious authority, congregationalism, confessionalism and mutual theological accountability."[92] Thomas Nettles concurred that Mullins led Baptists away from unity based upon doctrinal consensus. Soul competency denied the importance of doctrine and was an anthropocentric theological orientation that undercut "any meaningful emphasis on God's sovereignty." Mullins's emphasis on the "practical" life, according to Nettles, exalted "human consciousness" as the "final criterion of truth…Both the meaning and the truthfulness of the Bible recede in importance and give way to the authority of visceral sensation."[93]

Other Southern Baptists have added their voices to Mohler and Nettles. Sean Michael Lucas echoed one of Mullins's earliest critics, Princeton conservative J. Gresham Machen, when he criticized Mullins's modernist-like willingness to separate the spheres of religious and scientific truth.[94] Another recent Southern Baptist critic, John Hammett, claimed that Mullins shifted Baptists from a focus on "church competence" to "soul competence." Rather than relying on the church for doctrinal accountability, Mullins accepted the privatizing trend of democratic individualism. Hammett added that the radical individualism in *The Axioms of Religion* led Baptists to morph the corporate idea of the priesthood of all believers into the boundaryless subjective wilderness of the priesthood of the believer.[95]

---

[92] Mohler, "Baptist Theology," 19. See also pp. 8, 11–12.

[93] Thomas J. Nettles, "E. Y. Mullins—Reluctant Evangelical," *The Southern Baptist Journal of Theology* 6/4 (Winter 1999): 18–19.

[94] Sean Michael Lucas, "Christianity at the Crossroads: E. Y. Mullins, J. Gresham Machen, and the Challenge of Modernism," *The Southern Baptist Journal of Theology* 6/4 (Winter 1999): 71.

[95] John Hammett, "From Church Competence to Soul Competence: The Devolution of Baptist Ecclesiology," *Journal for Baptist Theology and Ministry* 3/1 (Spring 2005): 157–58. Writing earlier than Hammett, Timothy George suggested the trend toward the priesthood of the believer, but he did not explicitly blame Mullins. See Timothy George, "The Priesthood of All Believers," in *The People of God: Essay on*

Besides some American Baptist and Southern Baptist theologians, other critics include the theologians who issued the Baptist Manifesto (1997) and its call for Anabaptist-styled communal discipleship. In revisioning or redoing Baptist identity, they criticized individualism and private reading of scripture. These scholars attribute the ills of individualism to the Enlightenment focus on the autonomous individual and thus consider Mullins to be warped by its seductions. Freedom is not individual, they insist, but communal.[96]

Manifesto theologians seem to be evolving into Baptist-Catholics who increasingly affirm catholic community, the collective authority of the church fathers, and the historic creeds (e.g., Nicene) in opposition to any substantive role for soul competency in decision making.[97] Consequently, the legacy of Mullins must be overturned to develop a proper ecclesiology.

In addition to citing Winthrop Hudson and Paul Harrison, Baptist-Catholics rely heavily on the criticisms leveled at soul competency by literary

---

the Believers' Church, ed. Paul Basden and David S. Dockery (Nashville: Broadman Press, 1991) 85–95. George had no problem with the Baptist distinctive that each believer has the right to private judgment in Bible reading according to the dictates of conscience but he insisted that the community of priests can and should set their own doctrinal parameters. Mullins most likely would not have disagreed. Stan Norman is another Southern Baptist critic, who added, "Despite his best efforts, Mullins inadvertently placed greater weight on experience than the Scriptures, thereby giving Christian experience a new status within Baptist distinctive genre…The individual, as an autonomous being, was not the focal point for developing and interpreting Baptist distinctives. See Stan Norman, *More Than Just a Name: Preserving Our Baptist Identity* (Nashville: Broadman and Holman, 2001) 62–63.

[96] Mikeal Broadway, Curtis Freeman, Barry Harvey, James W. McLendon, Jr., Elizabeth Newman, and Philip Thompson, "Re-Envisioning Baptist Identity: A Manifesto for Baptist Communities in North America," *Perspectives in Religious Studies* 24/3 (Fall 1997): 303–10.

[97] Barry Harvey, *A Catholic Baptist Engagement with Ecclesiology, Hermeneutics, and Social Theory* (Grand Rapids: Brazos Press, 2008); Steven R. Harmon, *Towards Baptist Catholicity: Essays on Tradition and the Baptist Vision* (Waynesboro GA: Paternoster, 2006). Leaders in this movement also include Curtis Freeman, Ralph Wood, Beth Newman, and Philip Thompson among others. For an overview of the Baptist-Catholic perspective, see Cameron Jorgenson, "Bapto-Catholicism: Recovering Tradition and Reconsidering the Baptist Identity" (Ph.D. diss., Baylor University, 2008).

critic Harold Bloom and former Southern Baptist Charles Marsh. According to Bloom, Mullins—America's most neglected theologian—made soul competency a mystical focus on the inner light: each Southern Baptist was "alone in the garden with Jesus." Mullins's focus on the soul was "Gnostic" and "embodied a rough version of Emersonian self-reliance."[98] According to Charles Marsh, Southern Baptist preachers during the civil rights era hid behind soul competency and individualistic religion to avoid confronting racial segregation. While Mullins did not advocate the divorce of personal religious experience and social concerns, Marsh admitted, it became part of the Mullins legacy.[99]

Another part of the legacy, according to this perspective, is the inadequacy of Baptist higher education. Some scholars claim that soul competency and the Baptist insistence on personal freedom have meshed with American hyperindividualism to facilitate the secularization of Christian education. Consequently, the communal cohesiveness needed to develop an intellectual tradition was absent. These critics believe that the foundational theological identity of any Christian university and the backbone to an adequate ecclesial tradition should be "classic orthodox, ecumenical Christianity."[100]

---

[98] Harold Bloom, *The American Religion: The Emergence of the Post Christian Nation* (New York: Simon and Schuster, 1992) 195, 199, 203, 214, 231.

[99] Charles Marsh, *God's Long Summer* (Princeton: 1997) 91–92–112. Elizabeth Barnes and Molly Marshall cite Mullins and Francis Wayland for divorcing personal salvation concerns from social action. See Molly Marshall, "Exercising Liberty of Conscience: Freedom in Private Interpretation," in *Baptists in the Balance: The Tension between Freedom and Responsibility,* ed. Everett Goodwin (Valley Forge PA: Judson Press, 1997) 141–50; Elizabeth Barnes, *An Affront to the Gospel? The Radical Barth and the Southern Baptist Convention* (Atlanta: Scholars Press, 1987) 14.

[100] David Gushee, "Integrating Faith and Learning in an Ecumenical Context," in *The Future of Baptist Higher Education,* ed. Donald Schmeltekopf and Dianna M. Vitanza (Waco TX: Baylor University Press, 2006) 46–48. See also Ralph Wood, "An Alternate Vision for a Christian University," *Perspectives in Religious Studies* 34/4 (Winter 2007): 385–413. Non-Baptist analysts of Christian higher education follow Gushee's lead in criticizing Mullins. Robert Benne, "A Baptist Vision of Christian Higher Education or Better, A Lutheran Vision of Baptist Higher Education" (handout that accompanied lecture sponsored by the Institute of Faith and Learning, Baylor University, Waco TX, November 8, 2007). In a subsequent address, Gushee moved away from his earlier contention that Baptist colleges must root themselves in the Christian tradition. He now prefers "a more classically Baptist focus on Scripture"

Curtis Freeman is one of the strongest Baptist-Catholic critics of Mullins. He praised Mullins for steering "the Southern Baptist ship around the rocky waters of fundamentalism and past the swirling currents of liberalism." However, Freeman insists that soul competency provides no foundation for ecclesiology. Following Bloom and Marsh, Freeman calls Mullins a "Gnostic" whose heresy of individualism embodied a Southern mysticism that crippled the society's ability to address social issues. Freeman believed that soul competency mutated into "sole competency" when Baptist leaders asserted the right of individual conscience to read the Bible and answer only to Jesus.[101] Mullins's "rugged individualism" has no usefulness to a lonely postmodern age of moral strangers in need of community, Freeman concluded.[102] In response to the Manifesto/Baptist-Catholic agenda, Timothy Maddux says that these scholars are ironically guilty of what is attributed to Mullins—the bifurcation of the individual and community—but in their case they solely emphasize the community to the neglect of the individual.[103]

One of the most pointed criticisms of Mullins's focus on soul competency, articulated by Marsh but accepted by others, is the charge that he did not give significant emphasis to social ministry as part of his ecclesiological concerns. Thus, Southern Baptists hid behind a veil of hyperindividualism to avoid confronting social concerns in the twentieth century. This charge is true in part, but the Mullins story is more complicated. Mullins should be seen under the umbrella of the emerging emphasis on social Christianity and social reform in Southern Progressivism at the turn of the twentieth century.

While pastor of Lee Street Baptist Church in Baltimore, Mullins led the downtown congregation's involvement in a moderate-type social gospel. During the labor strife of 1894–1985, for example, Mullins normally

---

because it "enables us to critique tradition in the name of Scripture where Tradition went wrong, as it sometimes did." See David Gushee, "Theological Foundations for the Baptist University," Hester Lectures #1, sponsored by the International Association of Baptist Colleges and Universities (June 2007): 9.

[101] Curtis Freeman, "E. Y. Mullins and the Siren Songs of Modernity," *Review and Expositor* 96/1 (Winter 1999): 23, 34–36, 41.

[102] Mark Wingfield, "Mullins Scholars See Calvinism Behind Mohler's Speech," *Baptist Standard* 112/16 (April 17, 2000). http://www.baptiststandard.com/2000 /4_17/pages/calvinism.html (accessed June 15, 2007).

[103] Maddox, "Mr. Baptist," 87.

supported the grievances of laborers on strike. During his ministry at the more upper-class Newton Centre Baptist Church in Massachusetts, Mullins did not trumpet social themes, though he did encourage American Baptists to be involved in the education of African Americans in the South.[104]

Mullins facilitated a "moderate social gospel" orientation for at least the first half of his seminary presidency. Professor Charles Gardner offered courses in Christian sociology. His book, *Ethics of Jesus and Social Progress* (1914) contended for a progressive social application of the gospel.[105] The *Review and Expositor*, under Mullins's editorship, printed positive assessments of books by social gospel leaders Walter Rauschenbusch and Washington Gladden (1907 and 1908).[106] Mullins invited the more liberal social gospeler and Northern Baptist Samuel Batten to speak at the Southern Baptist Theological Seminary (1913). At the same time, Mullins hardly ever cited Rauschenbusch in his writings and critics have charged that he did not possess the "social passion" of Northern social gospelers.[107] At issue was probably Rauschenbusch's linking a social gospel to theological liberalism and socialism. Mullins ultimately decided that "the trouble with many a so-called modernist is that he has a fine moral and social program, but no adequate motive power."[108]

While not frequently, throughout his career Mullins spoke out against social problems. His *Baptist Beliefs* (1912), a book aimed at the laity, had a section on "social service." While not containing a "social gospel" section on corporate sin, Mullins commented that Baptists believed in every type of

---

[104] For an extensive analysis of Mullins's views on social ministry, see C. Douglas Weaver, "E.Y. Mullins: Soul Competency and Social Ministry," *Perspectives in Religious Studies* 36/4 (Winter 2010): 447–62. To place Mullins in Southern Progressivism, see Paul Harvey, *Redeeming the South: Religious Cultures and Racial Identities Among Southern Baptists, 1865-1925* (Chapel Hill: University of North Carolina Press, 1997) 197–226. Ellis, *Man of Books*, 25–29; Bryant, "Unifying Leadership," 9.

[105] Ferenc M. Szasz, *The Divided Mind of Protestant America, 1880–1930* (Tuscaloosa AL: University of Alabama Press, 1982) 63.

[106] Ellis, *Man of Books*, 87.

[107] Sydney Ahlstrom, "Theology in America: An Historical Survey," in *Religion in American Life*, vol. 1 of *The Shaping of American Religion*, ed. James Ward Smith and A. Leland Jamison (Princeton NJ: Princeton University Press, 1961) 307.

[108] E. Y. Mullins, *Faith in the Modern World* (Nashville: Sunday School Board of the SBC, 1930) 121.

righteousness, including "social righteousness or right living in society; commercial righteousness or right living in society."[109] In a 1923 address to the Baptist World Alliance, he exhorted that, as Baptists submitted to the Lordship of Christ, social problems like child labor, sweatshops, and graft would be confronted and broken by the power of the coming Kingdom of God. The Baptist World Alliance, with Mullins as president, expressed such concerns in an official statement: "The noble and self-sacrificing work of caring for the social wreckage of our time, the poverty-stricken and the outcast, must not cease."[110] Near the end of his career, Mullins still maintained that he sympathized with the social movements of the day and told ministers that preaching had social implications so they should be involved in the civic arena.[111]

Nevertheless, in the dominant evangelical fashion, Mullins supported social ministry as an outgrowth of redeemed individuals. The "panacea for social ills" was not any particular reform program, but regenerated individuals "loving their neighbors."[112] Mullins preached, "His (Jesus') business was to strike the human heart, and by striking the human heart he overturned the Roman Empire. If you adopt the method of reform merely, then you will have to have a new reform for every evil. It would be like trying to keep a hunting dog for every wolf or every bear which menaced the farm."[113]

It has been noted that Mullins's chapter on the social axiom, "Love Thy Neighbor," is the shortest in *The Axioms of Religion*. Length of the chapter aside, the *Axioms* provided a social element to Mullins's ecclesiological restatement of the New Testament church. According to Mullins, soul

[109] Mullins, *Baptist Beliefs*, 76.

[110] E. Y. Mullins, "The Lordship of Jesus," in *Baptist World Alliance: Record of Proceeding Congresses of 1905, 1911, 1923, 1928*, 377–92. For this quotation, see pp. 390–91. For the statement of the Baptist World Alliance, see E.Y. Mullins, "Message," 226.

[111] E. Y. Mullins, "The Modern Minister and His Task," *The Record of Christian Work* 46/10 (October 1927): 713.

[112] Mullins, *Faith in the Modern World*, 120; Mullins, *Christianity at the Crossroads*, 259, 266. See also the section on social service in the 1925 *Baptist Faith and Message*.

[113] E. Y. Mullins, "Christ's Law of Service," in *History of Southern Oratory*, ed. Thomas E. Watson (Richmond VA: Southern Historical Publication Society, 1909) 9:403.

competency did not lead to a hyperindividualism because God created individuals to be social beings. In a community of believers, "social relations are reconstituted in Christ." The social axiom "Love your neighbor as yourself" could then authentically occur.

Evidences of a moderate social gospel are manifest in the *Axioms*. Mullins cited the prevalence of graft in American business and political practices, the problem of child labor and the "competitive system," and the unfortunate fact that "the money-getter is the American hero." Mullins insisted that Christ could not be equated with any particular reform movement. Genuine Christian social ministry was still dependent upon converted individuals. Ultimately, Mullins believed that the spread of democracy from the church into the world would facilitate social improvement. Believers in churches that follow the simple nonhierarchical polity of the New Testament church would have more opportunities to engage in efforts to improve society.[114] While Mullins was evidently more socially conservative near the end of his career, he never ceased to affirm that social concern was a part of the church's ministry.

The Axioms of Religion: An Apology for the New Testament Church

Long before E. Y. Mullins, Baptists had affirmed an ecclesiology that highlighted local church independence, democratic congregational polity, and a focus upon the individual. Mullins intensified these egalitarian and democratic-friendly concepts in the context of Baptist battles and a cultural milieu that promoted the benefits of political democracy. In an era of intense denominational competition, Mullins wanted to clarify and maintain the historic claim that Baptists were the best hope to restore the New Testament church and its faith.[115] His attempt to do so resulted in the writing of *The Axioms of Religion*, a book that sought to explicate the "axioms," or universal principles, that embodied New Testament Christianity. Writing with the fervor of an apologist, Mullins's goal was to avoid the extremes of what he

---

[114] See chapter 12 of *The Axioms of Religion* for the material summarized in this paragraph. See also Mullins, *Freedom and Authority*, 41.

[115] The Baptist desire to be the New Testament church—evident throughout Baptist history—is a part of the larger "restorationist" theme prevalent in Christian history. See C. Douglas Weaver, *In Search of the New Testament Church: The Baptist Story* (Macon GA: Mercer University Press, 2008).

considered authoritarian threats to the restoration of "original Christianity."[116]

Landmarkism was Mullins's Baptist opponent concerning the quest for the New Testament church. Landmarkers claimed that Baptists were *the* New Testament church. Only Baptists had the correct polity, ordinances, and historical origins in the ministry of Jesus. Mullins opposed this "Baptist tradition" of Landmarkism that asserted Baptists were the New Testament church because they could trace an unbroken line of churches back to the apostolic era.[117] They were a "Roman Catholic party" among Baptists because they made their tradition of church successionism the same kind of sacred authoritative test of orthodoxy that Roman Catholics gave their understanding of apostolic succession. In doing so, they undercut the Baptist commitment to *sola Scriptura*. In the end, Landmarkers were rigid "Baptists and a half" who practically dechurched their opponents with persecuting personal rhetoric.[118] Without explicitly criticizing Landmarkism in his book, Mullins offered the *Axioms* as an alternative, a "fresh statement"[119]—not dependent on bad history or intolerance—to express Baptist convictions.

Mullins believed that his non-Baptist opponent was hierarchical religion, especially Roman Catholicism.[120] Protestant-Catholic rhetoric, on both sides, had been derogatory since the sixteenth century. The extensive immigration of Catholics to America by the turn of the twentieth century was a great concern to Protestants. Mullins and other Protestants were horrified by the doctrine of papal infallibility promulgated by Pope Pius IX at Vatican I (1870). Pius IX had also asserted that religious liberty was a "nightmare" and he had condemned the idea that each person had an inherent right to freedom of conscience. The next pope, Leo XIII, had censured "Americanism," a movement of some American Catholic leaders that advocated some American

---

[116] Mullins, *Axioms of Religion*, 65.

[117] Mullins wrote a Texas pastor that the historical evidence did not support Landmark claims. See Hinson, "Interpreter," 111.

[118] Mullins, "Roman Catholic," 1; Mullins, "Notes and Comments," 1.

[119] Mullins, *Axioms of Religion*, original preface.

[120] In *The Axioms of Religion*, Mullins also spoke against Protestant groups that promoted episcopacy and infant baptism, but he found Catholicism the most blatant denier of soul competency.

values like separation of church and state.[121] Writing during this era of Vatican I Catholicism, Mullins opposed the "Catholic tradition" of apostolic succession that emphasized an unbroken line of papal leadership back to the Apostle Peter in the New Testament. Mullins contended that the Catholic Church's centralized hierarchical leadership threatened and badly contradicted the simple polity of the New Testament church. It fostered "incompetence" of the soul in believers who were passively obedient to human authority. Mullins believed that Landmarkism and Roman Catholicism both erred by hiding behind bad tradition rather than relying on the lordship of Christ revealed in the scriptures.

Ultimately, Mullins believed that the key to restoring a New Testament church was to adhere to "the simple undeveloped polity of the New Testament."[122] By necessity and design, ecclesiastical polity was simple: a membership of professing believers, democratic congregational governance, local church independence, two symbolic ordinances, and the separation of church and state. A New Testament-modeled church was rooted in freedom. Consequently, the simple ecclesiology of the New Testament had no room for decision making restricted to ecclesiastical oligarchies (sacerdotalism) and had no room for anything that hindered the voluntary nature of faith (infant baptism and sacramentalism).

Mullins's plea for the restoration of "original Christianity" is more clearly seen in *Axioms of Religion* than in any of his other writings. It is revealing that he began his apology with two chapters on denominationalism and the kingdom of God—affirmations about the broader universal church—rather than restricting the church to a local body of believers or define the kingdom as the collection of local visible churches as Landmarkism did.[123] Mullins asserted that the "axioms" embodied the ideals of the kingdom of God. New Testament churches were the institutional embodiment of these kingdom ideals.

After two chapters (3 and 4) in which he defined soul competency and argued that it was the "historical significance of the Baptists," Mullins outlined his "axioms." These axioms, the essence of New Testament Christianity, highlighted the paradox of the lordship of Christ and the freedom of the

---

[121] Robert McAfee Brown, *The Ecumenical Revolution: An Interpretation of Catholic-Protestant Dialogue*, rev. ed. (Garden City NY: Doubleday, 1969) 250–51.

[122] Ibid., 229; Mullins, "Baptist Life," 301.

[123] Carrell, "Competency of the Soul," 54.

individual. The first axiom was the "theological axiom" of the sovereignty of God (chapter 6). The religious axiom, "All souls have an equal right to direct access to God," then provided the basis for cooperative fellowship in the community of faith seen in the ecclesiastical axiom, "All believers have a right to equal privileges in the church" (chapters 7 and 8). Soul competency demanded the spiritual democracy of congregationalism and avoided the coercive nature of hierarchical leadership and creedalism. The other three axioms (chapters 9, 11, and 12) built on the earlier foundational axioms and dealt with the dependence of morality on freedom, the separation of church and state, and social responsibility (love for one's neighbor).

Throughout the discussion of the axioms, Mullins strongly criticized the issue always found in Baptist apologetics of earlier decades and seen as a major hindrance toward the restoration of the New Testament church: infant baptism. For example, the insistence of the moral axiom that "to be responsible the soul must be free" included an emphasis on the "evil of infant baptism." Mullins also had a separate chapter (10) in which he critiqued the idea of "Christian Nurture" popularized by the nineteenth-century theologian Horace Bushnell, which affirmed faith in young children.

In two chapters (13 and 14), Mullins affirmed that the simple polity of a New Testament church still had some necessary ingredients. His criticism of ecumenical church union was that it would require Baptists to sacrifice what little church organization they had. They would practically become "a disembodied spirit."[124] If Baptists ignored the errors of infant baptism and "sacerdotal" authority, ecclesiastical integrity would be lost to an unbiblical church order. In an attack on "anti-institutional Christianity," Mullins wrote that the practice of open membership—accepting persons only baptized as infants as church members without administering believer's baptism—disparaged the New Testament church's insistence that ordinances gave it some indispensable institutional form.

In the final chapters of *The Axioms of Religion* (13–17), Mullins attempted to apply the axioms to larger issues. In "Baptists and General Organization," he re-affirmed that the voluntary principle, not hierarchical control, must characterize Baptist organizations. In "Baptist Contributions to American Civilization," Mullins again focused on liberty and said that his

---

[124] Mullins, "Baptists in the Modern World," 350.

"axioms" were analogous to the "political axioms" of the nation. In "Baptists and World Progress," he declared that the axioms "are fitted to lead the progressive civilization of the race."

It is not hard to understand why *The Axioms of Religion* became popular for Baptists worldwide. It functioned as an apology for Baptist ecclesiology and a call for the restoration of the New Testament Church. Baptist triumphalism still reigned in this "fresh statement" of Baptist principles. Yet, Mullins avoided the harsh intolerance found in Baptist Landmarkism. His understanding of Vatican I Catholicism found no strong rebuttal in his Southern Protestant world. He provided Baptists with an identifiable character in the midst of the rising ecumenical movement. His clear articulation of "axioms" was considered biblically grounded, but without reliance on "inferior" tradition. He emphasized that Baptists had always been a people of voluntaristic faith.[125] To readers who cherished freedom in the Bible, who realized how hard minority dissenting Baptists had fought to obtain freedom, and who lived in an era when religious liberty and political democracy were considered twins destined to prevail across the globe, *The Axioms of Religion* was simply old-time Baptist religion made fresh for future generations.

Conclusion

Is *The Axioms of Religion* a Baptist classic? As the most original and creative book of Southern Baptists' most influential theologian of the twentieth century, the answer is "of course." The book is a window to the Baptist past and offers much about Baptist theological attitudes of yesteryear. It is obvious, however, that the continuing relevance of E. Y. Mullins for contemporary Baptists is contentiously debated.

Mullins's reliance on a theology of religious experience will be rejected outright by those who describe scripture primarily in terms of doctrinal propositions. Even those less critical have noted the difficulties in an experiential-based theology and the tensions between affirming both the authority of subjective individual experience and written scripture. Mullins's smooth integration of spiritual and political democracy is quintessentially early-twentieth-century Americana. His harsh rhetoric against Roman

---

[125] Hinson provides a good summary of reasons for the popularity of *The Axioms of Religion*. See Hinson, "Interpreter," 117.

Catholicism, explainable because of the Protestant-Catholic relations of his day, is a barrier to modern readers.

Mullins's ecclesiology is too undeveloped for most analysts. He wrote about pastoral ministry much more than scholars have noticed, but still he never systematized his thoughts because of his focus on the "competence" of the congregation. His attacks against infant baptism, even when read by persons committed to believer's baptism, are historically dated by the intense denominational competition of earlier decades.

As Mullins's strongest critics have been quick to declare, his ecclesiology (or lack of one) will not meet the needs of those today who demand that freedom be for the community rather than the individual. His focus on individualism is indeed extensive—he reflected his Baptist heritage and his early-twentieth-century culture—but to discard him for hyperindividualism betrays the historical record revealed in his writings, his attachment to the scriptures, and his devotion to the church, local and worldwide. Moreover, to describe Mullins as a Gnostic is a "discussion stopper" and labels him with the heavy burden that the word "heresy" has been wont to evoke in Christian history.

While not affirming all of Mullins's attitudes or theology, other readers will continue to admire him because they believe that his focus on individual experience captures a part of the Baptist DNA—personal conversion via voluntary faith—and the Baptist historic insistence upon a "believers' church" that answers to the scriptures and ultimately to the lordship of Christ. Mullins's emphasis on soul competency will not be seen as "sole" competency—individual experience as sufficient unto itself—but as a vital foundation for preserving spiritual egalitarianism and the historic Baptist principle of the sacredness of an unfettered conscience before God.

In fact, Mullins was part of a long line of Baptist leaders who affirmed that there must be freedom for an individual to relate authentically to God — even if this meant lonely dissent. No church could tell a believer what to believe; each person would be judged by God at the Last Judgment. Where the right to dissent is acknowledged as a "dangerous" but "emancipating word,"[126] Mullins will remain relevant to the discussion about the relationship between personal faith and communal discipleship.

Does Mullins's stress upon the individual's relationship to God make "every man's hat his own church?" It can, of course. It does seem that contemporary Baptist ecclesiology in the twenty-first century will do well to incorporate an intentional balance between the individual and the community of faith. However, analysts will do well to remember that the Mullins legacy has rarely, if really ever, produced Lone Ranger Christians not connected to the ongoing life of the church. His contention that the nature of personal conversion "impelled" believers to recognize that they were a part of the body of Christ and were to share voluntarily in a community of faith could lead to relevant discussion of the event and process of conversion.

Is the Mullins legacy responsible for the divorce between personal faith and social action that has often been present in the Baptist story? An individualistic ethic can surely lead to social isolation, and can be seen as part of the slow Baptist response to social issues like racial segregation in the nineteenth and twentieth centuries. It is fair to say that the interpretation of Mullins contributed to this scenario. Mullins was evidently more progressive regarding social problems earlier in his career, but he always maintained that soul competency led to a social consciousness. However, blaming Mullins, soul competency, and Baptist individualism for social isolationism seems simplistic and distorts his legacy. Other factors were also at work; America was captive to cultural and economic forces that affected all denominations, including Baptists, long before and after Mullins's day.

Today, simple ecclesiology seems quaint and Baptist triumphalism about being the New Testament church is clearly embarrassing to most. Ecumenical dialogue, study of Christian traditions, and greater recognition of the universal church is readily accepted. Readers who appreciate Mullins realize his thought must be contextualized, broadened or revised in contemporary settings. Still, Mullins's focus on freedom for the individual—voluntary personal faith under a biblically understood lordship of Christ—and freedom for the Church to be a community of faith, sound applicable to any age.

---

[126] Mullins, "Baptist Life," 312. For the connection between individual conscience and the Last Judgment in the Baptist heritage, see C. Douglas Weaver, "E.Y. Mullins: Soul Competency and Social Ministry," footnotes 7 and 8.

The Axioms of Religion

By E. Y. Mullins

1

The New Test of Denominationalism

Each recurring season brings a new test to the trees of a forest. This oak perished because the foes which attacked it were too great for its powers of resistance. That pine was laid low because a fierce wind struck it at a new angle and thus discovered the one weak spot in its hold upon the earth. Under pressure of wind and snow that ancient elm was split in two. The next season some neighbors of these go down for kindred reasons, while others remain standing throughout many generations.

The centuries are to institutions what adverse conditions are to the forest trees. Changing circumstances bring fresh tests of endurance. The weak or decrepit succumb, the strong survive. Some are so modified by environment that they lose their original characteristics entirely. Others are purged of dross and purified and unfold more fully their distinctive life and power. Still others coalesce with kindred institutions and together under a new combination life and progress are achieved.

Since the Reformation denominationalism has been the characteristic expression of Christianity on its ecclesiastical side. The right of private judgment and freedom from ecclesiastical superiors, that priceless boon of modern believers, has led to great variety in the interpretation of the New Testament. The touchstone hitherto has been conformity to the teachings of the Scriptures. This battle has been waged long and it may be truly said that at length it is virtually at an end. At least this is true in the realm of scholarship and among thinkers generally, although on the popular side it progresses still. So far as explicit New Testament teaching is concerned there are no important points left unsettled among scholars as to the organization and polity of the church. Men do not hesitate, however, to reject New Testament teaching on these points in the interest of a theory of development or for other reasons when it suits their purposes, and they seek to justify the procedure in many ways.

New Test of Denominationalism

Practical conditions among us are today imposing a new test upon denominationalism. This test when fully applied will not, in the opinion of the writer, involve a rejection of New Testament teachings. It will rather supplement those teachings and corroborate them in a new way. The progress of events and the conditions of Christian work are the best interpreters of Scripture. Christianity is like a knife of many blades and other devices to be used in turn as need arises. There is this difference however. In Christianity many of the blades are concealed from view until new emergencies bring to light their presence and use. Every interpretation of Scripture assumes, or should assume, the divinely adapted fitness of Scripture to human need. History reacts upon and explains exegesis in many ways, just as the growth of a tree reveals what was lying potent in the seed, and as the progress of a building sheds light on the preliminary plans of the architect. Thus we are slowly obtaining an exposition of our exegesis. We are unfolding it into its implications and enlarging it into its logical and necessary outcome.

The nature of the practical test which we refer to may be understood by a brief glance at some of the problems and perils which confront all Christian bodies today. These are for the most part problems of adjustment of one kind or other.

Problems of Adjustment

One of the most important of these is the problem of doctrinal adjustment. In all denominations there is a pronounced movement of thought on doctrinal teaching. It has assumed acute forms in most of the evangelical bodies in heresy trials in recent years. The lines of doctrinal cleavage are as radical as at any time in the past, but the issues are new. As usual the extreme parties are doing most of the harm. On one side is the ultra-conservative, the man of the hammer and anvil method, who relies chiefly upon denunciation of opponents, and who cannot tolerate discussion on a fraternal basis; on the other is the ultra-progressive whose lofty contempt of the "traditionalist" shuts him out from the ranks of sane scholarship and wise leadership. The really safe leaders of thought, however, are between these extremes. They are men who have sympathy on the one hand with those who are perplexed by the difficulties to faith occasioned by modern science and philosophy, and on the other are resolved to be loyal to Christ and his gospel. Out of this situation arise two urgent questions. The first is this: What is the regulative principle of doctrinal growth and progress? The second is: What are the limits of doctrinal divergence within the pale of the denominational life?

As to the first of these two questions few will venture to assert that doctrinal statements are permanently stereotyped in any particular creed or book of theology which has appeared in the course of the Christian centuries; that the plates are, so to speak, in their final form, to be stowed away for safe keeping in the ecclesiastical vault and to be used for new editions when the old are exhausted. Such a claim would be tantamount to a claim that said plates are inspired and that God has withdrawn his Holy Spirit from modern investigators in so far as their labors are designed to enlarge or deepen or modify past interpretations of Scripture, or to discover new sidelights upon Scripture from any department of science. Respecting the second question, as to the limits of doctrinal difference, there is much divergence of view among the denominations themselves, and often within the pale of the particular denomination. It would be a great stride forward if our thinking on these two matters could be clarified.

Another question of adjustment presses, and that is of the denominations to each other. What shall be our attitude on the great question of Christian union? Are the denominations free to ignore this issue and in so doing can they remain loyal to the Master who prayed that his people might all be one? It has become clear that artificially devised union among the various bodies can never be permanently effected. Recent examples also warn us against premature attempts at union even among closely related bodies. And yet there remains before us the reproach of a divided Christendom and in many instances an apparent waste of resources in fields where churches are multiplied beyond the needs of the communities. So long, however, as the consciences of Christians revolt at compromise or surrender of what they regard as the will of Christ for them, we cannot hope for a radical cure of these evils. It behooves us, therefore, to recognize that permanent Christian union is to be realized only by training the conscience by means of the truth, and to ask what are the fundamental lines along which this training should proceed.

Christianity and Social Service

There is also the matter of the adjustment of our Christianity to social service. There are many who feel strongly that at this point has the church of modern times most deeply sinned. They think the church has been too much like a star blazing above men to show the way to the next life. They think it should seek to become a lantern in whose light men may walk in the dark. Accusations are frequent that church and ministry are indifferent to social conditions. Smug, prosperous, and contented church members, and genial ease-loving pastors, so we are told, live their lives and maintain their worship in oblivion of the tragedy and struggle of the masses, and careless of the cruelty and oppression of wealth. The charge is of course far from being the whole truth. It is in part a case of misunderstanding, due to a difference of view as to the relative values and of method.

To the best elements in the churches the material is not valued so highly as the moral and spiritual. Hence with them inequalities in economic conditions do not press so painfully upon consciousness as among those to whom the material is of primary importance. Those who are without the moral discipline to endure hard conditions with cheerfulness, or who see all things in the perspective of this life alone are at a serious disadvantage here. The misunderstanding is due in part also to a difference in view as to the method of ameliorating human conditions. The church has said, make the tree good and the fruit will be good. Give men spiritual natures and you will thus regulate society best; whereas the critics have insisted that she forsake evangelism for the other department of service. When all is said, however, it must be owned that a Christianity which is indifferent or callous to moral conditions of any kind is abnormal and imperfect, and it must also be owned that evangelism does not exhaust the program of the churches of Jesus Christ. We need, therefore, a clearer grasp of the nature and limits of the social duties of the church. We need a view on this point which can be intelligently advocated, propagated, and defended, and at the same time adjusted to other departments of duty and service. Is the church of Christ in relation to social questions a square peg in a round hole? Is it a misfit in social effort or is it unfit? If not, how can it be made to fit?

On the Foreign Mission Field

On the foreign mission fields a new situation has arisen in connection with the increasing growth and triumph of our missionary labors. What form of Christianity is best adapted to the civilizations of the East? Is it wise to attempt to urge our Western forms of ecclesiastical organization upon the

Orient? Should there be a fusion of the various Christian elements in India, China, and Japan, into as many national or racial organizations, which shall omit the distinctive features of the West? These are vital questions today in all these countries and will engage attention in increasing measure in the near future.

There is another matter of far-reaching significance. How are the various denominations to preserve a loyalty so intense as to make them compact and united in aim, and so inspired by a common spirit as to render them useful? When the modern denominations were in process of formation controversy was the bellows which kept hot the fires of zeal. Competition in missionary effort has played a similar part in more recent years. No one can question that controversy is a duty when circumstances demand it and truth is in peril. It will never, under earthly conditions, cease to be necessary within certain limits. But it is quite generally agreed in our day that propagandism through interdenominational controversy has in large measure served its day. The spirit of the age frowns upon such controversy, and the man who has no gift for other forms of service finds himself in a constantly narrowing field of usefulness. And yet as we face the situation created by a long delayed Christian union, and at the same time by a tendency to denominational dissolution we are in danger of resolving our Christianity back into a mass of unrelated and non-cohesive atoms. There is indeed a marked movement toward an anti-institutional, anti-ecclesiastical, and wholly individualistic Christianity. The period of the judges in Israel, of the little city democracies in the period of their anarchy and decline in Greece, and of the breaking up of Europe into feudalism in the Middle Ages, are historic analogues which suggest the possible outcome of such a movement. The man who is unattached to any religious organization, or equally attached to all, may of course exert some local influence for good combined with a very bad example of a false individualism. But he will lose all that splendid opportunity for service which comes of a life reinforced by thousands of others united and organized and aggressive in the pursuit of common ends. If the mass of individual Christians is to become simply a vortex ring of dancing atoms, each moving aimlessly around its own center, Christianity will soon spend itself.

A New Cohesive Principle Needed

There must be, then, some motive or incentive or cohesive principle strong enough to give unity to each of the religious bodies if these bodies are to continue their careers of usefulness. Denominational self-respect, a sense of a divine calling and mission, must possess any religious body which counts for much in the world. The prophetic mood, which implies that the soul is conquered by some great truth or truths, and seeks passionately and restlessly to propagate those truths, is a prime condition of power.

Now if the vigor and intensity of this prophetic burden can no longer be produced, as in the formative period of denominationalism, by the sense of discovery in the realm of truth and experience and by competition and conflict, we must somehow find another incentive. Some moral equivalent must be found which will serve to impel us forward with something like the pristine energy and persistence. The most intense denominationalists are often animated by this feeling in their assertive insularity and their feeling of re-pugnance toward suggestions of Christian union. They are afraid of lukewarmness and lack of force. It is certainly true that negative moods do not win in religion. None of the higher forms of spiritual religion have ever made wide progress merely as a leaven. Aggressive advocacy by deeply earnest indi-viduals is the sole condition. The hardest metals can be melted if you get a fire hot enough. All church problems are at bottom problems of spiritual tem-perature. God's Spirit supplies the flame. Earthly conditions furnish the fuel. Well-directed effort raises the temperature to the desired point.

Pressure Felt by All Religious Bodies

All the evangelical churches have felt the pressure of the problems and difficulties outlined above. Among Methodists, Presbyterians, and Episcopa-lians, there have been heresy trials which have attracted national if not worldwide attention in recent years, and all alike feel the urgency of the missionary, social, and other aspects of the problems. Baptists have also felt these conditions and experienced similar embarrassment at certain points. With the Baptists all the perplexities are dealt with in a more direct and simple way than is the case with the other more complex and highly organized bodies. But among Baptists there are conditions peculiar to themselves which call for attention. For one thing Baptists have increased in numbers and in wealth so rapidly that these two elements alone have created many problems.

How shall these vast numbers be made thoroughly homogeneous in spirit and aim? How may they be enlisted in the aggressive enterprises of a militant and conquering missionary gospel? How shall our vast wealth be drawn into the service of the kingdom of God?

Then too, out of our doctrine of independence, how shall we realize, in any adequate manner, the complementary principle of interdependence? Baptists must face this problem with renewed interest in order to avoid serious waste and great loss of power. We must work out patiently our problem of democracy and unity. Experiment has been demonstrating lately the startling energy of a wave of the sea. The power of the impact of the wave depends upon two factors apart from the impelling wind. One is the elevation of its center of gravity above the common level of the sea, the other is the rotary motion of the separate drops of water which enter into the formation of the wave. Baptist unity is like that, not of a block of granite, but of a wave of the sea. Individual energy answers to the rotation of the drops. The elevation of the common life of the churches fixes the spiritual center of gravity. The breath of the Spirit of God is the impelling wind. Our energy will prove resistless when all the conditions are fulfilled.

An Anti-Institutional Christianity

There is one extreme, although as yet quite small, group among us who are anti-institutional, or at least anti-ceremonial in their conception of Christianity. They are ready to sacrifice the ordinances and church order to the last possible limit in the interest of expediency. They want the spirit of religion without a body; or at least they want only an astral body which is unaffected by ordinances or forms. A few others would centralize our Baptist polity and adopt an approach to a Presbyterian or Episcopal church order. These parties are not large and there is little prospect of a triumph of their views in America at least. They are mentioned merely to indicate as completely as may be the currents and eddies of our denominational life.

It is unnecessary to enlarge further this outline of the present general situation of the various religious bodies. Enough has been said to indicate the gravity of the problems which press for solution, and the urgency and vastness of our immediate task as Christians.

Among those who recognize the authority of the New Testament there are two prevalent general views as to church order. One insists that the New

Testament gives final form to ecclesiastical organization; the other contends for a principle of development from New Testament beginnings. The congregational bodies represent the first view and the episcopal churches the development principle. Cardinal Newman has given the most consistent expression to the development idea in his well-known discussion of the subject. His principles of development are exactly adapted to relieve the conscience of the man who has left the Church of England for the Roman Catholic fold. They are an elaborate theoretical vindication of Romanism. One of their defects is that they do not conform to the facts of history but to an ideal. Another serious and vital fault is that they fail to show that in the Romish development the New Testament type is preserved. Newman's introspection led him into the subjective snare. By his speculations to relieve his inward distress he opened a trap door in his own floor through which he fell into the subcellar of an outgrown system.[1]

Two Issues

The real issues between the two theories, the congregational on the one hand and the episcopal and presbyterial on the other, are two. First, which best preserves the New Testament principles and ideals; second, which is best fitted to accomplish the enlarging task of Christianity in the world. On the side of the Scriptures the test is one of conformity. On the practical side the test is one of adaptation to changing and enlarging tasks. We inherit from the Reformation and the New Testament the first test. The second has been imposed upon us by the progress of events. The two tests are harmonious. Indeed they are mutually regulative of each other. It is a flagrant violation of the New Testament for a religious body to ignore conditions and the state of human need. In meeting these needs in any serious way we will be driven inevitably to the New Testament principles.

The practical test is the one which presses at present. It has a profound bearing upon the whole movement of an ever advancing civilization, as well as upon the deepest religious yearnings and aspirations of the human spirit. The issue is taking shape in modern thinking in many forms. It may be stated in

---

[1] John Henry Newman, *An Essay on the Development of Christian Doctrine* (London: James Toovey, 1845; New York: Longmans, Green, and Co., 1903). Newman (1801–1890) was a leading Anglican in the Oxford Movement which emphasized a return to Catholic teachings. In 1845, he became a Roman Catholic.

various ways. Will the widening tasks and increasing burdens of the churches result in the extension of the principle of episcopacy, or will the ever growing principle of democracy gradually undermine and dissolve episcopacy? Is the genius of Christianity best expressed in systems of corporate authority or in those of corporate freedom? Is the church a body of spiritual equals or shall it consist of a group of inferiors presided over by an authoritative group of superiors? Does it conduce to the progress of Christianity to entrust its great interests to the laity as well as clergy, or should the power of the laity be held within fixed limits by their clerical superiors?

Fresh Statements Needed

Now it is the conviction of the present writer that the time has come for the various Christian bodies to give a fresh account of themselves to the world, and in an entirely new way. The questions should be not one of past service merely, but of fitness for present service. The question of conformity to Scripture properly understood always involves the total question of conformity to racial needs and advancing civilization. Is there flexibility and elasticity or is there rigidity and petrifaction? Is Christianity conceived as a rule or as a principle? Are the tests those of life or those of the square and compass? Do the church polities contain in themselves heterogeneous and alien elements or are they in harmony with the genius and spirit as well as the express teachings of the New Testament? What contributions have the various polities to make to the subjects discussed in the preceding pages, such as missions, social service, Christian union, evangelism, civic righteousness, and family life, and others?

The aim of this book is to make this statement from the point of view of the Baptists. What is the distinctive message of the Baptists to the world? How far does our simple congregational polity embody the essential things in New Testament Christianity and to what extent is it adapted to the present and future progress of the gospel on earth? The question here is not primarily concerning baptism or the Lord's Supper or even church polity as these have been discussed in the past. The attempt is rather to state our case in the light of primary and universal principles, and to show the relation of the ordinances and polity to these principles. These principles of course are taken from the New Testament. The authority of the Scriptures lies at the basis of our plea. We do not believe any form of Christianity which breaks with the Scripture as the revealed and authoritative word of God can long serve the interests of God's kingdom on earth in any thoroughgoing way. Every position, therefore, which we assume in the following pages is either directly or indirectly grounded upon the revelation of God in Christ as recorded in the Old and New Testament Scriptures.

2

Denominationalism in Terms
of the Kingdom of God

A painted rainbow never equals a real one. An artificial diamond lacks the
brilliancy of one made in nature's workshop. The human touch always leaves
its mark of inferiority when brought into comparison with God's handiwork.
This is true in religion as well as in nature. We must constantly return to the
divine standard in dealing with religious organizations.

Church Polity and Spiritual Law

It is proposed in this chapter to examine denominationalism in the light
of the New Testament ideal of the kingdom of God; or, what amounts to the
same thing, to consider ecclesiastical polity as over against universal spiritual
laws. We are to seek first the distinctive ideals and principles of the religion of
Christ, and then to ask whether or not church polity bears any relation to
them, or whether, on the contrary, polity is solely a question of expediency.
Or, recurring to the figure, letting the rainbow answer to the great New
Testament ideal of the kingdom of God, do the religious bodies reproduce its
seven colors and its curve? Or is there any necessary relation between the form
of church organization and the ideal of the kingdom? Do the churches need
the kingdom in determining their polities? We approach our subject by
analyzing the ideal of the kingdom into some of its constituent parts.

The first point to be noted is that the kingdom of God brings to us a
personal as distinguished from a positive religion. That is, it is not a set of
legal enactments put down in a book, like those of Mohammed in the Koran,
to be obeyed as external statutes. It is, on the contrary, a personal religion. It
teaches that a Person—God—took the initiative in salvation, and that a
person—man—responds to it. Primarily then, Christianity is a relation
between persons—God and man. The method of all legal religions is that of
the command and the prohibition. They say "Thou shalt," and "Thou shalt

not," with the result that human nature revolts, or else tends to obey mechanically rather than through love. "When the commandment came sin revived and I died," says Paul. Human nature is made much after the disposition of the old woman in the walled city who had never desired to go outside the walls until her friends urged her to remain inside until death that it might be told of her. Thenceforth she was irresistibly impelled to go outside and at length did so. A religion which commands awakens revolt, if there are only commands. Christianity as a personal religion begins with faith. Its method of growth is fellowship with God, entering into his plans, grasping his aims.

The Emphasis on Personality and Love

A second point is that this religion of the kingdom and of personal relationships very naturally puts much emphasis upon the divine personality and love, or the Fatherhood of God. The idea of the kingdom teaches that the realm of salvation is an ordered sphere—that in it laws prevail. The idea of Fatherhood shows that the realm of salvation is more than mere law; that it is the sphere of the highest, deepest, and tenderest of known relationships—that between father and son. Those in the kingdom call God Father, and those who call God Father are swayed and molded by the laws which are of the essence of the kingdom. These two conceptions, therefore, are not contradictory but supplementary. Each is an exhaustive statement of the contents of Christ's religion in its own way and from its own point of view; one from the point of view of constituted order, the other from the point of view of personal relationships.[1]

The next note which distinguishes the kingdom is the principle of revelation. Revelation is the method and guarantee of intercourse between the persons who enter into the religious relationships, God and man. Revelation implies the kinship between God and man, that God can communicate and man may receive messages. Revelation implies human capacity for God.[2]

The fourth distinctive thing in this religion of the kingdom is that Christ himself is the medium of revelation and redemption. He brings God near. God comes to us in and through Christ; we approach God in and through him. He is the revelation of God to us. The soul cannot thrive on abstract

---

[1] Mullins cites Matt. 10:20; 6:5–15; 10:7–8; and John 3:3, 16.
[2] Mullins cites Matt. 11:25–27; and I Cor. 2:6–16.

E. Y. Mullins

notions about God, just as a bird cannot fly in a vacuum, or a tree root itself in a bank of mist, or as a vine cannot climb a moonbeam. Christ made the idea of God concrete. Christ is God's message to man. It is at this point that the authoritativeness and regulative value of the Scriptures come into view. The Scriptures alone enable us to maintain contact with the Christ of history. His image grows dim, his authority over the soul inevitably wanes when detached from the historic records. So far are the Scriptures from hindering the free intercourse of the soul with Christ, as some allege, that we may assert on the contrary their indispensableness to that free intercourse. These records are the sheet anchor of Christian experience and of Christian theology.

Now the above fundamental qualities and attributes of Christ's religion determine by necessity and beforehand its methods and the laws of its practical development in the world and the forms it will assume.

The Practical Unfolding of Ideals

Observe then the stages in the practical unfolding of these ideals. As personal it will be the intercourse of persons, one person speaking to another. As an ordered kingdom it will require exposition of its laws. As fatherhood and sonship it will involve an attitude of filial obedience on the part of man. As revelation it will require intelligence and a responsive moral nature.

What then will be the initial stage in its development on earth? It will take the form of a word of God—a gospel. The first gospel was the incarnate Word of God, and afterward the "good news" of salvation to which the incarnation gave rise. Observe that it is the word which is the fivefold symbol of all the marks of the kingdom outlined above. The word is the symbol and means of intercourse between persons. It is the symbol for the constitution of an ordered kingdom among intelligent beings. Laws cannot be enacted without words. Through words fatherhood reveals itself and by them develops and unfolds sonship. It is the only fitting symbol and means of a revelation of truth from above. It is taken by the Evangelist John as the descriptive name of Christ himself in his function as revealer of God. "In the beginning was the Word."

This prominence of a gospel, or a word of God, will emphasize the importance of prophecy and preaching, of evangelism and teaching, in the progress of the kingdom. For these all find the reason of their existence in the idea of the word. Thus the word becomes personalized in the human agent of

51

redemption. This is the way of the kingdom. In Gilbert Parker's novel *The Right of Way*, Charlie Steele the drunkard struggled in vain against his appetite until a human love and a human will came to his rescue reinforcing his own feeble will.[3] In *Les Miserables* Victor Hugo exhibits a like insight into the divine method. The criminal who stole the candlesticks from the bishop was apprehended and made to face the owner, but was released upon the assertion of the good bishop that the candlesticks were the rightful property of the thief. You no longer belong to yourself, was the bishop's declaration, but to God. Afterward the thief passed through a tragic struggle, alone with God, which led to his spiritual regeneration. But in that struggle the bishop's forgiving face was omnipresent in the guilty man's imagination and conscience, and had for him almost the value of God.[4] Thus in the kingdom of God the human mediator does not come through sacraments and exclusive religious privileges between the soul and its God, but enters by the truth and love into the life to redeem it. Thus man again incarnates the word, and becomes a sort of burning bush of divine manifestation to save, and not a priestly and exclusive manipulator of sacraments.

Man's Response to the Word

What, then, will be the answer on man's part to this proclamation and incarnation of the word? The answer is faith. Not faith in the sense of blind acceptance of hidden mysteries; not implicit faith in the sense of acceptance of the total body of teachings of an infallible church, but faith in the biblical sense of an intelligent response to the revelation of truth from person to person. This faith arouses the entire being, the intellect, the emotions, the will, and the moral nature. The intellect grasps truth, the emotions are drawn out by trust and affection, the will yields to the commanding will of another, and the moral nature by an intuition of right and wrong puts the stamp of its approval upon the soul's act. Christ is the object of the soul's trust, and he thus inducts it into the kingdom, and reveals to it God's fatherhood.

Observe now that the first and immediate result or attendant circumstance of the act of faith is regeneration and redemption. The immanent

---

[3] Canadian novelist Gilbert Parker (1862–1932) published *The Right of Way* in 1901.

[4] French author Victor Hugo (1802–1885) wrote *Les Miserables* (1862), one of the best-known novels of the nineteenth century.

Spirit of God employs the word of truth as instrument, and the soul, fully aroused in all its parts, is brought forth into a new life—is constituted spiritually a son of God, and translated into the ordered spiritual realm of God's kingdom.[5]

As this spiritual life begins in a believer so it continues. "As ye received Christ Jesus the Lord so walk in Him" [Col. 2:6], is Paul's injunction. Faith is not only the initial act of the soul in response to the word it is also generic and representative of the soul's permanent attitude. All the after-life of the believer is a projection or continuation of the first act of faith. The open mind and cognition of truth, the obedient will trusting Christ, the moral intuition of the excellence of the Christian way—that is, all those elements of the first act of faith are implicit in all the believer's relations to God in the life which follows. Thus by repetition of the initial act of faith we work out our salvation. It is like making a dotted line on a piece of paper with a pencil. First the dots are wide apart. Then we fill in the blank spaces by greater fidelity to duty, and at length we make the line black and continuous. In other words, faith is no longer an interrupted and occasional but the permanent attitude of the soul.

Growth in grace is a progressive apprehension of the grace which came when the soul was regenerated. Salvation and sanctification move forward in parallel lines with faith until both are consummated in the salvation to be revealed at the last time. Faith then at the beginning, in the midst, at the end of the Christian life is the characteristic Christian attitude. It is the response of the entire spiritual nature of man aroused in all its parts to the approach of God the Father, through the revealing Christ, constituting men members of his kingdom through his word. The above set of forces and ideals operating in the manner indicated is the kingdom of God on earth. This is the kingdom everywhere proclaimed by Christ.

Spiritual Affinity Leads to Church Organization

Now the individuals who thus respond to God by faith and who are regenerated by his grace are inevitably drawn together by spiritual affinity into fellowship with each other through Christ, the revealer of God the Father. And in this way the church arises. It comes into being in a sense just as a diamond mine comes into existence. Diamonds are usually found, not scattered broadcast over continents, but collected at certain points. This is be-

---

[5] Mullins cites Mark 1:15; John 3:3; and Rom. 5:1.

cause the heat and pressure necessary to produce them were felt at these particular points. Each diamond was born, so to speak, of an experience common to all the rest. What shape it bore in its previous state of existence matters nothing. By some wondrous act of change nature transformed it. Thus by a common experience of God's regenerating grace the church arises.[6] It is the social expression of the spiritual experiences common to a number of individuals. The basis of their associations together is the common sense of need due to sin—a common experience of forgiveness and regeneration through the common exercise of faith. The same divine heat and pressure acted upon them all. Identity of need, identity of grace to meet it, identity of privilege in their direct fellowship with God, and identity of obligation to make known to others the good news of God's grace—these constitute the inner side of the church's justification of her existence. Christ's command and action in bringing the church into existence is the external authority which constitutes the ultimate ground of its life and being.

The relations of the church to the kingdom are now apparent. The kingdom precedes the church in the order of time. But the laws and ideals of the kingdom give form to the church. The kingdom and the visible church are not identical. But the kingdom imposes upon the church its constitution and prescribes its laws and determines the nature of its ordinances and organization. It has been said that the contour of every leaf bears a certain resemblance to the contour of the tree from which it is taken. This may or may not be true. It does contain a possible analogy for spiritual truth. The local church is like a leaf on the tree of the kingdom of God. As such it must reproduce in its own measure the outlines of the kingdom. The motion and the forces which produced the solar system operated in a uniform manner. The heavenly bodies all became spheres. The planets are smaller than the sun, but like the sun, their source and center, they are spheres. The church may be described as the institutional embodiment of the principles and ideals of the kingdom for practical purposes. The church is a divine contrivance for realizing the ends of the kingdom of God. It becomes evident thus that we may not estimate the church apart from the kingdom. We can only find the criteria for judging the church by carefully analyzing the essential principles revealed in Scripture as constitutive of the kingdom of God.

---

[6] Mullins cites Acts 2:47.

A False Assumption

It is often assumed in discussions of the church that these relations to the kingdom are non-existent, as if church organization and polity were purely matters of expediency or of historical development. On the contrary, as the church is the institutional embodiment of the principles of the kingdom of God, and the only adequate embodiment, it is altogether possible that a question of polity may under certain conditions involve the very life of Christianity itself. If any one doubts the vital bearing of the institutional side of Christianity upon human welfare and ordered progress let him turn his eyes to those countries where Roman Catholicism has sway, and let him observe the stagnation and blight which have fallen upon those peoples. There are ecclesiastical polities which quench the spirit of Christianity. A living faith is at once suffocated when it seeks freedom for expansion under them. It will always be found, moreover, that this repressive tendency of the polity is in direct ratio to its divergence from the principles and ideals of the kingdom of God.

Spiritual Laws of the Kingdom

Keeping in mind, now, the foregoing outline of the fundamental principles of the kingdom of God and its relations to the church, we may gather up the New Testament teachings as to the kingdom in the form of a series of spiritual laws which must be respected in any and every ecclesiastical polity which can in any sense lay claim to biblical warrant. These laws, it will be observed, are inherent in the very essence and idea of the kingdom. They constitute the colors and reveal the curve of the rainbow of the divine kingdom.

The first is the law of Salvation: Faith in Christ the Son of God. This excludes meritorious works, the acceptance of a formal creed, or entrance merely into a visible church organization, or grace through humanly administered sacraments, as conditions of salvation. Any one of these substitutes for faith would destroy the religion as personal and bring it into the class of positive religions. Moreover either would dim if not destroy the sense of sonship and of Fatherhood, which would empty Christianity of its essential contents. The church which obscures this law is out of harmony with the kingdom.

The second is the law of Worship: freedom of intercourse between the Father in heaven and the child. This excludes of course the limiting of acceptable worship to particular places, or through human mediators, or by means of physical appliances. One of the most striking things in the teachings of Jesus was the absence of dependence upon such things. His religion is the foe to the idea of the holy place, the holy person, and the holy thing, in any such sense as would give these peculiar sacredness or as possessing an inherent sanctity or efficacy in communicating grace. "The hour cometh and now is when the true worshippers shall worship the Father in spirit and truth" [John 4:23–24].

The third is the law of Filial Service. This is of course the idea which answers to that of the Fatherhood of God. The church is the filial society. Its form of government, its ordinances, its rules and regulations, must be molded on this principle. Whenever a church interposes between the child and the Father, through sacrament, through human priesthood or hierarchy, through centralized government, through authoritative oligarchies of any kind in spiritual affairs, it ceases to conform to the kingdom of God, and becomes a juvenile court or orphanage instead. Christ founded an institution to bear the name of church with no such marks.

The fourth is the law of Liberty. As the kingdom comes always in the first instance to the individual and can only so come; as fatherhood and sonship are relations expressive of individual and not of corporate experiences; and as there is in every regenerated life an element of privacy; as personality indeed is in every case an inner circle where outside feet may not enter, so the life of the kingdom must forever be a life of free service "under the eye and in the strength of God."[7] This autonomy of the believer's life is inherent in the very idea of grace, which means that God comes into the soul to raise it into a state of moral power, and transform it into his own image. To deny the liberty and autonomy of the soul under God is to impugn grace itself.

The fifth is the law of Interdependence and Brotherhood. The free soul is not an isolated soul. Other free souls enter in manifold ways into its life. But these all are regulated and ruled by the same grace of God the Father in Christ by which these associated souls may influence each other. The common Lordship of Christ over all and the sufficiency of grace toward all are the two

---

[7] Adolf Harnack, *What is Christianity?* (New York: Putnam's Sons, 1903) 8.

facts which forever exclude lordship of the one over the other. Their relations to each other are those of brothers, and not of masters and servants. Every ecclesiastical polity must recognize this fact.[8]

The sixth is the law of Edification. This requires that Christian growth and nurture be conducted on lines consonant with the essential principles of the kingdom. As the word is the instrument of the Spirit in the regenerating act wherein faith is the human response to God, so also in the sanctifying process. Truth apprehended and obeyed is the way of God's kingdom in making men holy. "Sanctify them through thy truth, thy word is truth" [John 17:17], was the prayer of Jesus. To make of ordinances sacraments possessing spiritual efficacy in themselves is to change the nature of faith and to degrade the entire process of sanctification. The *opus operatum* of the Roman Catholic Church involves a theory of the ordinances which is subversive of the spirituality of the kingdom.[9] Ordinances as symbols of truth assist faith and explicate the ideals of the kingdom. Ordinances as sacraments obscure both. Baptism and the Lord's Supper as symbols of truth with the explicit sanction of Christ for perpetual observance, taking their places in the kingdom of truth along with other things and operating upon intelligence and faith after the manner of the word, are one thing; but transformed into channels of grace limiting and restricting God's love in any degree to the human mediators who administer them, they are a reversion to a lower type of religion. The ordinances are vocal with truth, not magical with occult power.

The seventh is the law of Holiness. This implies that all the means adopted in the church must be adjusted to the ends of personal and social righteousness. Nothing is more terrible in Christ's teachings than his arraignment of merely ceremonial righteousness and empty orthodoxy.

Church Order Not Subject to Ordinary Laws of Expediency

All these principles will receive further statement under other forms in later chapters. They are set forth as the ground work for what shall follow. The chief point at present is to show that ecclesiastical organization and life are not to be conceived as subject merely to ordinary laws of expediency. Nor are they to be regarded solely as so many attempted interpretations of a particular set of

[8] Mullins cites I Cor. 12:12–31; II Cor. 11:7–11; and Eph. 4:16.
[9] According to the Council of Trent (1545–1563) the efficacy of a sacrament is dependent upon Christ rather than the merit of the minister or the recipient.

proof texts in the New Testament. They are rather under the sway of a group of universal and fundamental principles which inhere in the very essence of the kingdom of God itself. J. H. Newman in his work *Development of Christian Doctrine* sought to show that the Roman Catholic is the only existing modern representative of the New Testament church.[10] He seeks to establish this by his theory of ecclesiastical development from New Testament Christianity with its seven tests, viz.: "preservation of the idea," "continuity of principles," "power of assimilation," "early anticipation," "logical sequence," "preservative additions," and "chronic sequence."

I have no intention of discussing this theory at length but simply ask the reader's careful attention to the preceding exposition of the essential nature of the kingdom and the laws thereof as criteria for estimating the claims of any church. It will then be perfectly apparent that Newman's application of his own theory to the Roman Catholic Church breaks down at many points. Romanism certainly fails to preserve the New Testament "idea" in the law of Salvation and of Edification as well as in other respects. It can in no just meaning of the words be said to exhibit a "continuity of principles" from the New Testament times. It is indeed at most points a system totally at variance with the New Testament ideals of religion.

In closing this chapter we recur once more to our figure of the rainbow, by way of gathering up our conclusions. The kingdom of God is the rainbow of human hope formed by the sunlight of divine revelation in Jesus Christ. Its colors represent the primary elements of truth which that revelation brings. Church organizations have it in their power to reproduce or obscure those colors. Sacramentalism dims the great truth of God's direct dealing with the soul of man. Episcopacies and hierarchies obscure the truth that all souls are free and individually responsible to God. In succeeding chapters we shall seek to make these statements good and to elaborate many other aspects of our subject.

---

[10] Mullins cites John Henry Newman, *An Essay on the Development of Christian Doctrine* (London: James Toovey, 1845; New York: Longmans, Green, and Co., 1903) 62–64.

3

The Historical Significance of the Baptists

Baptists have a noble history. It is fitting to ask the question: What is their historical significance? What is their distinctive contribution to the religious life and thought of mankind? In this chapter an answer is given to these questions somewhat different in form from that ordinarily heard. It is different, however, not in the sense that it is contradictory to answers previously given, but rather that it seeks to sum them up in a single principle.

Baptists certainly have a consistent record. In their advocacy of soul freedom in its completest measure, and of the principle of the separation of Church and State, in their insistence upon believer's baptism and a regenerate church membership, there is not a fleck or stain upon the fair page of their history.

Baptists in Rhode Island and Virginia

As to the doctrine of soul liberty and separation of Church and State they have so far outstripped all other religious bodies in modern times that without doubt the impartial historian in the future as in the past will accord to them the palm of leadership. In their first Confessions of Faith in England in the seventeenth century this principle was clearly and distinctly avowed. In Rhode Island under Roger Williams they planted the seed in American soil long before the other colonies were prepared for it. In Virginia there occurred about a hundred years after the founding of Rhode Island the most typical and interesting struggle for religious liberty which the world has ever seen. The interest of this Virginia struggle warrants our dwelling upon it a moment here.

I have said it was typical. That is, the successive stages of the conflict appear. The ground was won inch by inch. Imprisonment and persecution in other forms had but one effect upon the zeal of the fathers; it fanned it into an intenser flame. In Rhode Island there are but two stages, the banishment of Roger Williams from Massachusetts, and at length the new charter and the beginning of the new era in the world's spiritual career. In Virginia on the contrary the darkness was driven back more gradually. There was the contest over the question of freedom of worship, over the general assessment, and the glebes. At length after many hardships and struggles Virginia Baptists conquered and the established church was overthrown.

Virginia Baptists were alone in this struggle so far as other religious bodies were concerned. There were indeed great statesmen who championed their cause who were not Baptists. Madison and Jefferson and George Washington were enlightened men on this great theme as on others, men with new "spiritual empires" in their brains. But without the ceaseless agitation, the continuous stream of petitions and protests, which poured into the halls of legislation from the Baptists, no statesman could have stemmed the tide in favor of perpetuating religious privilege through an established church. In those days our Methodist brethren were not yet free from alliance with the established church and hence could not enter the lists in the cause of complete separation of Church and State, and as a matter of fact were not found there. The Presbyterians at certain stages of the conflict rendered fine service and made some notable deliverances, but their record is an inconsistent one. At times also they were on the side of legalized ecclesiastical privilege. The Episcopal Church, of course, held the reins of power and tightened its grip as danger of disestablishment loomed on the horizon. They were in those days particularly hostile to the Baptists. Happily we have fallen upon better times and there is a growth of the spirit of brotherhood and cooperation among the various religious bodies. But Baptists would be untrue to themselves and to the cause of truth if they failed to recount for the generations of the present and the future the brilliant achievements of their Rhode Island and Virginia fathers, achievements which, as the world now admits, had enfolded within them the most precious spiritual hopes and treasures of all mankind.

Soul Freedom Always Held by the Baptists

There is no evidence that Baptists came to their view of soul freedom and separation of Church and State gradually. There is nowhere a wavering note on this great theme. It seems to have been a divinely given prophetic insight into the meaning of the gospel and the implicit teaching of Scripture. Mark the phrase, implicit teaching. For Scripture nowhere enjoins in so many words separation of Church and State. It required spiritual discernment to discover the doctrine, prophetic insight of a high order, and yet when once discovered by the unbiased mind it was accepted as a self-evident truth.

We need only to consider the historic background in order to estimate at its true value this great insight. After Constantine until Pope Gregory VII there had been a struggle for supremacy between Church and State. In Gregory the spirit of the Roman Church became incarnate and conquered. He made the Emperor Henry do penance by standing in the snow with bare feet at Canossa, and he wrote his memorable letter to William the Conqueror to the effect that the State was subordinate to the Church, that the power of the State as compared with that of the Church was as the moon compared with the sun. For many generations the figure of Gregory filled the imagination of Europe, and even today he is a potent force there.[1] Neither Luther nor Calvin hesitated to resort to the arm of civil power when they deemed it necessary to enforce religion. The great Reformers did not rise to the conception of separation of Church and State. In those days it was left to the persecuted Anabaptists to make this prophetic deliverance. But they were hounded to death, and in Europe seemed almost to disappear from the face of the earth.

In England even today our Baptist and Nonconformist brethren are battling for religious equality; and so recent and able a statesman as Gladstone wrote a book to prove that the propagation of religion is a function of the State.[2]

Religious Toleration Not Liberty

In the American colonies apart from Rhode Island and Virginia, where Baptists led the way, the nearest approach to the true ideal was one form or another of religious toleration. The story is a familiar one and need not be recited again here. Suffice it to say that in no American colony save in the two mentioned was there even an effort made to establish religious liberty in the true sense. In the founding of Maryland the Calverts secured a charter from England which granted a certain measure of toleration. This, to these Roman Catholics, seemed indeed a great stride forward. In comparison with their usual insistence upon an ironclad church authority and their exclusive claim to apostolicity, it was a real step in advance. But the Baptists stood for a more

---

[1] Pope Gregory VII (1020–1085) was pope from 1073 to 1085.
[2] William Gladstone (1809–1898) was a prime minister of the United Kingdom and author of *The State in Relations with the Church* (1838).

thoroughgoing principle than Romanist or Protestant in their doctrine of complete separation of Church and State. Everything is relative. A snail complained of a tortoise: "You travel too fast for me!" A clod nearby said to the snail: "You go so fast you make me dizzy!" While this colloquy was going on an eagle swept past overhead; but his proximity and flight never dawned upon clod, tortoise, or snail. Toleration and religious liberty are the poles apart.

Common as was religious oppression in those days even the Declaration of Independence fails to mention it as a thing to be cast off along with other forms of tyranny therein enumerated. It was as Madison, Adams, and others said, the conception of a free Church in a free State was foreign to the general philosophy and social theories of the age. Men imagined that to adopt the principle would be to open the floodgates to infidelity in a thousand forms. It was not until after the promulgation of the federal constitution that Congress was awakened to the danger of perpetuating the un-American theory of the union of Church and State. The Baptists of Virginia again took the lead. They sent their well-known memorial to George Washington, then president of the United States, and from him received assurance that the liberties of the people in religious matters would be protected. Soon afterward the first amendment to the Constitution was enacted, forever forbidding religious tests or special privileges in the United States.

The Historical Significance of the Baptists

But it is time we take up the answer to the question: What is the historic significance of the Baptists? What great principle have they contributed to the religious thought and life of mankind? Or to state the question in a slightly different form: What interpretation of Christianity do they represent, which distinguishes them from all other Christian bodies?

In replying to these questions we shall find that there are a number of great elementary truths, of the nature of axioms, which lie at the heart of the Baptist conception of Christianity. It is the aim of this book to show that these universal and self-evident truths are simply the expression of the universal elements in Christianity and thus serve as the best statement of what the religion of Christ is in its essential nature.

What then is the distinguishing Baptist principle? Is it separation of Church and State? Or is it the doctrine of soul freedom, the right of private judgment in religious matters and in the interpretation of the Scriptures?

Assuredly these are distinctive Baptist principles, which have been held by no religious denomination so consistently. And yet they are scarcely an adequate statement by themselves. Separation of Church and State may be an accomplished fact and yet Roman Catholicism remains as the form of Christianity which survives. This of course means the survival of spiritual tyranny in the church, although the church itself be untrammeled by the civil power. Soul freedom too is but a partial statement. Freedom alone is not the end but the means. Self-realization through Christ is the end. Until freedom is thus directed toward its end it remains negative in meaning, it simply points to the broken fetters, from which it has escaped. Freedom by itself does not imply capacity for self-government, and any adequate statement of the New Testament teaching must include this.

Again, can we claim that individualism is the peculiar teaching of the Baptists? Here again we touch upon a great truth which Baptists have insisted upon in a manner more thoroughgoing than any others. But individualism alone is inadequate because man is more than an individual. He is a social being. He has relations to his fellows in the Church, and in the industrial order, and in the State. We must comprehend these relations in our fundamental view.

Justification by faith was a central principle in Luther's teaching, and has become a part of the common Christian heritage of the succeeding centuries. Baptists here share with others the possession of a great truth. This cannot therefore be regarded as a doctrine peculiar to the Baptists.

Obedience to Christ's will as revealed in the Scriptures has been urged as the all inclusive Baptist principle. Dr. W. C. Wilkinson's admirable work on *The Baptist Principle* sets forth this conception in its fullness.[3] There is a great truth here. Baptists rightly insist on obedience at all points. There are portions of Scripture which others have ignored or set aside. And yet it may be questioned whether the principle of obedience is quite sufficiently comprehensive to cover the case fully. Historically, at least, there are aspects of the Baptist position which come into view more clearly under another conception as we shall see. As a force in history they have borne a

---

[3] William C. Wilkinson, *The Baptist Principle in its Application to Baptism and the Lord's Supper* (Philadelphia: American Baptist Publication Society, 1881). See chapter 1, "The Principle Defined," pp. 23–29. Wilkinson (1833–1920) was an American Baptist and a founding faculty member of the University of Chicago.

distinguishing mark which will become evident enough when duly considered. All evangelical denominations claim to obey, and in theory adopt the principle of obedience, however much they may depart from it as regards infant baptism and immersion as the sole New Testament baptism. The Roman Catholics, however, deny entirely the believer's right or capacity to interpret and obey the Scriptures for himself. He maintains that the principle of individual initiative here leads to ecclesiastical anarchy. Another aspect of obedience is that it may be stated in a form which ignores the necessity for intelligence. Obedience may be blind, or fanatical, and thus far from the New Testament ideal. The idea of obedience, therefore, would seem to require some qualification in order to answer all the ends of a comprehensive definition.

What shall be said of regeneration? Is the doctrine of regenerated church membership the sufficient statement of the Baptist view? It is a view peculiar to Baptists, and far reaching in its significance. And yet it is conceivable that the doctrine of a regenerated church membership might co-exist alongside of a priestly or an episcopal system of church government. The fundamental statement should be at the same time duly inclusive and exclusive, and regeneration alone comes short.

Democracy and the priesthood of all believers, again, have been urged as the fundamental Baptist view. Unquestionably they are of vital importance and grow directly out of our fundamental position. But they are corollaries to a prior truth. They are not original but derived.

The sufficient statement of the historical significance of the Baptists is this: The competency of the soul in religion. Of this means a competency under God, not a competency in the sense of human self-sufficiency. There is no reference here to the question of sin and human ability in the moral and theological sense, nor in the sense of independence of the Scriptures. I am not here stating the Baptist creed. On many vital matters of doctrine, such as the atonement, the person of Christ, and others, Baptists are in substantial agreement with the evangelical world in general. It is the historical significance of the Baptists I am stating, not a Baptist creed.

This conception of the competency of the soul under God in religion is both exclusive and inclusive in a measure which sets forth the distinctive contribution of Baptists to the religious thought of the race. It is of course a New Testament principle and carries at its heart the very essence of that conception of man's relations to God which we find in the teaching of Christ.

Observe then that the idea of the competency of the soul in religion excludes at once all human interference, such as episcopacy and infant baptism, and every form of religion by proxy. Religion is a personal matter between the soul and God. The principle is at the same time inclusive of all the particulars which were named above and more. It must include the doctrine of separation of Church and State because State churches stand on the assumption that civil government is necessary as a factor in man's life in order to a fulfillment of his religious destiny; that man without the aid of the State is incompetent in religion. Justification by faith is also included because this doctrine is simply one detail in the soul's general religious heritage from Christ. Justification asserts man's competency to deal directly with God in the initial act of the Christian life. Regeneration is also implied in the principle of the soul's competency because it is the blessing which follows close upon the heels of justification or occurs at the same time with it, as a result of the soul's direct dealing with God. The necessity for a regenerated church membership follows of necessity from the doctrine of the regenerated individual life. The doctrine of the soul's competency, however, goes further than individualism in that it embraces capacity for action in social relations as well as on the part of the individual. The church is a group of individuals sustaining to each other important relations, and organized for a great end and mission. The idea of the soul's competency embraces the social as well as the individual aspect of religion.

Let it be noted further that the steps we have already traced lead directly to democracy in church life and the priesthood of all believers. The competency of the regenerated individual implies that at bottom his competency is derived from the indwelling Christ. Man's capacity for self-government in religion is nothing more than the authority of Christ exerted in and through the inner life of believers, with the understanding always, of course, that he regulates that inner life in accordance with his revealed word. There is no conceivable justification, therefore, for lodging ecclesiastical authority in the hands of an infallible pope or a bench of bishops. Democracy in church government is an inevitable corollary of the general doctrine of the soul's competency in religion. The independence and autonomy of the local church, therefore, is not merely an inference from a verse of Scripture here and there. It inheres in the whole philosophy of Christianity. Democracy in church government is simply Christ himself animating his own body through his Spirit. The decisions of the local congregation on ecclesiastical matters are the "consensus of the competent."

The priesthood of all believers, again, is but the expression of the soul's competency on the Godward, as democracy is its expression on the ecclesiastical side of its religious life. No human priest may claim to be mediator between the soul and God because no possible reason can be assigned for any competency on his part not common to all believers.

The principle of obedience also takes its place as a very important particular under the general conception of the soul's competency. The principle of competency itself meets the Roman Catholic plea against direct individual obedience to the Scriptures on the ground of the man's incapacity to interpret Scripture for himself. The right of private judgment as to the meaning of the Bible is of course another aspect of the same great truth.

General Summary

The reader will observe that what we are maintaining is that the doctrine of the soul's competency in religion under God is the *historical* significance of the Baptists. We may restate the Baptist position in the various relations as follows: The biblical significance of the Baptists is the right of private interpretation and obedience to the Scriptures. The significance of the Baptists in relation to the individual is soul freedom. The ecclesiastical significance of the Baptists is a regenerated church membership and the equality and priesthood of believers. The political significance of the Baptists is the separation of Church and State. But as comprehending all the above particulars, as a great and aggressive force in Christian history, as distinguished from all others and standing entirely alone, the doctrine of the soul's competency in religion under God is the distinctive historical significance of the Baptists.

It thus appears that the doctrine of the soul's competency in religion is a comprehensive truth. It unites and concentrates in itself indeed three great streams of tendency in modern times. The first is the intellectual principle of the Renaissance, man's capacity and right in the exercise of mental freedom. The second is the Anglo-Saxon principle of individualism which has been so potent a political force in modern times. The third is the Reformation principle, justification by faith. Baptists, however, have changed all these tendencies and modified them by elevating them into nobler forms and made them more fruitful. In their insistence upon man's competency in religion they have saved intellectual freedom from all forms of human repression and at the same time safeguarded it by relating it to man's true goal, the Intelligence behind the visible universe. Human intellect illumined by the Divine intellect is the Baptist view. In their advocacy of individualism they have saved the Anglo-Saxon principle from the ruthlessly selfish tendency by defining it as a moral and religious impulse under the direct tutelage of the moral leader of mankind—Jesus Christ. Moreover, they have carried the Reformation principle of justification by faith far beyond the dreams of Luther and the other reformers. All that is implicit in the justification principle they have advocated. The long struggle for religious liberty and separation of Church and State which Baptists have led, has been the unfolding consistently of a greater ideal than that cherished by Luther, which has gathered up into a larger unity all the moral and spiritual treasures of the Reformation itself.

Now this principle of the competency of the soul under God in religion, like all other radical views of man or nature has its underlying philosophy. For the present we may indicate that philosophy by asserting that the principle of competency assumes that man is made in God's image, and God is a person able to reveal himself to man, or Christian theism. Man has capacity for God, and God can communicate with man. This philosophy of course underlies the total Christian movement. The incarnation of God in Christ is the one great historic expression of it.

4

The Soul's Competency in Religion

It is in order now to point out how the claim in the preceding chapter may be made good. If the principle of the competency of the soul in religion under God is a distinctive Baptist contribution to the world's thought, a vital element in the Baptist message to the race, then it ought to appear to be such when compared with the points of view of various other Christian bodies. Under this process of comparison I think the candid reader will recognize without difficulty that this is a distinguishing mark of the Baptists. He will also perceive its simplicity, and indeed universality as an underlying assumption in New Testament Christianity, while at the same time he will discover in it a comprehensive criterion of judgment for classifying the various existing ecclesiastical bodies of Christendom.

Romanists and the Soul's Competency in Religion

First, then, compare the principle of the competency of the soul in religion with Roman Catholicism. It can be shown historically without the slightest difficulty that the formative principle of the Roman Catholic system is the direct antithesis to the doctrine of the soul's competency. Romanism, in other words, asserts at every point the soul's incompetency in religion. From beginning to end Romanism conceives of the human spirit as dependent in religion upon other human spirits. It regards the soul as incompetent to deal alone with God. This is not only the outward expression and practical result of the Roman hierarchical system; it is also the avowed theory of the church, proclaimed without hesitation. The laity are dependent upon the priesthood. Each lower order in the hierarchy is dependent upon the next above it, and all together are under the necessity of drawing instruction for the intellect and the rule for the moral and religious life from the infallible head of the church in Rome.

In every particular of the ecclesiastical and religious life of the Roman Catholic, the soul's incompetency is assumed. All the seven sacraments illustrate the statement in a striking way. The soul's capacity to deal with Christ and receive revelation at his hands is denied in baptism. For through baptism alone as administered by the authorized priesthood (save in certain emergencies) can the regenerating efficacy of Christianity reach the soul. Outside the church is no salvation. Christ and the soul alone are not equal to the redemptive task. The only competent hands are human and priestly. The same principle inheres in the administration of the Lord's Supper. Its power is nothing until the elements are changed by the priestly touch into the body and blood of Christ. Communion with Christ is thus taken out of the realm of spirit and transferred to the realm of matter, and the material elements necessary to the communion are held in the form of an ecclesiastical monopoly by a human priesthood. Auricular confession also assumes that in prayer man is incompetent to deal directly with God. A human priest must pronounce absolution. The penance also which the priest imposes raises a barrier between the broken heart and the forgiving Father in heaven, and asserts that his pardoning love instead of rolling in like a tide upon the penitent soul expands and contracts in accordance with the severity or leniency of an erring human mediator. Again, Christ cannot call a man into his ministry, and no man can respond to that call, outside the line of apostolic succession. The sacrament of orders limits Christ's ministry to an ecclesiastical chain which at no point must be broken, and at once pronounces the decree of condemnation upon all others, and asserts that the alleged direct call into the ministry from Christ himself is a delusion.

The sacrament of extreme unction, which is applied to the dying is another form of the Romanist assertion of the soul's incompetency. God's grace in the heart cannot fit a man for the exodus through death out of this life into the next. Not until the priest, with oil consecrated by the bishop, has anointed the dying in the figure of the cross, on eyes, ears, nostrils, mouth, the palms of the hands, and soles of the feet, is the soul prepared to make its exit. The soul is thus made competent for death only through priestly mediation. The fetters of this bondage to a mortal and human priesthood are not broken even when death has severed spirit from body; for even then the gates of purgatory fly open only through priestly intercession upon earth.

And finally the doctrine of papal infallibility combined with that of an authoritative tradition forbids all private or divergent interpretations of Scripture. To discover and proclaim an interpretation of the word of God which contravenes in any essential particular that which bears the stamp of traditional or papal approval, is for the Catholic to invoke upon his head the anathema of the church.

Thus from beginning to end and throughout its very fiber Romanism rears its ecclesiastical structure on the denial of the soul's competency in religion. There is not a leaf on this vast tree which is not ribbed and modeled in rigid obedience to its one constructive ideal, the soul's incapacity to attend to religion for itself. While not desiring in the slightest measure to abate the value or importance of the good Roman Catholicism has done in its benevolent and philanthropic work, one is compelled to say that in its ecclesiastical theory it is not only against the spirit of human development and progress, but it is inconsistent with the Christianity of Christ. If there is any one thing which stands out above others in crystal clearness in the New Testament it is Christ's doctrine of the soul's capacity, right, and privilege to approach God directly and transact with him in religion.

Protestantism Also Inconsistent

We look next at the Baptist principle of the competency of the soul in religion in its relation to Protestantism in general. We find here, of course, important modifications of the case as it stands with Roman Catholicism. But all the churches which adhere to infant baptism or episcopacy in any form come short of the New Testament principle in certain important respects. These bodies in fact represent a dualistic Christianity. They attempt to combine the Romish principle of incompetency with the antithetic principle of competency. In insisting upon the doctrine of justification by faith they recognize the principle of competency; but in retaining infant baptism or episcopacy they introduce the opposite view. Infant baptism takes away from the child its privilege of individual initiative in salvation and lodges in the hands of parents or sponsors the impossible task of performing an act of religious obedience for another. Such a view is as an axe laid to the root of obedience, and destroys its essential nature as such.

It thus appears that current Protestantism attempts to harmonize two principles which are essentially contradictory to each other. There are in other words two ways of being saved, and two ways of entering a Presbyterian or Episcopal church. One way is by personal obedience. The applicant for church membership who has not been baptized relates a Christian experience which of course involves justification by faith in Christ. He is received and baptized upon this profession of faith and thus obeys for himself. Another, who was baptized in infancy, also applies for church membership and is received on the strength of that baptism. In the one case the candidate obeyed for himself, in the other his sponsors obeyed for him. The two principles are fundamentally opposed. It is not surprising, therefore, that Pedobaptist churches have great difficulty in explaining the status of baptized infants in the church. Are they church members or not? New England Congregationalists struggled over the question for a long time in colonial days, and they have never attained a satisfactory solution of the problem as we shall see in a later chapter.

The same difficulties exist today in all Pedobaptist denominations. No intelligible view of the status of baptized infants in the church can possibly be set forth which does not contradict the doctrine of justification by faith and personal obedience which is also held by these same churches. The reason is that in the one case the competency of the soul in religion is affirmed—that is, in justification by faith and personal obedience; and in the other that competency is denied—that is, in infant baptism and sponsorial or parental obedience.

The New Testament principle of the soul's competency is violated also in all forms of church polity which retain episcopacy and any other form of ecclesiastical oligarchy. But as the principle of democracy in church government is to receive attention in later chapters, further discussion of this point is omitted here.

In concluding our remarks on the relation of the Baptist doctrine of the soul's competency in religion to Pedobaptist ideas, it is only necessary to remark that the latter adopt at one point and contradict at another a principle which reaches its fullness in the Baptist polity and general view of Christianity. The Baptists have consistently applied the principle at every point. Their aim is to restore original Christianity in its completeness to the human race.

The Soul's Competency and Modern Progress

We must consider next the relation of the doctrine of competency to modern life and progress. This also will be discussed in later portions of the book. Meantime a few words by way of general outline. Properly understood the doctrine of the soul's competency in religion is the summary of our progressive life and civilization. The religious principle is always the dominant force which gives its leading characteristics to any civilization. The competency of man in religion is the competency of man everywhere. Every significant movement of our day is one form or another of that high purpose of man to make his way back to God. Art is simply the assertion of man's inherent capacity for beauty, the claim that he is competent to trace out in time all the subtle lines of grace, all the varied hues and forms of a manifold and wonder-crowded universe. Art is simply the march of the beauty lover along the highways of a variegated creation, forward and upward until he stands face to face with Him who is the infinitely Beautiful.

Science is the corresponding quest for truth, the assertion that the soul was made for truth, its competency to find and its capacity for truth, its death-less struggle for truth until it stands in the presence of Him who is the Truth.

Agnosticism: A Belated Philosophy

Philosophy also simply asserts the competency of man in the realm of speculative thought. Christian theism is the only possible philosophy for the man who accepts our fundamental principle of the soul's competency. For it asserts God's ability to communicate a revelation to man and man's capacity to receive it and to communicate with God. Agnosticism, which denies the competency of the human intellect, is the Roman Catholicism of philosophy, and is a belated view of human ability in the intellectual sphere. Many who lean toward agnosticism in their theological attitude need to reexamine their foundations and discover its real intellectual and spiritual affinities.

Again, politics and government and the social institutions assume man's moral competency, his capacity for moral progress under God in a well-ordered society. Society is the bold assertion that under God's leadership eternal right will be attained in the human sphere. If you let the gold and the pearl stand for the highest moral values; if you let the walls of jasper and their twelve foundations stand for the reign of moral law; if you let the sunless yet resplendent heavens above stand for the light and glory of truth in its triumph in the human soul; and if you let the hallelujahs of the tearless and shadowless and triumphant multitude in white stand for a purified social order, then you have in the unmatched glory and beauty of the New Jerusalem which the prophet saw descending from heaven to earth, the fitting symbol of what is going on in the world all about us—man under God achieving for himself an ideal social order. The absence of the temple from the perfected city means that all life will become a temple, all its manifestations an act of worship. The absence of the sun means that all light and all truth are now ours through the indwelling God. The absence of labor from the city means that now achievement is spontaneous. Culture, religion, morality, are all blended into a perfect harmony of achieving and progressing humanity.

The Fountain of Discontent

It is man's deathless conviction of his competency to achieve this goal that opens in his bosom the fountain of eternal discontent. A symbol of his progress toward his goal is a sculptor carving out of the marble his vision, rejoicing in it for a time, and then destroying it or setting it aside and beginning his work on another block and making a better statue; forever achieving and yet forever repudiating his achievement until he achieves the image of God in himself through God's grace. All this and more is implicit in our view of the competency of the soul in religion. America is the arena which God has supplied for the free and full play of the principle, and from here it is destined to spread until it covers the earth.

It will be observed that man's competency as thus outlined is a competency under God. In religion the counterpart of this truth is God's revelation in Christ, the divine competency, so to speak, to approach man on the basis of his divinely constituted human nature, and in keeping with his mental and moral faculties. All the history of religion shows that without the divine initiative, without revelation, without grace, man failed to find God. His competency, therefore, is not apart from God's approach to him but only in and through that approach. The Scriptures are the record of God's approach to man in Christ. These become to us the medium through which truth finds us, and without them Christ would inevitably pass into eclipse, and men would wander helpless, like a rudderless ship driven by tide and tempest. He would thus repeat the sad failures of the past, seen in all the superstitious, and ceremonial, and speculative attempts to find God.

5

The Axioms of Religion

Having examined the principles of the kingdom of God in their broad outlines, and having sought to discover the general significance of the Baptists in history, and having summed up that significance in the doctrine of the soul's competency in religion, we come next to examine in a more extended way the essential elements of the Baptist message to mankind. Hitherto in our Baptist literature there has been exhibited a vast amount of minute and careful exegesis of the New Testament passages which support our claims as to the form and meaning of baptism, the nature and significance of the Lord's Supper, and the constitution and order of the church, and related subjects. The exegetical basis for our plea has been wrought with such success, indeed, that we may assert with the utmost confidence that the scholarship of the world, taken as a whole, stands with us in our conclusions.

We have reached a point in our history, however, at which it is fitting that our message and our mission be interpreted anew. This is not because the older plea has lost its force or that it will cease to be necessary in the future, but rather because we have come to a period of Christian thought in which another kind of plea will appeal to many minds with far greater force than the old, and because the inner logic of our Baptist principles demands unfolding into their larger implications.

Baptists Often Misunderstood

Another thing: Baptists are, even yet, quite too generally misunderstood. For example, one charges: "The Baptists invert the pyramid of Christianity and try to make it stand on its apex instead of its base, by holding as their chief interest the question of whether there is much or little water in baptism." A Baptist smiles at this misconstruction of our views, but it is quite prevalent. Another says: "Baptists evince a lack of the sense of proportion in their exaggerated emphasis of their doctrine of communion." This of course is also erroneous, a misconception of us and our real position.

A recent speaker has said that in our claim that the New Testament teaches the congregational polity we have relied in our exegesis on a very few questionable passages; that we have taken a very small bit of exegetical dough, so to speak, and, with our controversial roller, we have flattened it out so thin that it is scarcely strong enough to form the crust of our denominational pie! So that we are, according to these various objectors, deficient in religious architecture, spiritual art, and theological cookery. All of which are serious charges.

Now let me say at once that the Baptists have won their contention on the following points: Baptism by immersion, believers' baptism, and congregational polity. The scholarship of the world is practically a unit in the view that the New Testament teaches just what the Baptists hold on these points. Our plea falls sometimes on unresponsive ears because men have lost interest in the baptismal and communion question in some communities.

Now it may be questioned whether the Baptists have ever set forth all the contents of their message to the world. At the bottom of our Pandora's box there may lie neglected greater things than those which have been taken out. The pressure of controversy has kept two or three things to the front to the exclusion of greater things.

A Fresh Analysis Needed

What, then, do we need? We need a transfer of emphasis. We need a fresh analysis of our fundamental principles. We need to reverse the shield of our denominational beliefs and see what is on the other side, and then we need to proclaim what we find there with the same earnestness and zeal which have marked our conduct in the past. This does not mean of course that we are to abandon the old positions, or cease our plea for baptism and church order, but only that we must enlarge our message and make it complete.

I propose, then, as a new defense of our Baptist position a restatement of our views from a higher standpoint, or to go back to the former figure, to look on the other side of our denominational shield. I will put my plea in the form of six brief propositions, and I will predict for them at the outset three things. First, that the reader will concede that they accord with the teachings of the New Testament. Secondly, that they will be so simple and self-evident that our

Methodist and Presbyterian and Episcopalian friends will all accept them. Indeed they are self-evident. They are the axioms of religion. The instructed religious consciousness cannot and will not repudiate them, however inconsistent men may be in applying them. The third thing that I predict is that you will recognize that these axioms of Christianity grow out of the mother principle for which Baptists have stood through the ages, as set forth, viz., the competency of the soul in religion under God. These six simple propositions are as six branches from that one trunk of New Testament teaching. Let us come, then, to the axioms. I will give them all first, and will follow the statement with remarks about them.

The Axioms of Religion

1. The theological axiom: The holy and loving God has a right to be sovereign.
2. The religious axiom: All souls have an equal right to direct access to God.
3. The ecclesiastical axiom: All believers have a right to equal privileges in the church.
4. The moral axiom: To be responsible man must be free.
5. The religio-civic axiom: A free Church in a free State.
6. The social axiom: Love your neighbor as yourself.

Now my claim is that these are axioms; they are to those who accept Christianity at all self-evident. Indeed, they will not be denied so far as they are general principles by any evangelical Christian or intelligent unbeliever. They are the very alphabet of the Christian religion. Understand me. They do not exhaust the specific beliefs as to the Scriptures, Christ, the church, the ordinances. They are not an exhaustive creed. They are rather the great New Testament assumptions, which are the very basis of our Baptist faith. What we wish the world to see is that our conception of the church and of Christianity rests upon an impregnable foundation.

I remark further that no religious organization so consistently embodies all these axiomatic principles in its life and doctrine as the Baptists.

In calling the above statements axioms the intelligent reader will understand that I do not employ the word in its strict mathematical sense. The truths set forth, however, are in the moral and religious sphere what axioms are in mathematics. That is to say, when the meaning of the various terms is clearly grasped there will be no protest or objection in the reader's mind. I make bold to say that in America no member of any of those churches known as "evangelical" will dissent from any of the principles enunciated in this list of six axioms. Indeed, it is believed that the great multitude of unbelievers—men who reject Christianity as held by the evangelical bodies, but who are theists, believers in a personal God to whom man is responsible, will also admit these axioms. I do not of course suppose that all Roman Catholics will yield assent to these propositions save in a most abstract and general way. Romanism forbids more. Such of them as grasp clearly the principles of Romanism will combat them just as they do the whole Protestant standpoint of the right of private judgment in religion. Romanism, against the whole modern view of man, assumes the incompetency of the soul in religion. Doubtless also those in European countries who are wedded to the theory of a union of Church and State will repudiate the religio-civic axiom. But the cases of the Romanist and of the man who favors a religious establishment may for the purpose of our discussion be treated as exceptional. On the other hand it may be asserted freely that the religious and intellectual growth of the great Protestant world since the Reformation has been such that, with the qualifications just made, the six axioms will meet with a hearty and favorable response.

A Basis of Agreement

It will doubtless come as a surprise to many to be told that on the basis of the universal assumptions of the gospel of the kingdom of God as revealed through Christ, Baptists can set forth their distinctive and fundamental positions in terms which are acceptable to all evangelical believers. The author rejoices that this is true for several reasons. He is glad that there are so many of the essential and fundamental things of the gospel on which there is at least theoretical agreement. These things ought to serve as a fresh starting point for the consideration of the whole subject of Christian union; and if they may in any measure serve this end I shall feel that a real service has been rendered. The sequel will show, however, that in the application and interpretation of these axioms of religion there is radical and wide divergence of view among the various Christian bodies. The chief task of the chapters which follow will be to show that Baptists have more consistently than any other evangelical body carried out these principles in their polity and life. It will appear, indeed, that the plea of Baptists is a plea for the religious rights of mankind. No body of people is farther in essential spirit and aim from a narrow sectarianism. Everything which they hold as distinguishing them from others is, so to speak, a plank in the platform of the chartered religious rights of mankind, as revealed in and through Jesus Christ. The six axioms, taken in connection with the fundamental general principle out of which they spring—the competency of the soul in religion under God—may be regarded as the platform of human rights in religion.

Axioms Embody Laws of the Kingdom

This last statement is justified by the fact that all the axiomatic truths announced are in complete harmony with the ideals of the kingdom of God as outlined in a previous chapter; indeed they are an interpretation in universal terms of the contents of the laws of the kingdom. The law of Salvation, the law of Worship, the law of Edification, the law of Liberty, the law of Brotherhood and Interdependence, the law of Filial Service, the law of Holiness, all these find interpretation and explication in the "Axioms of Religion." All this, I think, will become increasingly clear as we proceed. Meantime we submit our axioms as the "Principia," the first truths of the Christian religion, just as the laws of the uniformity of nature and of universal causation are among the first truths of science. They are to religion what the alphabet is to literature, what the law of affinity is to chemistry, and what the law of gravitation is to astronomy. The essential meaning of these truths in relation to our Baptist position and in relation to universal Christianity will appear as we study them from various standpoints in the chapters which follow. As "first truths" in the proper sense of the word, that is, as fundamental assumptions, they will appear to be harmonious with all other truths including the cardinal doctrines of the incarnation and atonement of Christ and related teachings.

In conclusion we remark that the conception of the competency of the soul in religion under God, along with the axioms of religion, express the truths and ideals which lie at the heart of all man's higher strivings today. These truths are so obvious when once understood, so inspiring, so self-evident, that the hungering spirit of man seizes upon them as upon the pearl of great price. They shine in their own light. Men can no more deny them than they can deny the beauty of an orchid, or gainsay the transparency of a crystal, or criticize the note of a nightingale, or deny the splendor of the milky way. They fall under God's blessing, like notes out of a seraph's song upon the ears of men. They catch and enrapture us and are destined to lead the race to greater heights than any yet attained.

6

The Theological Axiom:
The Holy and Loving God Has a
Right to Be Sovereign

In view of the fact that various meanings are often attached by different people to the same religious terms it is necessary to explain, as concisely as may be, the meaning and development of the axioms in their order. This we shall attempt in the next few chapters.

We begin with the theological axiom:

Character the Basis of Sovereignty

A holy and loving God has the right to be sovereign. Men have ever stumbled at the doctrine of God's sovereignty, chiefly because they have not understood it. They have thought it meant that God was merely a predestinating omnipotence, that he is capricious lightning, a meteor God, moving across the heavens of man's hope in a lawless manner, smiting one and saving another, without regard to moral law. They have thought of him as sovereign omnipotence or as sovereign omniscience instead of sovereign fatherhood, as he is. If he is holy and loving, if he has character, he has a right to be sovereign. We may say indeed that men find little or no difficulty in accepting the idea of the sovereignty of God so soon as they recognize character behind sovereignty. Indeed, as a matter of logic there is not standing room in the intellect of man for any theory which is opposed to the idea of God's sovereignty. Men have revolted at a sovereignty which seemed to them to be unfair in its choice of some to salvation to the exclusion of others. But that this objection was not directed against the idea of the sovereignty itself, but against the results of its operation in saving some men and not all, is seen in this, that the doctrine of the sovereignty has been made to do service in the interest of a universal salvation. Dr. George. A. Gordon in his book *The Christ of Today*, and elsewhere, expounds a doctrine of divine sovereignty which is avowedly drawn from the teachings of Jonathan Edwards.[1] But Edwards would, if he could behold Dr. Gordon's application of his doctrine, be far from accepting it. For it is in the latter's hands made to operate as the principle of a universal salvation. Thus we see that so soon as sovereignty takes the form of love, and particularly a love which saves all, men do not object to it, but rather hail it with delight. That is to say, character vindicates sovereignty.

There are two sides, however, to God's character. He is holiness as well as love. There are conditions also wrapped up in human freedom, the mark of moral character in man correlative to sovereignty in God, which affect the operation of God's sovereignty. Dr. Gordon ignores these in his argument to show that sovereign love must necessarily result in the salvation of all. Nevertheless it remains true that character is the vindication of sovereignty.

Nature and Man

We may approach the same truth from another side. Modern philosophy and science have emphasized in a remarkable manner the helplessness of man in the order of nature. He is an atom played upon by irresistible forces external to himself. The reign of law in nature and the inviolability of the natural order have greatly enhanced the plausibility of this view. Thus many hold to a most rigid form of determinism based on natural law. The idea of the freedom of the will is scouted. Man is the puppet and the sport of a sovereignty of material forces. He is a bit of matter, serving as a brick in the temple of nature, with other material bricks above and below him. From that perpendicular and rigid wall there is no escape.

Matthew Arnold improved slightly upon this idea when he described the mighty force outside of man which played continually upon him, as "the power not ourselves which makes for righteousness." The element of progress in Arnold's view is that it recognizes that the power not ourselves is moral. This is a step toward making it personal. For an impersonal power can scarcely

---

[1] George A. Gordon, *The Christ of Today* (Boston: Houghton Mifflin & Co., 1895). Gordon (1853–1929), a Congregationalist pastor in Boston (of the influential Old South Church), was a modernist theologian associated with liberalism at Harvard. Some scholars today deny that he was a Universalist because of his emphasis upon the freedom of the will which could resist God's love.

be regarded as "making for righteousness." Righteousness is an attribute of personality.[2]

The Mohammedan makes of God a personal being but leaves him immoral. "God is great" is the sum of the Mohammedan ideal of God. To the Moslem, therefore, God is a predestinating omnipotence merely.

It is seen at once what an immense stride forward is made in the idea of God when the conception of an external force urged by science and philosophy, plus the attribute of righteousness as advocated by Arnold, plus the omnipotent Person of Mohammedanism, has added to it the idea of holiness and love, and the idea of God becomes that of the holy and loving Person.

The process, however, is not yet completed. For this analysis of the idea of sovereignty into its constituent parts of holiness, love, and personality, finds strong corroboration in the experience of the spiritually mature. No demand of the mature Christian life is more imperious than the demand for a sovereignty in God which takes the form of holy and loving fatherhood. The mature Christian consciousness not only tolerates, it demands it. Life, in its blindness and helplessness, in its sorrow and its suffering, would be intolerable without the solace of the belief in holy and loving and sovereign fatherhood. The eye of faith discerns clearly that the only safe hands into which the affairs of the universe may be entrusted are those of God himself.

The Incarnation and Sovereignty

Now sovereignty expressed in terms of love and righteousness is the outstanding fact of the gospel. The incarnation of God in Christ is the greatest of all conceivable expressions of that sovereignty. It is the expression of a sovereignty of power, indeed, but it is most of all an expression of the sovereignty of character, the sovereignty of holy and loving fatherhood. Its very essence is that the Father gave the Son, and that the Son came to reveal the Father. Thus God manifests his sovereignty in the first instance by taking the initiative in salvation, and this initial expression of sovereignty in which he

---

[2] Mathew Arnold (1822–1888) was an English poet and literary critic. He believed that authentic religion was personal and moral and lauded Jesus' stress on individual rather than national conduct. He disapproved of literal readings of scripture that led to bibliolatry. His works included *Literature and Dogma* (1873) and *God and the Bible* (1875).

approaches man and reveals himself and pleads with man to be reconciled unto himself through the revealing Son is the index to all his sovereignty, a sample, so to speak, which reveals what sovereignty is in its deepest essence. A dewdrop on the grass is like other drops of water until seen from the right angle of observation. Then it mirrors and reflects the sun. Christ's spotless humanity as a finite drop of dew reflects the glory of sovereign holiness and sovereign love taking the initiative in saving men.

In discussing our moral axiom there will be occasion to make our plea for human freedom. At present we anticipate it sufficiently to say that any doctrine of divine sovereignty must safeguard man's freedom. The sovereignty of holy and loving character, indeed, expresses itself in constituting man as a free moral being. Sin came in and human nature became so biased that, without God's prevenient grace the will inevitably chooses evil. But neither prevenient nor regenerating grace, nor grace in any of its forms acts upon the will by way of compulsion, but always in accordance with its freedom. The will responds and man chooses for himself God's freely offered gift of salvation. Grace conforms to the structure of the will, pursues its windings, inflates but never forces it, fills it out as a human hand fits or fills a glove, the two forever distinct and separate, yet identical in shape and united in destiny.

God's Method Necessarily Slow

Now it is because of this necessity for the response of the human will that God's sovereignty in saving men must needs pursue a slow method. He might save all men outright by a nod, if salvation were merely a question of power. But it is also a question of holy and loving character in God and of freedom in man. Persuasion is necessary to convince men. Human agents of redemption, preachers and teachers of the gospel of his grace, are organically bound up in the process of redemption. Moral and spiritual laws, by their very nature, are only by slow degrees incorporated into human character and human society. The process is like the slow knitting together of the parts of a broken bone, or the weaving, thread by thread of a delicate and beautiful fabric on a loom, or like the slow unfolding of the first germ of life in the seed into the stately and beautiful plant. Only where these require hours or days the spiritual process requires millenniums.

Now God's election of men to salvation is not the arbitrary or capricious thing which some of the older and extreme forms of the doctrine of sovereignty taught. It is infinite wisdom, grace, and skill, seeking to save the world by the method which will reach the greatest number in the shortest time. This explains the fact that election is a widening process. From generation to generation the horizon broadens and increasing numbers enter the kingdom. Holiness thus vindicates itself in that God refuses to violate man's moral nature, even in order to save him; and love vindicates itself in that the process of saving men is accelerated as much as possible at every stage. The limitations upon God are imposed by a threefold necessity: first, of saving man and at the same time leaving him free, which really means that salvation is a moral process and not a mere physical act of power; second, the necessity of reaching the human will while it is in such a state of sin as will certainly lead it to exercise its moral freedom by the choice of evil unless restrained therefrom; and thirdly, the necessity of employing human agents as channels of his saving grace. Unless God does so employ human agents he takes man's moral task away from him, robs him of his chief birthright. If God should save men and sanctify them directly, if there were no interdependence among men in moral and spiritual effort, no struggle, no suffering, no toil and effort to save others, the mainspring of real moral growth would be broken. If salvation were a direct miracle, and sanctification God's immediate act upon each saved man without the necessity for the various agencies and appliances of the kingdom as we know it, it is quite true that many a heartbreak would be avoided, and the long drawn agony of a creation which groaneth and travaileth in pain together would cease. But it would be at fearful cost. Man's moral freedom, man's privilege of growth, the cultivation of the social virtues, in short man's opportunity for achieving through God's grace a righteousness of his own in addition to God's imparted righteousness would be gone forever. Thus the race would become spiritually bankrupt, and remain forever in a state of spiritual childhood. The redemptive enterprise is God's spiritual gymnasium where giants are made. Only an apparatus which provides for grappling with sin develops the highest spiritual power. The ability to wield planets and stars would be child's play in comparison.

Man's Freedom and Election

Recurring now to the threefold necessity which limits holy and loving sovereignty in saving and sanctifying men—man's freedom, his inevitable choice of evil, and the necessity for human agents of redemption—we may say that election was the only method left to God under the conditions imposed by these necessities. This method of election is relieved of all appearance of arbitrariness or of unfairness, when it is seen that it alone would meet the situation. If, in addition, we suppose that God began the electing process at the most favorable period in the world's history, and placed the objects of his choice most favorably for making use of them in reaching others, and if in widening the circle of his electing love he gave it the direction most favorable to the speediest and most effective evangelization of the whole world; then it will appear that holy and loving sovereignty has ever presided over the process of election, and that at every stage of the process we may vindicate the declaration of Scripture that he willeth that none should perish but that all should live.

Strategic Men in History

All these conditions are met in the call and choice of Abraham, in the establishment of his descendants in Palestine, the highway of the nations; in the dispersion of the Jews, who carried the truth abroad with them to prepare the way for the gospel; in the call of Paul the apostle to the Gentiles; in the westward course of evangelization under Paul toward the aggressive and missionary Western races rather than toward the passive Orientals; in the lodging of modern missionary effort in the hands of the cosmopolitan people of the West rather than in the exclusive races of the East, and in other ways which might be indicated if space allowed. Looking at human history as a whole, and assuming God's sincere love for every man, and recognizing the limitations imposed upon his action by the nature of human freedom and sin, we need only two factors beyond those ordinarily recognized to show the loving as well as the holy character which is behind the electing sovereignty in redemption. Those factors are the selection of the opportune time in which to act, and the choice of strategic men through whom grace might flow to the world at large. Abraham and Paul and hundreds of others may illustrate the principle of choosing strategic men, and the New Testament in many ways recognizes the principle of the "fullness of times" in God's action. In the bowling alley the aim of the bowler is to hit the king pin. If this is done at the proper angle he knocks down all the other pins. God is the Master Bowler in human redemption and chooses men with a view to the largest results consistent with the conditions and limitations under which he must work These have been pointed out and grow chiefly out of human freedom and sin.

Strategic men are not moral men necessarily in the first instance, and their choice rather than others has no reference to their moral merit. Paul called himself the "chief of sinners," and perhaps on this very account he was a strategic man—a man through whom grace might flow to the greatest number. Indeed, Paul expressly asserted this. We conclude therefore that God's electing love is his effort to save the greatest number in the shortest time under the conditions imposed by human freedom and the necessarily slow processes of moral growth.

In closing this part of our discussion it should be said that the acceptance of our theological axiom is not necessarily dependent upon the reader's acceptance of the various subordinate points in the above very brief outline of an exceedingly difficult subject. The essence of the axiom I am sure will commend itself to every thoughtful reader, viz., that character in God is all we need to vindicate his sovereignty. Assume that God is holy and that he is also loving and the human heart rests in the idea of his sovereignty, indeed demands it as the only possible ground for security and peace and the ultimate triumph of holiness and love among men.

We may now briefly summarize the foregoing.

The Key to Sovereignty

What is the key to God's sovereignty in creating the universe? The key is the garden of Eden, his desire to create beings capable of holiness and happiness. What is the key to the sovereignty of God in the incarnation of Christ? Why this, that sovereign omnipotence desired to become sovereign sympathy and sovereign patience and sovereign suffering to redeem. Not the God sitting on the circle of the heavens contemplating a perishing world is the most winsome God, but God in Christ in the upper chamber girding himself with a napkin and washing disciples' feet.

What is the key to God's sovereignty in providence? Simply this, that his sympathy and patience would provide an arena and time for slow pupils to achieve character for themselves and society. Human society is as yet but a splendid sketch with a column here and portico there, a cornerstone yonder. Give it time, says sovereign holiness and sovereign love, and you will see a fair structure. Then too, there is that image of the prophet, so repugnant to many, which likens God to the potter and man to clay. But look at the image.

The potter has in his mind's eye a beautiful image which he would reproduce, and he molds it on the wheel which is before him, and if it is yielding and plastic the result is as he wishes. But if the clay is refractory, the vessel is marred—all of which means that God will not do violence to the will of man. His sovereignty is holy and it is loving; it respects human freedom. And so everywhere. The sovereign God is the holy God and the loving God. He will reproduce in human life and society the order and the beauty, the majesty and power of the material heavens, with its glittering constellations and flashing suns; he will communicate to men his own blessedness until they reflect in themselves the harmony and melody, the might and the glory of the angelic hosts which continually encircle his throne. But he will be sovereign; he holds the reins of power that none of the winged horses which draw his mighty chariot, though coursing across the sky on flaming hoofs, shall become unruly or bring on disaster. Even sin will he overrule, so that in a deep, true sense it is true,

> That nothing walks with aimless feet,
> That not one life shall be destroyed
> Or cast as rubbish to the void
> When God hath made the pile complete.[3]

---

[3] Mullins is quoting Alfred Tennyson's "O Yet We Trust" (1850).

7

The Religious Axiom:
All Men Have an Equal Right
to Direct Access to God

There needs to be little said in explanation of the terms of our religious axiom. It will scarcely be denied by any. It simply asserts the inalienable right of every soul to deal with God for itself. It implies of course man's capacity to commune with God. It assumes the likeness between God and man. It is based on the principle of the soul's competency in religion. It asserts that on the question of spiritual privilege there are no such differences in human nature as warrant our drawing a line between men and claiming for one group in this particular what cannot be claimed for others. It denies that there are any barriers to any soul to any part of the Father's grace. There can therefore be no special classes in religion. The spiritual belong to God's family. They all have equal access to the Father's table, the Father's ear, and the Father's heart.

Conversely this religious axiom implies and carries with it the truth that to deprive any soul of the privilege of direct access to God is tyranny. For one soul to assume the religious privilege or obligation of another is a contradiction in terms. Religion by its very nature forbids such assumption.

This axiom of course does not forbid the setting apart of ministers or officials to perform certain specified duties for the sake of convenience or expediency in the church. It is only when such officials presume to monopolize for themselves the privileges or appointments of the Lord's house, or when they, through spiritual usurpation, become lords over the faith and life of others, that there is violation of the axiom. Nor does our axiom stand opposed to all those manifold forms of sympathy and helpfulness in the religious life from one to another among the non-official members of the churches. Here again it is only when the one life trenches upon the spiritual rights or duties of the other that the axiom raises the finger of warning.

The Principle of Individualism in Religion

The axiom, of course, asserts the principle of individualism in religion. Primarily the religious relation is a relation between God and the individual man. Religious privilege and religious duty subsist between men and God in the first instance in their capacity as individuals and only secondarily in their social relations. On the social side of their religious life there is nothing which can properly destroy the freedom of access which all men have to God, or in any way mar that fellowship.

As Christ is the mediator between God and man, man's religious life is established and maintained through Christ. "No one cometh unto the Father but by me" [John 14:6], is Christ's own word on the subject. Indeed this point is too clear from all the New Testament teachings to require elaboration here. Its connection with our religious axiom is clear in this: Direct access to God through Christ is the law of the Christian life. It is a species of spiritual tyranny for men to interpose the church itself, its ordinances, or ceremonies, or its formal creeds, between the human soul and Christ. This will become increasingly clear as we proceed. For the present we mention it as a part of our statement of the contents of the religious axiom. Some have erroneously supposed that Baptists make a saving ordinance of baptism. Such a conception is radically at variance with our religious axiom and with the whole Baptist standpoint.

Since the Reformation this axiom has found expression in nothing more than in the exercise of the individual's right of private interpretation of the Scriptures. It guarantees the right of examining God's revelation each man for himself, and of answering directly to God in belief and conduct.

New Testament Teachings

How vital the religious axiom is to the Christianity of Christ appears from numerous very striking teachings. The soul's direct relation to God and God's immediate contact with the soul's life appear from the following scriptures. Christ said to Peter that on him he would build his church after the latter had confessed him as the Messiah, and Christ had spoken to him the memorable words, "Flesh and blood hath not revealed it unto thee, but the Spirit of my Father in heaven" [Matt. 16:17]. Intelligent personal grasp of truth and inner illumination of the Spirit are a part of the structural law of the church. Without these the church is not a church. It is in the same context that Christ gives to Peter the keys of the kingdom and the power of binding and loosing [Matt. 16:19]. Experimental knowledge of the truth as revealed to the heart of the individual directly by the Father is the only possible key to the kingdom of God.

In harmony with this is Christ's saying in connection with his parabolic teachings, "Unto you it is given to know the mysteries of the kingdom of heaven but to them it is not given" [Matt. 13:11]. Here the relation of knowledge to spirituality is manifest. Ceremonialism in any form apart from knowledge is alien to the spirit of the gospel. Quite in keeping with this requirement of knowledge is Paul's striking statement [I Cor. 2:4] that his ministry took the form not of sacerdotalism or the administration of ceremonies, but that it was a message which he delivered and which went to its mark in the hearts of men "in demonstration of the Spirit and of power." Here again the primacy of the word of God as the instrument of the kingdom is entirely clear. Spiritual truth addressed to the soul and demonstrated directly to it by the Spirit is of the essence of Christianity. Then too, in Hebrews the nature of the new covenant is set forth in terms which for substance are the same as the passage just cited. The law of God is written on the heart. "I will put my laws into their mind, and on their heart also will I write them...and they shall not teach every man his fellow citizen, and every man his brother, saying, Know ye the Lord; for all shall know me from the least to the greatest of them" [Heb. 8:10–11]. Here again personal knowledge, derived from God himself, and not even from the brethren is the characteristic mark of the members of the kingdom. And this knowledge is the possession of all, from the least unto the greatest. None in the kingdom are too young or too ignorant to partake of the knowledge revealed therein.

Perhaps most suggestive of all is the passage regarding the unpardonable sin. That sin is hardness of heart which takes the form of opposition to or blasphemy against the Holy Ghost. Refusal to receive the "demonstration of the Spirit"—that is, the distinctive evidence supplied by the Spirit within the soul and in mighty works without—is the unpardonable sin. Such resistance to the Spirit, which there is not space to define more fully, indicates that the soul has passed the supreme spiritual crisis, from which there is no recovery. The sphere in which the unpardonable sin takes place is the sphere of the inner relations between God's Spirit and man's, and the form it assumes is resistance to the truth which the Spirit reveals.

Summary of the Scripture Teachings

We may now sum up the contents of the five passages as follows: In Christ's words to Peter it is clear that the characteristic confession of the kingdom is the confession of the Messianic truth; in the next passage the characteristic privilege of the kingdom is knowledge of its mysteries; in the third passage the characteristic method and ministry of the kingdom is "demonstration" of the truth by the Spirit; in the fourth the characteristic description of the kingdom is of men on whose hearts the truth has been written by the inner demonstration of the Spirit. In the final passage the characteristic and unpardonable sin of the kingdom is resistance to the work of the Spirit who conducts the spiritual demonstration within.

These teachings of Scripture simply give in striking form from the New Testament itself the essential contents of the religious axiom. They disclose to us the peculiar and distinctive quality of Christianity as a religion which asserts as inviolable the direct relation of the soul to God, and the universal necessity of truth as the instrument of God's intercourse with man. It must follow from these facts that certain things are excluded from Christianity by virtue of its essential nature. One is the assumption on the part of one of the religious obligations of another. It is clear that one man cannot repent or believe or obey for another. It is clear that to attempt thus a vicarious repentance or faith or obedience is a contradiction of the elementary principles of the Christian religion. No soul can on any ground perform these acts for another on the one hand, nor on the other can one soul perform such acts for another as will exempt the other from obligation to perform them for himself. The most intimate of all human relationships do not avail for this purpose. Family ties are the closest. Yet Jesus repeatedly asserted that family ties must be broken, if need be, in order to realize the ideal of direct dealing with God through him. "He that loveth father or mother more than me is not worthy of me" [Matt. 10:37]. "I came not to send peace but a sword" [Matt. 10:34]. "A man's foes shall be they of his own household" [Matt. 10:36]. "My mother and my brethren are these which hear the word of God and do it" [Matt. 8:21].

The Principle Not Annulled by Covenant Relations

So vital is this principle of the direct relation of the soul to God under Christianity that no covenant relations growing out of the theocracy of Israel can annul it or affect it. Other things were preparatory to it and led up to it. The Old Testament records especially in the later prophets give evidence of a relaxing of the principle of family solidarity which prevailed in the earlier periods. In Ezekiel and Isaiah individualism in religion is proclaimed as the law of the soul's relation to God and, as we have seen, the Epistle to the Hebrews asserts that this individualism is the distinct mark of the new as contrasted with the old covenant.

The religious axiom, then, is that all souls have an equal right to direct access to God. It is now in order to trace in outline the violation of the principle contained in this axiom in the course of Christian history. We shall devote the greater part of the present chapter to infant baptism as the most striking illustration of a departure from Christianity, still prevalent among many evangelical bodies, into whose doctrine and practice it came from Roman Catholicism, and with many of whose essential principles it is directly at variance. It is in direct contradiction of the religious axiom. Infant baptism really has no logical place in Presbyterianism or Methodism, or Congregationalism, if we are to draw conclusions from the light of history. Or if these bodies insist that it has a logical place in their systems, they thereby cast away in principle the chief part of their spiritual birthright. My plea in this chapter is not merely a polemic against infant baptism. It is far more an appeal to evangelical denominations, with noble histories behind them, to cast out an alien element and conform to their own higher principles and ideals. If the reader will not prejudge the case I think this will become clear before we have finished. All evangelical bodies which practice infant baptism erect in their church life a double Christianity, a twofold conception, the parts of which are in radical and irrepressible conflict.

The Departure of Early Christianity

But first we must glance at the departure of the church in the early Christian centuries from the principle of our religious axiom. Here we are on undisputed ground, as to the historic facts themselves, at least among Protestant historians of all names. There is substantial agreement among them, with variations in details of course, on all the leading facts which follow as to early modifications of New Testament Christianity.

There were four leading forces which had a share in the corruption of early Christianity. These were paganism as a religious force, Gnosticism,

Judaism, and Roman imperialism. The resultant corruptions or modifications of the New Testament teachings may be summed up as episcopacy and sacerdotalism, or in terms which are equivalent, as ecclesiastical imperialism and sacramentalism. Episcopacy is not the same as sacerdotalism. The bishop is for government, the priest administers sacraments. Of course the two overlap and constantly tend to be merged, the one in the other. For present purposes we confine our attention for the most part to the development of the priest and the sacrament. For it was here, perhaps more than in episcopacy, in its earlier stages, that the religious axiom was obscured or ignored.

The simplicity of baptism and the Lord's Supper, the two ordinances instituted by Jesus Christ, was only gradually corrupted into the elaborate sacramentalism of the later Roman Catholicism. The facts are substantially as follows: Paganism had certain rites and ceremonies which were analogous in some respects to baptism and the Lord's Supper. With these rites certain mysteries were connected. Weak and carnal Christians lately won from paganism would naturally bring over some of their heathen conceptions with them. These rites and their corresponding mysteries would in a measure color their views of baptism and the Supper. Another idea of paganism, almost ineradicable indeed, was the necessity of the priest and the priesthood in religion. A religion of direct and immediate relations between God and man seemed to the pagan mind inconceivable. This of course would make easy the transition to a sacerdotal Christianity. Judaism and Old Testament teachings would lend color to the idea of a human priesthood, and its ceremonialism would tend to foster corresponding practices in the church. All these tendencies would combine to obscure the one sufficient sacrifice and the sole priesthood of Jesus as the author of salvation, and the universal priesthood of believers as the subjects of salvation.

Baptism and Heathen Rites

It was but a single step to transfer the idea of magical efficacy in the heathen rites over to baptism and the Lord's Supper. Accordingly, in the second and third centuries men began to connect remission of sins with baptism. This early view still required repentance and faith as conditions of remission, although actual remission occurred only at baptism. It was the first step toward the conception that magical efficacy resides in baptism. Justin Martyr in his *First Apology* taught that we are regenerated in baptism. Slowly the view that baptism has a magical power gained ground. It was greatly aided by the Stoic philosophy of the period especially in the hands of Tertullian.[1] The chief element in this philosophy was its idea of substance (*substantia*). The essence of all things is a substance. Nothing exists which is not corporeal. What is without body is without being. Spirit is a kind of body. God is body-substance. Now, it is not difficult to see how this philosophy would affect the growing tendency to ascribe a magical and sacramental efficacy to the material elements of baptism and the Lord's Supper. Thus arose a philosophic and apparently rational vindication of the sacramental view.

The doctrine of original sin was made use of to the same end. This sin affects infants as well as others. Baptism has inherent power. Hence its application to infants cleanses them from sin—regenerates them. Infant lustrations were practiced among the heathen, and this would prepare the way for infant baptism. Thus generally were the ordinances transformed from symbols into sacraments with saving power. Without baptism there was no salvation.

A Great Abuse of Human Power

But a priest was needed to impart its sacred character to the sacrament and to administer it. Tertullian is the first who called ministers priests. But the idea develops rapidly after him. Cyprian completed the conception.[2] The priesthood now becomes the depositaries of the mysteries and the grace of God. The hierarchy is slowly evolved. The "power of the keys" is transferred to an exclusive priesthood. The church consists of the hierarchy. Outside of the church is no salvation. Thus the church, the priesthood, and the sacraments are all interposed between the soul and God. Christianity slowly crystallizes under the action of the new principle and all its faces and angles are changed.

---

[1] Mullins cites a reference to Justin in Baptist historian A. H. Newman, *A History of Anti-pedobaptism* (Philadelphia: American Baptist Publication Society, 1897) 4. The writings of Justin Martyr of Rome (100–165) and Tertullian of Carthage, North Africa, (ca. 155–230) can be found in the *Ante-Nicene Fathers*. See www.ccel.org. Justin is considered the most prominent of the second-century Christian apologists. Tertullian was the significant Latin theologian who coined the term "Trinity" but also said Christians should not mingle with non-Christian culture in any way.

[2] Cyprian of Carthage (d. 258) wrote *On the Unity of the Church*. He emphasized unity in the episcopacy: "the Church is in the Bishop" and "there is no salvation outside the Church."

Faith passes into a long eclipse. Direct relations to God are unknown. Forgiveness now becomes absolution; prayer becomes confession to a priest. Regeneration takes place in baptism, and baptism is administered in infancy, lest death ensue before the sacrament is applied. The whole machinery of religion passes over into the hands of a human priesthood with its terrible power of spiritual tyranny. The sacraments are multiplied from two to seven, and each adds a resistless weapon to those already possessed by a set of priestly lords of the consciences of men. The priestly power culminates in the interdict by virtue of which a man of clay, like other men, sitting in Rome yonder, can exclude whole cities and countries from the grace of God, can shut the gates of heaven to millions of fellow mortals and fellow sinners. The great elemental truth that all souls have an equal right to direct access to God passed out of human thought so far as the Roman Catholic Church was able to influence that thought. If it survived it was confined to those in monasteries and among the despised sects and was inoperative in Christendom at large.

The above sketch is of course exceedingly brief and necessarily inadequate. But it will serve to indicate the direction of ecclesiastical development until the Reformation. But the Reformation ushered in a new era for mankind, which I cannot here discuss save in so far as its principles are applicable to the subject in hand.

What Luther found confronting him at the outset of his great movement, therefore, was an ecclesiastical closed system in which the sacraments, the priesthood, the hierarchy, the church, and the pope, were the central influences and agencies. The people were relegated entirely to the background. The whole of Christian theology had been economized and modified in the interest of the sacramental idea. Man is incapable of transacting directly with God. Human mediators were essential to the theory and the practice of religion. Luther's battle was directed not merely against evils in the church, nor was it, of course, the result simply of a quarrel among priests about doctrine. In its deepest and essential meaning it was a revolt against spiritual tyranny, it was the assertion of the fundamental truth of our religious axiom that all souls have an equal right to direct access to God. As is well known Luther did not at first think of leaving the church of Rome. Essentially it was Christ's church but it needed reforming, was his early thought. He was like the man who remarked: "If you were to give me a fine peach and it was so decayed that it could not be eaten, I would not throw it away, I would plant it and from the seed I would get a tree that would yield me a crop of fine peaches every year." Luther thought he would plant the decayed Romish peach and obtain a new harvest of fruit. But, alas, he soon discovered that the seed itself was bad and neither tree nor fruit could come therefrom.

There are, of course, various ways of stating the principles of the Reformation, but they all come practically to the same thing. Dr. Schaff, in his *History of the Christian Church* sums them up as follows: "There are three fundamental principles of the Reformation, the supremacy of the Scriptures over tradition, the supremacy of faith over works, and the supremacy of the Christian people over an exclusive priesthood."[3] These are the objective, the subjective, and the social principles of the Reformation. Each of these principles accentuates in its own way our religious axiom. The objective principle of the authoritative Scripture asserts that every man has a right to read and interpret the word of God for himself, under the guidance of the Spirit, untrammeled by human tradition. The subjective principle of faith in God and justification through Christ restores to the soul its spiritual birthright of individual responsibility and privilege in direct dealings with God. The social principle accents the priesthood of all believers against the claims of an exclusive priesthood, which means of course that there can be no priestly class in the church of God. All are priests alike. This, then, was the threefold plea of the Reformers, the supremacy of the Scriptures, justification by faith, and the priesthood of all believers. In short, Romanism stood for indirect and the Reformation for direct access to God on the part of man. At every point this one principle was the kernel of the issue. The inner logic of the Protestant movement, its implicit law, is this idea of the direct relationship between the human soul and God, just as the inner logic and implicit law of Romanism is the principle of the indirect relations between God and man.

The Troublesome Question of Infant Baptism

We consider next one of the most troublesome questions of the Reformation, that which related to the baptism of infants. As is well known the Reformers retained the practice, while the Anabaptists and other radicals rejected it. No one today claims any direct and explicit teaching of Scripture

---

[3] Mullins cites Philip Schaff, *History of the Christian Church*, 6:16. The entire *History* can be found today in eight volumes; the last two were completed by David Schaff, Philip's son; see the 1910 edition published by Charles Scribner's Sons.

for infant baptism. It is based by those who practice it on inferences and deductions rather than explicit teaching on the subject. It is not our purpose here to deal with this aspect of the matter. Exegesis has won the day in favor of believers' baptism. But it will be profitable to examine infant baptism in the light of our religious axiom.

Luther and the other Reformers found infant baptism the universal practice in the Roman Church. Under the principle of *opus operatum* it was regarded as efficacious in regenerating the soul even in the absence of faith. The principle involved in the *opus operatum* was that the sacraments conveyed grace always unless mortal sin were interposed as a barrier. Infant baptism therefore was a logical and consistent custom. Infants do not and cannot have faith. But then the sacraments do not require faith. This was the Roman Catholic view. It was at this point that the Reformers encountered trouble. The faith principle was of the essence of the whole Reformation movement. Without it the entire fabric fell in ruins like a house of cards. Yet the Anabaptists pointed out that infant baptism had no place in New Testament Christianity because there could be no faith. Luther retorts in a manner which provokes a smile: "How will they prove," said he, "that infants do not believe? Because forsooth they do not speak and show forth faith. Very well. By this reasoning how many hours will we ourselves not be Christians, while we sleep and do other things? Cannot God therefore in the same manner throughout the whole period of infancy, as in a continuous sleep preserve faith in them?"[4]

Melancthon had serious misgivings on the subject, and Zwingli's clear mind perceived distinctly that the Reformers' principle of faith necessarily excluded infant baptism and so taught in his earlier career. Under pressure of ancient custom, however, and for expediency's sake he finally decided to retain it, and sought to find Scripture warrant for it.

Thus it was that the Reformers admitted into the Reformation an alien principle which led to endless difficulty. The necessity for faith they could not deny, and yet infants had no faith. The Roman Catholic doctrine of the sacrament that it is *opus operatum*, a thing efficacious without faith, they could not admit. They retained infant baptism nevertheless, and from that day to this have struggled in vain to naturalize it in Protestantism. The struggle continues today in Europe and America with no hope of solution, for the

---

[4] Mullins cites Newman, *A History of Anti-pedobaptism*, 72.

reason that there is an irrepressible conflict between the principle of justification by faith and infant baptism. One principle holds to the direct the other to the indirect access of the soul to God, and in all Protestant bodies which practice infant baptism the two principles exist side by side in a state of unstable equilibrium, because they are irreconcilable with each other.

Contradictions in the Protestant System

We proceed now to trace briefly this conflict in some of the Protestant churches. We begin with the Lutheran Church in Germany. In a recent volume Professor Lutgert of Halle has given an instructive sketch of this controversy inside of the Lutheran body.[5] As already indicated Luther resisted the Catholic doctrine of sacramental efficacy without faith. On the other hand he sought to meet the Anabaptists who denied faith in infants, by asserting the objectivity of baptism, i.e., faith does not create the baptism but baptism creates faith. God through baptism thus communicates faith to the infant. Faith of course gives rise to the new birth and so in baptism the infant is born again. But the matter did not rest here. Gradually the Lutheran teachers drifted back into the Catholic view, and Hollaz and Baier asserted that grace and faith are communicated always where no evil will is raised in opposition to God,[6] without faith. Slight as this variation is from the orthodox Lutheran view Chemnitz and others denounced it as a return to the Romanist view of the *opus operatum*.[7]

The danger of this view was that it made faith mere passivity and it became one of the leading causes of passive churches. Conversion, the awakening of faith, was no longer the task of preaching or of Christian nurture. The reaction was inevitable. It came in a pietism which sought the conversion of men and made this its chief task.

The Lutheran doctrine was attacked from another side by those who yet held to infant baptism. Calvin asserted that God could give an inner illumina-

---

[5] Mullins cites Wilhelm Lugert, *Gottes Sohn und Gottes Geist* (1905) 126ff.

[6] Ibid., 135.

[7] David Hollaz (1648–1713) and Johann Wilhelm Baier (1647–1695) were Lutheran theologians. Baier wrote *A Compendium of Positive Theology* (1877). Martin Chemnitz (1522–1586) was a Lutheran reformer who studied under Martin Luther and Philipp Melanchthon. He helped put together the *Formula of Concord* (1577), an important Lutheran confession.

E. Y. Mullins

tion to the baptized infant without the preaching of the word. Calvin did not assert with Luther that infants became believing in baptism, but asserted that through a secret energy of the Spirit the seed of faith and repentance is planted. Thus arose the distinction between the seed of faith and faith itself. The Lutherans objected vigorously. The danger in Calvin's view is in recognizing through this inner illumination a new birth where there is no faith. Faith is expressly denied and yet the new birth asserted.

But in the nineteenth century, Lutherans in a noteworthy manner attached themselves to Calvin's view. W. Hoffman, and Martensen, and Hofling under the pressure of pietism and other influences, asserted a view practically identical with that of Calvin.[8] Baptism communicates, they said, not the new birth itself, but the power of the new birth. In the infant this power of the new birth was not in consciousness itself, but in the subconscious part of the soul. It lies there germinally, so to speak, below consciousness. But orthodox Lutheranism rejected this as subversive of the baptismal teaching which asserts that the sacrament is nothing without faith. They opposed this later doctrine also as a return to the Roman Catholic *opus operatum*, which denies the necessity of faith in order to the efficacy of baptism.[9] Thus we come to the present time in which the orthodox Lutherans assert that neither faith, nor repentance, nor the word of God, nor forgiveness can be separated from baptism. In the case of infants the vicarious faith and prayers of the parents take the place of the personal faith of the child.

Lutheran Difficulty Easily Understood

Now it is easy to understand this long controversy among the Lutherans regarding infant baptism. The orthodox doctrine asserts and denies in the same breath respecting the same thing. Baptism without faith is nothing they assert, and at once assert that the baptized infant has no faith. By a sort of spiritual fiction they assume that a vicarious faith in the parents is sufficient. Clear thinking inevitably detects the radical departure in this from the Reformation doctrine of justification by faith and the direct relation of every

---

[8] Johann Christian Konrad von Hoffman (1810–1877) was professor of history and theology at Erlangen. He and Johann Wilhelm Friedrich Hofling (1802–1853) were a part of the "Erlangen School" of "Neo-Lutheranism." Hans Lassen Martensen (1808–1884) was a Danish theologian.

[9] Mullins cites Wilhelm Lugert, *Gottes Sohn und Gottes Geist* (1905) 138.

soul to God. Infant baptism is irreconcilable with the Reformation. And as we have seen each attempt to modify the orthodox Lutheran doctrine led straight back to the *opus operatum* of Roman Catholicism. Lutheranism then, attempts to maintain a dualistic or twofold principle of salvation directly and radically contradictory of each other. Early Lutheranism asserted, as the standards show, that faith was actually wrought in infants in baptism while modern Lutheranism seems content with asserting only vicarious faith in the parents. Intermediate Lutheranism dissatisfied with both speaks with Calvin of a seed or germ of faith in baptism. But this latter is rejected by the orthodox as Romanism. One party rejects the orthodox view as meaningless, and the orthodox reject the rival view as Romish. The conclusion is that there is no satisfactory explanation of infant baptism except on Roman Catholic grounds, which all evangelicals of course reject as subversive of New Testament Christianity. The antithesis, sharp and clear, between Romanism and the principle of the Reformation comes out nowhere more distinctly than in this matter of infant baptism, and historic Lutheranism furnishes no satisfactory method of explaining it or naturalizing it in Protestantism. If personal faith is the cardinal principle of the Reformation there is no standing room for a rite which completely ignores it. To retain it is to set up a double principle of salvation whose parts are gold and clay and incapable of fusion or union of any kind.

We seek in vain among the great religious denominations which practice infant baptism for any more satisfactory vindication of it. In the Church of England the High Church party holds a doctrine practically identical with that of Romanism. In baptism a germ of life is implanted in the soul, which may remain undeveloped for a long time, but which may in the end be either unfolded or destroyed. This of course is also practically the same as Calvin's conception of the germinal regeneration and faith. Bishop H. U. Onderdonk of the American Church maintained the doctrine of a twofold regeneration, one in baptism which was a new birth in the sense that it changes the state or relation constituting us as sons of God; the other without baptism and directly through the Holy Spirit giving to us a new moral nature, and thus constituting a new birth morally and spiritually. This theory of Bishop Onderdonk is simply one of the possible logical devices for escaping the evil results of a consistent application of the principle of baptismal regeneration. It is a very bold assertion of the duplex principle of salvation implicit in all

Protestant doctrinal systems which favor infant baptism. The sacramental or magical and the moral and spiritual principles appear in quite sharp contrast in Onderdonk's theory.[10]

The Presbyterian View

We note next the Presbyterian view as expounded by Dr. A. A. Hodge in his *Outlines of Theology*. Two things are included in every sacrament, says Dr. Hodge; "First, an outward visible sign used according to Christ's appointment; second, an inward spiritual grace thereby signified."[11] The relation between the sign and the grace signified is simply moral, i.e., it is established only by the authority of Christ; and it is also real, so that when properly administered and "received by the recipient with knowledge and faith they do really, because of the promise of Christ, seal the grace signified and convey it to the recipient."[12] The grace thus conveyed, however, is due not to the sacraments themselves nor to the administrator, but to the Holy Spirit who as a free personal agent uses them sovereignly as his instruments. In the case of adults grace is conveyed only where there is a living faith.[13]

Dr. Hodge expressly adopts a twofold principle in the baptism of adults and infants. For adults the prerequisite to baptism is a "credible profession of their faith in Jesus as their Savior."[14] This is a clear recognition of New Testament individualism and of the Reformation doctrine. It accords with the religious axiom, that direct access to God through faith is the soul's birthright. But Dr. Hodge at once departs from this principle. He asserts that "the family and not the individual is the unit embraced in all covenants and dispensations," and that everywhere "the free will of the parent becomes the destiny of the child."[15] He then postulates a series of principles nowhere warranted in the New Testament, as that the church (of which Christ spoke in the future tense, saying, "I will build my church") already existed when

---

[10] H. U. Onderdonk, *Episcopacy Examined and Re-Examined* (New York: Protestant Episcopal Tract Society, 1835).

[11] Mullins cites Archibald A. Hodge, *Outlines of Theology* (New York: Carter and Brothers, 1880) 590. Hodge was one of the influential Calvinistic/Reformed "Princeton theologians."

[12] Ibid., 592.

[13] Ibid., 596.

[14] Ibid., 616.

[15] Ibid.

Christ came; that in the absence of explicit command the church that was before continues to be the church after Christ; that as the family was the unit under Judaism so it is in Christianity; that baptism under the new is the same as circumcision under the old covenant, a circumcision which, we may remark, continued to be practiced in the New Testament after baptism had been instituted. These positions are well known and have been frequently answered most successfully. I do not propose to go over the same ground here. I mention them to indicate how elaborate the logical machinery is to justify infant baptism. I remark simply that consistently carried out it leaves nothing distinctive in the new covenant at all. It really converts Christianity back again into Judaism. Yet some such argument must be devised if infant baptism is to be supported; for modern exegesis has settled the point that there is no explicit teaching and no New Testament instance of the baptism of any others than believers. Inferences which are contrary a universal usage and fundamental law can scarce serve to justify infant baptism.

Dr. Hodge, however, insists that faith is necessary in the baptism of infants. But it is vicarious faith, a thing unknown to the New Testament and destructive of its teachings. The faith of parents and the covenant with parents are urged by Dr. Hodge in the case of the baptism of infants. The effect produced by baptism upon the infant is not very definitely set forth by Dr. Hodge. The infant is capable of receiving regeneration and "of receiving from the Holy Ghost the habit or state of soul of which faith is the expression."[16] He quotes Calvin approvingly: "The seed of both repentance and faith lies hid in them by the secret operation of the Spirit."[17] This will be recalled by the reader as the teaching of Calvin adopted by certain Lutherans and rejected by orthodox Lutherans as Romish, as the anti-Protestant *opus operatum*, containing the obnoxious doctrine of regeneration without faith. It is not for us of course to attempt to reconcile these contradictions. Our sole purpose here is to show that Presbyterianism, like Lutheranism, and other Protestant systems, seeks to maintain a dualistic Christianity, a Christianity rent and torn by two irreconcilable principles of grace and salvation.

---

[16] Ibid., 624.
[17] Ibid. See *Calvin's Institutes*, Book IV, Chapter XVI, Section 20.

Doctor Hodge's Inconsistencies

The contradictions of Dr. Hodge's position appear at numerous points. We indicate a few: For one thing he insists upon baptism before and baptism after faith; in infants before, in adults after. The New Testament will be searched in vain for support of this teaching. He teaches another contradictory in his doctrine of the need of personal faith in adults along with the doctrine of vicarious faith for infants. On this also the New Testament is silent. Again, he admits infants to one of the ordinances, baptism, without faith, and excludes them from the other, the Supper, because they are without it. The vicarious principle thus operates in the case of the one ordinance, but breaks down in the case of the other. Dr. Hodge excludes infants from the Lord's Supper. There is no logical ground for baptizing without personal faith and then excluding from the Supper for the lack of it. To support this position, however, another contradictory principle is introduced, viz., that in baptism the recipient is passive while in the Supper he is active. Infants cannot be spiritually active, hence the Supper is withheld from them.[18] But this even does not exhaust the contradictories in Dr. Hodge's doctrine. For in the same discussion he lays down the general principle that the "conditions of admission to the Lord's table are identical with those requisite for baptism."[19] If this be true it is difficult to see how infants can be admitted to the one and excluded from the other. If a passive state in the baptism of adults does not exclude them, why should it operate to exclude infants? There is not the slightest warrant in the New Testament or in the nature of Christianity for the assertion that the recipient is spiritually passive in baptism and active in partaking of the Supper. Faith is active in both ordinances. Once more, Dr. Hodge's doctrine exhibits the irrepressible conflict in this, that baptized infants are thus admitted to church membership and then excluded from the dearest of church privileges, partaking of the Lord's Supper.

Upon occasion, indeed, Dr. Hodge reasons very much like a Baptist. Hear him: "Faith and repentance are prerequisites to baptism." "In Christ Jesus neither circumcision availeth anything nor uncircumcision, but faith that worketh by love...but a new creature." "Faith alone is said to save, the absence of faith to damn." "The entire spirit and method of the gospel is

---

[18] Hodge, "Outlines of Theology," 624.
[19] Ibid., 616.

ethical, not magical. The great instrument of the Holy Ghost is the truth, and all that is ever said of the efficacy of the sacraments is said of the efficacy of the truth. They are means of grace therefore in common with the word and as they contain and seal it."[20] This language is fatal to infant baptism as the reader has already discerned. A religious rite applied where faith is not, where the word of truth is not grasped, is alien to a religion whose essential nature is thus described by Dr. Hodge. But how explain this language which is so fatal to infant baptism? The explanation is that he is there asserting the essential nature of Christianity against the Roman Catholic doctrine of baptismal regeneration. Thus he expresses our religious axiom that all souls have an equal right to direct access to God; thus he maintains that Christianity is spiritual and personal, not magical or sacramental. Infant baptism in its Romish or modified forms is radically at variance with Christianity. It is alien and not native to the Christian soil. It has no logical place in the great Reformation movement. Presbyterianism, with its great history, will become far greater when it surrenders this alien element and consistently stands for the inalienable rights of the human spirit in this as it has done in so many other things.

The Methodist Teaching

In the Methodist body also the same contradictory views prevail as to baptism. The *Book of Discipline* enjoins upon pastors that they "exhort all parents to dedicate their children to the Lord in baptism as early as convenient."[21] Later, however, it becomes clear that they are regarded as members of the church after baptism. The baptismal prayer for the infant is that God will grant to the child "now to be baptized with water that which by nature he cannot have; that he may be baptized with the Holy Ghost; received into Christ's holy church, and be made a lively member of the same." Also the minister prays "that he being saved by thy grace, may be received into the ark of Christ's church."[22] It thus appears that Methodism also adopts a double standard of church membership, one for the non-believing infant through the

---

[20] Ibid., 628.

[21] Mullins cites Jno. J. Tigert, ed., *The Doctrines and Discipline of the Methodist Episcopal Church, South* (Nashville: Publishing House of the M.E. Church, South, 1898) 92.

[22] Ibid., 235.

vicarious faith of parents and another for the believing adult. It is not surprising, therefore, that Methodists are not entirely agreed among themselves as to the status of baptized infants. A body of Christian people with as much spirituality and life as the Methodists possess was sure sooner or later to have misgivings regarding so incongruous a custom as the baptism of infants.

Congregationalists also have had their struggles over this apparently insoluble problem of infant baptism. In Massachusetts in colonial days the baptism of the infant did not entitle it to the exercise of the franchise as was true of those who were church members in the full sense of the word. The "Half-way Covenant" [of 1662] was an expedient adopted by them for settling the question whether children of parents who had themselves been baptized in infancy, but who were not discharging their duty as church members, were entitled to the privilege of baptism. The "Covenant" provided that such parents could transmit to their children the right of baptism, with its implicit church membership by covenant. This "Half-way Covenant" was never universally endorsed by Congregationalists because of its illogical and inconsistent position. In reality under the "Half-way Covenant" there were four sorts of qualifications for church membership: One for the man who obeyed in baptism for himself upon relation of Christian experience; another for parents who were in good standing in the church and for their children, all of whom were baptized in infancy; a third for parents not in fellowship with the church although baptized in infancy; and a fourth for the children of this last class of parents.

We will next examine briefly a recent volume entitled *Democracy in the Church*, which sets forth many important considerations in favor of Congregationalism. The author's utterances regarding infant baptism are very frank and he faces the difficulties involved without evasion, although he fails to satisfy the reader's mind as to the legitimacy of that institution in the Christian church.

A Recent Congregational Writer

This Congregational writer grants freely that as to the form of baptism, "there has been since the discovery of the *Didache* a quite general agreement among competent historians."[23] "The baptism practiced by the Jews, by Christ's disciples, by the whole Christian Church for about thirteen hundred years was baptism by immersion." The author is not certain but thinks it probable that infant baptism was practiced in the New Testament church. He concludes with Professor Fisher, however, that perhaps it is best to say that "the baptism of infants is neither explicitly required nor forbidden in the New Testament."[24] This, of course, confirms what we have already said that modern exegesis has rendered its verdict in favor of believer's baptism by immersion. Our aim in this volume does not include a restatement of the entire argument from exegesis. It can be found in many books. Our aim is to show that infant baptism is alien to the very genius of New Testament Christianity and violates its fundamental ideas.

The author of *Democracy in the Church* says that the baptism of children among Congregationalists "is a custom more honored in the breach than in the observance. A haze surrounds the whole subject as from our past history was perhaps inevitable." We quite agree with him as to the inevitable haze which surrounds the subject. He sets out to restate the doctrine and theory of infant baptism in order to justify it. We condense his views. He urges, as usual, the vicarious faith of parents, insisting on the necessity of faith to the efficacy of baptism. In the case of adults personal faith is required. But this author departs from the views of Bushnell and others on the point of infant church membership.[25] Baptized infants he says are not members of the church until they exercise personal faith. Here he expressly joins the Baptists in insisting upon the voluntariness of church membership. He distinguishes between the covenant of grace and the church covenant. Infant baptism takes

---

[23] Mullins cites Edgar L. Heermance, *Democracy in the Church* (New York: The Pilgrim Press, 1906). Mullins draws from pp. 155–68 for his material in this section.

[24] Professor Fisher is the Congregationalist George Park Fisher (1827–1909). His works of history and religion included *The Christian Religion* (1882) and *History of the Christian Church* (1887).

[25] Horace Bushnell (1802–1876), a Congregationalist theologian, is best known for his work, *Christian Nurture* (1847). See the reprint, *Christian Nurture* (Grand Rapids MI: Baker Book House, 1979). Bushnell, who criticized revival-type conversion experiences, believed that children could be nurtured so that there never was a time that they did not know they were Christian.

place under the former, he thinks; voluntary church membership under the latter. New Testament warrant for this is lacking of course. This writer's instinct for the voluntary principle in religion, for the religious axiom, leads him to assert that baptism may occur twice, in unconscious infancy and when years of discretion have been attained. In many ways the struggle of the contradictory conceptions of Christianity manifests itself in this work with a decided tendency to surrender sacramentalism and the indirect for the spiritual, voluntary, and direct approach of the soul to God.

The Early Congregational Struggle

In colonial days, as is well known, the Congregationalists had a serious and protracted struggle over the status of infants in the church. Were those baptized in infancy members of the church or not? The Congregationalists were divided on the subject, and neither the "Cambridge Platform" nor the "Half-way Covenant" [of 1662] cleared the matter up in any satisfactory manner.[26] There is no possible mode of conceiving or defining the church which shall include infants and adults without introducing fundamentally contradictory views. A church thus inclusive of both would embrace in its membership conscious and unconscious members; believing and unbelieving; those who came by vicarious and those who enter by personal faith; those who come to Christ directly and those who come indirectly; those who are spiritually passive and those who are spiritually active; those entitled to commune and those who, without personal sinful acts, are disqualified for communion. To adopt the view of the author of *Democracy in the Church* involves a double Christianity at every point when baptism is in question. Baptism in order to church membership for believing adults, baptism without church membership for unbelieving infants; baptism without faith and baptism with faith; and in some cases two baptisms, the first without, the second with faith.

We must bring this long chapter to a close. We have made good our plea. Infant baptism has no place in New Testament Christianity and no logical place in the churches of Protestantism. In such churches it involves the presence of contradictory and radically inconsistent views of religion, one a spiritual fiction the other a spiritual reality. It makes current in the religious

---

[26] Congregationalists of colonial Massachusetts produced *The Cambridge Platform* (1649) which became the official polity statement of the "New England Way."

world spiritual coins of coordinate value bearing the same stamp and passing for the same ends, one of which is pure gold and the other an alloy which under any just standard of spiritual values would have to be rejected as counterfeit. Such contradictories in religion inevitably lead to one of two results: The base and the genuine metal come to be regarded as equivalent to each other; or they both become equivocal in meaning and value. The rule is for the higher value to become obscured or set aside and the lower to flood the market, as in the commercial world. Of one thing we may be sure, whatever may be true in the fiscal world, the kingdom of God cannot permanently endure a spiritual bimetallism.

The plea that infant baptism is necessary to Christian nurture assumes falsely that any real element of parental duty or Christian nurture is impossible without it. Every parental duty in the matter of religious teaching and training is possible without the use of a rite which anticipates and forestalls personal action, robs the child of the joy of conscious obedience to Christ in his own appointed ordinance; in short which does despite and violence to individuality and personality, the choicest gift of God to our children, and that which we should above all things protect and conserve. No one can join the church for another; no one can perform any act of personal religious duty for another; no one can without usurpation choose for another in religion. If the principle of vicarious faith and obedience is valid in the case of infant baptism there is no reason why it may not be applied in every part of the Christian life. Heredity and Christian nurture are one thing. They are the law of God for man. But neither heredity nor Christian nurture admits vicarious choices in religion. Even God's elective decree never executes itself in the soul apart from a persuaded will which chooses for itself so far as we have explicit teaching on the subject. Yet parents and sponsors elect and decree and perform for their children in the matter of infant baptism, where there is no slightest response of the will, and thus do despite unto God's grace as revealed in Christ and contaminate the fountainhead of Christian truth.

8

The Ecclesiastical Axiom:
All Believers Have a Right to
Equal Privileges in the Church

A few words in explanation of the terms of this axiom will be sufficient. Equality of privilege in the church of course has no reference to the mental and spiritual capacities of men. No one regards all men as possessing equal natural ability or learning. Nor does the axiom assume that one man is as well fitted as another for official position in the church. Diversities of gifts and offices and administrations are clearly recognized in the New Testament churches and as clearly set forth for our guidance.

The Ecclesiastical and Religious Axioms

The ecclesiastical is best explained by the religious axiom. It is because men have an equal right to direct access to God that they are entitled to equal privileges in the church. Equality before God makes men equal in their ecclesiastical standing. The church is a brotherhood because it is a family of which God is the father and in which Jesus Christ is the elder brother. There is, with respect to the members of the church, no law of ecclesiastical primogeniture by which favored sons receive special and disproportionate parts of the Father's inheritance, and no law of hereditary lordship by which spiritual dynasties are established through imposition of hands or otherwise. The methods of the church are those of a spiritual brotherhood of equals. Personal adjustment of offenses, not judicial decisions, is Christ's preferred way in all private grievances and nowhere does he establish a court other than the local congregation. Apostles even, who were especially inspired for their tasks, exerted their authority not as lords of the conscience but as brothers.

The nature of Christ's church is determined by the twofold relationship of the believer, one to Christ himself, the other to the brethren. Christ is Lord. The believer in Christ belongs to an absolute monarchy, the most absolute indeed the world ever knew. But the monarch is in heaven and relates himself to his subjects through his revealed word and through his Spirit. The subject has fellowship directly with the monarch. All his dealings with his subjects are individual. He delegates his authority to none. But the first and finest expression of Christ's lordship over the individual believer is in the gift of autonomy to him. Christ discovers each man to himself and starts him on an autonomous career, but never for a moment does he relax his grasp upon that man's conscience or life. Yet nothing thrills men into such a sense of freedom and power.

The above is a paradox: The lordship of Christ and the autonomy of the soul. Against such a soul there is no law, as Paul declares. It incarnates the law of Christ. But the paradox of the individual and Christ involves a paradox of the spiritual society and Christ. Because the individual deals directly with his Lord and is immediately responsible to him, the spiritual society must needs be a democracy. That is, the church is a community of autonomous individuals under the immediate lordship of Christ held together by a social bond of common interest, due to a common faith and inspired by common tasks and ends, all of which are assigned to him by the common Lord. The church, therefore, is the expression of the paradoxical conception of the union of absolute monarchy and pure democracy. This we might say is the formula of the church. Every form of polity other than democracy somewhere infringes upon the lordship of Christ. I mean direct lordship. There is no indirect lordship known to the New Testament. An ecclesiastical monarchy with a human head, like the Roman Catholic Church, radically alters the very nature of Christianity. Baptist congregationalism is the exact antithesis of the Romish hierarchy. Modified ecclesiastical monarchies, or aristocracies, or oligarchies, are less objectionable but they too violate one or the other of the organic laws of the church, the direct lordship of Christ, or the equality of all believers in spiritual privilege.

The Human Body and the Church

The favorite New Testament figure to set forth Christ's relations to the church is that of the human body of which Christ is the head. The church members are the members of the body of Christ. Repeatedly this image is employed, especially by Paul. The blood flows directly from head to members. The will issues its mandates directly to the members of the body, and they respond. Church members are members one of another and also of Christ. Thus in the figure of the body we have a striking exposition of the twofold relationship of the believer which determines the nature of the church, viz.: a direct relation to the head and a relation of equality to other members of the body.

Now, it is because of this twofold relationship, this union of absolute monarchy and pure democracy in the church, that analogies to human government cannot hold in fixing a church polity. No such relationships exist in human government. All, or nearly all, human governments are indirect.

The town meeting is an example of pure democracy, but in extending human government over large areas the central authority must be localized. It cannot act everywhere and immediately upon its citizens or subjects. Moreover, legislation on matters of general interest must be through delegated powers, for the reason that the total citizenship cannot assemble, unite, and deliberate for this purpose. Centralized authority is also necessary in the State for the exercise of force, a function always improper for the Church. On the contrary the central authority in Christianity cannot be localized. Christ said it was expedient that he go away in order that the Holy Spirit might come. Thus he "exchanged his presence for his omnipresence." It might be a logical procedure for a given community owning a large body of real estate in common to delegate the control of its mines and the distribution of the coal to a commission. The nature of the case would require some such administration perhaps. But it would be absurd to appoint a commission to control and distribute the sunlight. In this respect the inhabitants would only need to keep out of each other's light. Every man would simply have to avoid building his house or ordering his life so as to obscure the sun from his brother. As the Baptist sees it, papacies and episcopacies are commissions to control the sunshine.

Legislation Not Needed in the Church

We may now add that legislation is not needed. The Scriptures are the rule of faith and practice and the omnipresent Spirit the interpreter. Republicanism, therefore, or representative government, or indirect democracy, cannot take the place of the pure democracy and the absolute monarchy of the New Testament church.

We conclude therefore that pure democracy in church polity is the only institutional expression—the only expression in the form of church organization—of our two axioms, the religious, or the soul's right to direct dealing with God, and the ecclesiastical, or the equality of believers in spiritual privilege in the church. It thus appears that the question of church polity is more than a question of a few detached proof-texts from the New Testament. The question of the constitution of the church enters vitally into the question of the constitution of the kingdom of God.

Our position will become even more abundantly clear if we now institute a contrast between the two methods by which church polities have been developed, or the laws by which their forms have been determined. These we will call on the one hand the spiritual and on the other the temporal. This contrast will exhibit to us the very suggestive fact that two environments have operated upon the churches in ecclesiastical history, and that each environment operates in a way of its own and with results corresponding.

The first line of development is the spiritual. This we find in the New Testament. Baptists sometimes define a church as "a voluntary association of believers united together for the purpose of worship and edification." Dr. A. J. Gordon has criticized this definition. "It is no more true," he says, "than that hands and feet and eyes and ears are voluntarily united in the human body for the purposes of locomotion and work." Dr. Gordon's emphasis is upon the sovereign agency of the Holy Spirit in creating the church.[1]

Now as a matter of fact both the definition and Dr. Gordon's criticism are correct and valid, because each supplies a needed element. The voluntary principle enters essentially into the constitution of a church. But prior to human choice in the matter was the initiative of the Holy Spirit. The spiritual environment from above acted upon men. They were regenerated. Their renewed spiritual natures then impelled them to associate themselves together as a church. The religious and ecclesiastical axioms both came into play; a direct relation to God first, then a voluntary association on terms of equality.

---

[1] Mullins cites A. J. Gordon, *The Ministry of the Spirit* (Philadelphia: American Baptist Publication Society, 1894) 53–54. Pastor of Clarendon Street Baptist Church in Boston, Gordon was a recognized participant in the nineteenth-century "holiness" movement which emphasized sanctification and the gifts of the Spirit.

Church Organization from Within

This was precisely the way in which the New Testament churches arose. First came Christ's call and the response of the individual. Then came a group of individuals attached to his person. When the Spirit came at Pentecost after Christ's departure to the Father the process indicated in Dr. Gordon's criticism of the current definition of a church began, under the leadership of the Holy Spirit. Individuals were drawn together. The indwelling Spirit began to organize the membership of Christ's body into his church.

I am not here concerned to cite the texts which prove that the New Testament churches were democracies. It may be fairly claimed by the advocates of a congregational polity that scholarship has decided in their favor. There was neither priest nor bishop in the medieval and modern sense of the word in the New Testament churches. These were pure democracies. But what I am concerned in particular to show is that democracy alone accords with the nature of the kingdom of God; that the direct relations of men to God and their equality as brethren require a democratic church polity. No other polity leaves the soul free.

This last statement is susceptible of historical proof. Whenever men are acted upon directly by the spiritual environment they tend to the free and self-governing congregation, and when untrammeled by external bonds they always adopt it. The reader will recall the many sects of Christian history whose offense was the freedom of the Spirit. The Donatists[2] were suppressed in the early centuries because they insisted upon prophesying. This meant that they asserted their direct relation to Christ through the Spirit as against the indirect relation through the priesthood. So with many other sects which the Roman Church sought to suppress.

Monasticism illustrates the same principle. At its outset monasticism was the revolt of the soul against the tyranny of external authority and an effort to come into direct relations with God. Readers of church history will recall at once the struggle between the bishops and the monasteries. The latter were little self-governing communities which were intensely jealous of their

---

[2] The Montanists (late second century) are most often cited for emphasis upon the Spirit; the Donatists (fourth century) are usually cited for their focus upon the holiness required for a pure church, holiness being achieved through faithfulness during times of persecution.

spiritual freedom, and for a long time they maintained that freedom within the limits of a general subordination to the pope at Rome. This was not ideal but it illustrates the truth we maintain that democracy is the law of church organization whenever and wherever the soul enjoys its spiritual right of direct access to God. The effort of the Romish hierarchy to suppress this spontaneous and beautiful life of the Spirit, by imposing its iron authority instead, was very unwise. It was the church authorities laying waste their own vineyard. It reminds us of the ignorant Indian soldier who found a leathern pouch containing pearls. Not knowing the value of pearls he threw these away but kept the pouch as a convenient receptacle for his tobacco.

Puritanism Perpetuates Monasticism

Puritanism in England was, according to Prof. A. V. G. Allen, the continuance of monasticism in its essential principle. Professor Allen maintains that the various Nonconformist churches in England today are modern equivalents of monasticism in the Middle Ages, in that they stand for individualism, for soul freedom, for the spiritual and direct relation of the soul to God as against the ecclesiastical lordship of the Established Church.[3]

Another interesting illustration of the same law of ecclesiastical democracy in response to spiritual impulse and environment is seen in the rise of Baptist churches where men have only the New Testament for guidance. A striking instance was that of Oncken and his friends in 1834 in Hamburg, Germany.[4] Coming into the new life in Christ they were without ecclesiastical guides. They shut themselves up to a study of the New Testament. A Baptist church resulted and to this single congregation the Baptists of Germany in large part trace their origin. Baron Uixkull of Russia, who has recently visited America in the interest of the Russian Baptists relates a similar story of the origin of the Baptists within the Czar's dominions. Lutheran missionaries came and preached and left Bibles and then departed. With no guide but the Holy Spirit and the New Testament the flourishing Baptist movement began in Russia. The Baptists of Russia now number many thousands and are growing rapidly. Other instances of the same principle are numerous in modern

---

[3] Alexander A. V. Allen, *The Continuity of Christian Thought* (New York: Ward, Lock and Bowden, 1895). See p. 246.

[4] Johann Oncken is considered the "founding pioneer" of German and European Baptists.

Baptist history. In Mexico and Brazil and elsewhere, Baptist churches have sprung spontaneously into being, so to speak, as a result of the simple study of the New Testament under the sole tutelage of the Holy Spirit.

Church Organization from Without

If now we look at the various modifications of church polity throughout Christian history we find that another environment and another group of forces were at work. Thus, modifications through the temporal as contrasted with the spiritual environment took place. We can of course only look at this development within present limits in a most general way. Yet this will suffice to make clear the point.

The preeminence of the Roman See came about as a result of the operation of many forces. Geographical location at the world's capital was no small factor. The tradition of a visit by the Apostle Peter to Rome assisted. The need for a central and powerful machinery for the suppression of heresy cooperated. When the empire was destroyed the need for a strong temporal head offered the bishop of Rome an opportunity. We have already in a previous chapter pointed out how the sacerdotal and sacramental idea arose in large part from heathenism. The factors were nearly all temporal. It is easily seen that they reversed the principle of church organization. That principle was no longer inward, the Spirit forming for itself a body in accordance with its nature, but outward. The temporal and political environment imposed its laws upon a spiritual body. Thus the church ceased to be an organism and became a mechanism. It was a contrivance for achieving temporal ends rather than a spiritual body adapted to the ends of a life-giving Spirit. Hitherto the church had been a tree of life, full of sap and power and yielding abundant fruit for mankind. Now the tree was cut down and fashioned into a battering ram for warlike purposes. Battering rams are useful in their time and for the purposes for which they are built, but they have no roots and bear no fruit.

The Reformation did not cure this evil. Both Calvin and Luther resorted to the temporal environment for aid in the creation of the new churches. Calvin's community became a theocracy. Luther turned over the government of the church to the temporal power, and this in turn placed it in the hands, not of a hierarchy indeed, but of a consistory made up from the clergy. Luther admitted that the real church and real authority is the local congregation. Indeed the seventh article of the *Augsburg Confession* defines the church thus.

But Luther said in his characteristic fashion that the "wild Germans" were not yet ready for congregationalism.

In England the king had always been prominent in church affairs from the earliest days. Even Wycliffe championed the prerogative of the king in the church.[5] This helps to explain the tenacity with which English thinkers have prosecuted the attempt to justify a religious establishment on theoretical grounds. Hooker's was one of the most forcible and impressive of these efforts. It asserted that Church and State were one society. There follows a long list of theorists and theories, including Coleridge, Chalmers of Scotland, Gladstone, Macaulay, and others.[6] These need not be dwelt upon here further than to indicate how church polity was being determined not on grounds deduced from its own nature, but on those drawn from the temporal environment.

Opportunism in Control

There was indeed a sort of opportunism which seemed to control in the formation of the many polities which took their rise after the Reformation. The point of view and the exigencies of the hour nearly always determined which side of the scales would go down. Romanism even in the earlier ages asserted the Church's independence of the State when it was in danger of becoming subject to the temporal power. It reversed this position when under Hildebrand and his successors the Church gained the ascendancy over the State.[7] In the sixteenth century the Jesuits taught that in the State the power all belonged originally to the people; thus, as Dr. Fisher remarks, anticipating the

---

[5] John Wycliffe was a "pre-reformer" in fourteenth-century England who criticized many Catholic tenets such as transubstantiation and emphasized the authority of Scripture.

[6] Mullins is referring to Anglican theologian Richard Hooker (c. 1554–1600) who was Anglicanism's most prominent defender (*Treatise on the Laws of Ecclesiastical Polity*, 1594–1597). Hooker said the church and state were united and related like two sides of a triangle: the same line can be both a base and a side. Samuel Coleridge (1772–1834) was a romantic poet and author of *On the Constitution of Church and State* (1830); Thomas Chalmers (1780–1847) was founder of the Free Church of Scotland; William Gladstone (1809–1898) was prime minister of the United Kingdom and author of *The State in Relations with the Church* (1838); and Thomas Macaulay (1800–1859) was a British politician and author of *The History of England* (1848).

[7] Hildebrand (1020–1085) was Pope Gregory VII from 1073 to 1085.

democratic ideas of Rousseau and Jefferson.[8] Their aim was to weaken the power of the king. They still held to an opposite theory as to the church, that is, the spiritual despotism of the pope.

In England in the sixteenth century the Anglicans denied and the Puritans affirmed the divine origin of church polity. In the seventeenth century the positions were reversed, the Anglicans affirming and the Puritans tending more and more to deny New Testament warrant for a fixed polity.[9] Presbyterians and Congregationalists in America today are firm believers in separation of Church and State. But it is well known that in the Massachusetts Bay Colony a theocracy was set up in which civic privileges were limited to church members. The history of Presbyterianism in England and Scotland makes it clear that originally in this body there was no inherent principle forbidding a union of Church and State. Chalmers, indeed, formally promulgated the view that the State should adopt and maintain some one form of Christianity. Methodism in like manner in its earlier history was identified with the fortunes of the Church of England and in the struggle for religious freedom in Virginia cast the weight of its influence in the scale with the established church.

Lessons from the Past

The above sketch is not given merely to recall outgrown conceptions of the church, nor to question the wisdom and greatness of the men who founded the great denominations referred to; nor am I blind to the difficulties they had to encounter. I rejoice in their mighty influence for good and the power of those forms of organized Christianity which they have left. It is proper, however, to gather gems of wisdom amid the ruins of the past, and to observe what flowers of truth blossom by the wayside of a pathway untraveled by pilgrims of today. It is entirely clear from the foregoing that in a very large part of modern Christendom the polities which survive are the result of the operation in very large measure of the temporal rather than the spiritual environment upon the church life and growth. The spiritual method may be

---

[8] George Fisher (1827–1909) was a Congregationalist historian who wrote *The Christian Religion* (1882) *History of the Christian Church* (1887) and *A Brief History of the Nations* (1896).

[9] Mullins cites Alexander V. G. Allen, *Christian Institutions* (Edinburgh: T&T Clark, 1898) 13.

likened to the action of a flame which played upon the material until its nature was changed and it was shaped into a new unity. The temporal was like the action of a mold which received the material unchanged and impressed upon it externally its own form.

I shall probably be met at this point by an objection. Some one may say, "You ignore the principle of development in Christianity; you are right in asserting that the earliest form of Christianity was democratic, but you forget that the pure democracies of the New Testament were necessarily subject to modification by changing circumstances. You must allow room for church organization to take the form demanded by changing conditions from age to age." To which we reply: There is no evidence of any such principle of development in the New Testament itself. The objection is based upon an inference not from the principles of the New Testament but from the course of events.

The Test of Development

It is not difficult, however, to test any theory of development. Ecclesiastical development is permissible within the limits of the religious and ecclesiastical axioms. So soon as development carries the church beyond the boundaries of free and direct intercourse with God—beyond the limits of equality and brotherhood—it becomes subversive of the fundamental principles of the kingdom of God. This comes to light in a striking manner in J. H. Newman's theory of development, outlined in a previous chapter. Newman's quest was for a religious authority. He rejected conscience which might serve a natural but not a revealed religion; he rejected the Church of England as having no unity of expression and no central organ of authority. He rejected the Scriptures because they required an interpreter. He found his authority in the Roman Catholic Church with its authoritative head in Rome. He became a Catholic. His doctrine of development was the logical attempt to vindicate his action. Of course all Protestants reject the papacy as the vicegerent of Christ. They look to Christ himself as the supreme authority in religion.[10]

Now every doctrine of development which passes beyond democracy and autonomy in the church repeats Newman's mistake in greater or less degree, because it localizes authority somewhere outside of Christ. It may be in a

---

[10] See John Henry Newman, *An Essay on the Development of Christian Doctrine* (London: James Toovey, 1845; New York: Longmans, Green, and Co., 1903).

bench of bishops or in a synod or general assembly, but in any case it makes the soul responsible to Christ through other men and not directly. It cuts off the direct access of men to God in all matters delegated to a human authority.

We remark further that the "developed" polities which incorporate in any degree the principle of authority of the indirect kind are all needless in the Christian program. There is no room for human legislation of the authoritative kind in Christianity. What about creed-making? Creeds are useful as interpretations of Scripture at any particular period but so soon as they become binding they become divisive. The Scriptures are the guide of the church under Christ's Spirit. Laws of any kind—those which affect the faith or the life—inevitably lead to mischief in the church. The reason is that they introduce a double principle of authority—that of Christ and that of ecclesiastical superiors.

Judicial Functions and the Local Congregation

There is likewise no place for any judicial functions apart from the local congregation. In the local congregation it is not so much a legal and judicial procedure as it is a life process, the healthy organism sloughing off unsound parts. All high ecclesiastical courts for the trial of heretics bring scandal and confusion and schism to the church of Christ. In fact the only aspect of the organization of Christianity which requires or admits development is the administrative. In this particular New Testament Christianity is susceptible of indefinite development, without doing any violence to the Christian principle of authority.

The question may be asked whether democracy as the form of church polity would have been adequate to the task of the past centuries, whether it could have preserved Christianity in the long night of the Dark Ages. Usually a negative answer is given. The question is, of course, in large part speculative and no certain conclusion is possible. But something may be said. If infant baptism and sacramentalism had been kept out of the church and the doctrine of a regenerate membership maintained steadfastly, the occasion for centralized ecclesiastical authority need not have arisen. If the gipsy moth had never been brought across the sea and introduced into New England, the authorities of Massachusetts would not have been called upon to organize a campaign for the protection of the trees. When the tide of the unregenerated began to flow into the church through infant baptism, the gipsy moth of medieval Christianity, then the secular ideal and method became necessary for government. The papacy was the result. Of course the direct spiritual authority of Christ could not be exerted over men whose loyalty to his religion was merely external and formal. Loring Brace, as we shall see in a later chapter, has declared that the most unfortunate thing for early Christianity was the loss of the simple democratic polity of the New Testament.[11] For when this occurred and religion took the form of an establishment supported by the State, Christianity ceased to be a leaven of spirituality and righteousness permeating society everywhere, and became instead a political force operating after the manner and with the ends of such a force. In fact we may say that from Constantine onward the destiny of Christianity was guided by a new law. The State and Church like Diomed and Glaucus in the opposing armies of Homer's story, had exchanged weapons. The State henceforth would seek to wield the spiritual power and the Church the temporal. But alas, as in the exchange of weapons on the Trojan battlefield, for brass arms of mean device the church gave her own "of gold divinely wrought."[12]

Democratic Polity Successful

As a matter of fact the democratic polity has always worked successfully when fairly tried, among barbarians or civilized men. It is working well today in many mission fields. It is peculiarly the polity of the intelligent and the spiritual, it is true. But then its fundamental assumption, as Baptists hold it, is that every member of each congregation is a regenerated man. We do not realize our ideal of course, but our doctrine and practice are a bulwark of protection against evils from without. Luther's objection to congregationalism for the Germans was that they were "wild" and "turbulent." But Baptists assume at least, and seek to embody the assumption in church life, that church members have been "tamed" by the Spirit of God. Certainly the congregational polity was quite suited to the New Testament age and ere long the beacon fires of a new hope for mankind were kindled all around the shores of the Mediterranean. Spiritual power waned as these democracies were left behind and Christianity went forth into the wilderness of the Dark Ages to meet the giant of sin, not with the spiritual weapons of the earlier days, which under

---

[11] C. Loring Brace, *Gesta Christi* (New York: Hodder and Stoughton, 1882).
[12] Homer *The Iliad* 6.294.

God had conquered the Roman power, but with the carnal weapons which she had wrested from the hands of her conquered foe.

It will be in order now to look for a moment at the equipment of democracy for its spiritual tasks. It can be maintained that as Baptists hold it this form of polity is eminently fitted for the work which Christianity is to perform in the world. This is by no means to overlook the fact that centralized polities possess certain advantages for doing some things. But where there is gain in one respect there is loss in another.

Be it said at once then that Baptists have no creed-making or other legislative power. They hold that all men are directly answerable to Christ, and that the Scriptures are a sufficient revelation of his will. Neither have they any courts to try heretics. They believe the local church, with the help of a council of wise advisers, can attend to all judicial matters. As a result they have never lost any time or energy over the question of creed revision. Their general bodies do not require weeks to transact the Lord's business chiefly because they are unencumbered by complicated systems of legislative and judicial machinery. Baptists sometimes express surprise that their general conventions are not more widely exploited in the secular press. A reporter recently gave the true answer. "The reason is," he said, "you Baptists have no church politics in your conventions."

Baptists and Organization

Baptists, however, can and do organize their forces efficiently. We have the district Associations or voluntary assemblies of messengers from local churches covering a limited district. We have our State Conventions which include messengers from all parts of the State, and our general conventions among English and Continental and other Baptists. Our organization, therefore, in its amplitude and geographical extent is equal to that, say, of our Presbyterian brethren, but without imitating them in the introduction of the principle of indirect authority. None of these bodies is legislative or judicial. Christ is the sole authority in all. They are for advisory and administrative purposes.

Then too, our superintendents and secretaries of missions perform the work of bishops without any of the authority of bishops. They visit the fields and lend a helping hand by means of suggestion, and in other ways. But they have no semblance of authority over any congregation however small.

We have also a great variety of Boards and councils. Congregationalism is capable of great diversity in this respect. These are not rigid in form that they may not be changed when occasion arises. Thus there is all needful flexibility.

We must of course frankly recognize our shortcomings. There is often an over-emphasis of individualism. Demagogues have occasionally taken the place of wise leaders over limited areas and for a brief period. Questions of administration have sometimes led to temporary schism and unwholesome controversy. But as there is no legal solidarity of the denomination, so also there is no way to split it into two or more parts on general questions. When divided we remain in a state of unstable equilibrium and can reunite at any time. There is no chemical law operative among us which leads to crystallization of separated parts on permanently antagonistic lines. If a local church becomes worldly and dies spiritually it may also pass out of existence as a visible organization. It cannot remain as a burden to its sister churches. It is simply insulated from the rest by its own worldliness. The spiritual churches, however, may unite in their Associations and Conventions for mutual helpfulness.

An Evil to Be Corrected

There is another really great evil which may be but which has not yet been corrected. Members leaving one church frequently refuse to put their leaving letters in the church of the community in which they live. Our pastors are sometimes to blame here. They encourage their members too often not to call for church letters. "Parochial selfishness" is the name which has been given to this tendency. Baptists ought to correct it.

The freedom and autonomy of Baptist churches give rise to another fact which is evil in one aspect and good in another. As unity among us is voluntary and not enforced it sometimes comes slowly. Intelligence and spirituality, or common sense and the grace of God, are the only unifying forces at our command. Sometimes, therefore, there are two or three or four denominational papers where there should be but one. The same is true of denominational schools and once in a long while of Associations and Conventions. This, however, while it is an element of weakness has its good side. It is our way of carrying out the principle of live and let live. Time, however, nearly always corrects the divisive tendencies for the reason that there are no permanent barriers to unity which any one can erect, and slowly common sense and duty assert themselves. It is a prime merit of our polity that conscience and judgment can never be permanently ruled out of court. In centralized polities the hands of common sense are sometimes bound by the red tape or chartered powers of institutionalism, while the voice of conscience is stifled by authority.

9

The Moral Axiom:
To Be Responsible The Soul Must Be Free

This axiom scarcely needs comment of any kind so far as its terms and general meaning are concerned. It is the basis of all ethics. No system of morals or of theology attempts now to repudiate or even to question it. As we have seen, God's sovereignty respects it. No gardener with a passionate love for growing things ever dealt so gently and skillfully with a delicate vine in training it to climb its trellis as God deals with the human will. We should imitate God in this. The gospel message is never forced upon the will. Indeed the will cannot be "forced." The ideas of the will and of force are incompatible and incommensurable.

The appeal of the moral axiom is to our self-consciousness. This is what gave it power when the theologians after the Reformation urged it against the extreme Calvinism of the day. Men knew they were free, and therefore no theory of God's decrees which ignored this fact could permanently hold its place in the doctrinal system. The reaction went too far, but it was wholesome and necessary.

It is our own consciousness of freedom which fortifies us against the modern doctrine of heredity. On one side, of course, heredity contains a great and profoundly significant truth. But man's moral sense will here stubbornly guard the citadel of freedom. The soul may not be able to defend its freedom in a speculative or metaphysical way. But it shuts itself in its castle, closes the drawbridge and every other avenue of entrance, and defies the foe. It knows there is something wrong with any metaphysics which denies freedom, and if metaphysics cannot overcome the difficulty it is merely bad for metaphysics.

Freedom against Heredity and Materialism

Our consciousness of freedom, again, repudiates materialism. When materialism asserts that moral choices are the product of chance combinations of atoms and molecules in the dim past, the soul denies. When a Christian gives a cup of cold water to another in the name of Christ, or spends his life as a spiritual hero in the effort to redeem the islands of the sea, and materialists tell him his entire conduct was predestined by the dancing atoms before chaos had become cosmos, the Christian enters his quiet but none the less emphatic denial and passes on.

Of course there are good and sound defenses of freedom on theological, metaphysical, and psychological grounds, as well as on moral and religious. Our purpose here does not require that we present them even in outline. We are dealing with an axiom. It is because this is an axiomatic truth that it holds its place in human thought and experience in spite of all metaphysical objections. If a luminous object holds place in the firmament through a period of thousands of years and is observed by the entire human race except a few men of defective vision, surely we are warranted in asserting that it is a fixed star and denying that it is a meteor.

Jesus taught the moral freedom of man. Not only so, he asserted it for himself. The first recorded event in his life after the story of the birth is an account of an act of self-assertion when he was twelve years of age. This was the temple experience. He did not disobey his parents, but he evidently had come into a sense of his heritage of individual responsibility. He declared later that he "came" into the world, that he would "go" to the Father. He asserted that he would "lay down" his life and that he would "take it" again [John 10:17–18]. In all his intimate union with the Father there is never on the Father's part the slightest movement or impulse to override the voluntary choice of the Son.

Christ and Free Choices

Jesus inveighed against the idea of heredity as giving spiritual rights or privileges apart from personal choice and corresponding character. The Jews were no true sons of Abraham because they were simply physical descendants of Abraham. Heredity did not bind the will, and heredity did not exempt the will from moral choices and personal obedience in the New Covenant.

Now freedom is self-determination. Of course it does not mean that the will is without bias, or that human choices are uninfluenced by external forces or other human personalities, or by divine influences of grace. It only means that when a man acts he acts for himself. The choice is his own. He is not compelled but impelled. He is self-determined. This is the core of manhood and personality. This is the inner glory of our being. It is the one spark of fire which kindles about our humanity its unique splendor.

In all spheres freedom is self-determination. In civic life political freedom is self-government. A government of the people by the people for the people is a free government. The individual is politically free only when he exercises his function as citizen without artificial or unjust extraneous hindrance. A man is intellectually free when he is intellectually self-determined. His beliefs are not imposed by authority but accepted as his own free act. Industrial freedom is the privilege of self-determination in the economic world. Unjust discriminations, class legislation, inequitable adjustments of the industrial machinery at any point impair or subvert industrial freedom. In morals freedom is self-determination in conduct. In religion freedom is exemption from State compulsion, social compulsion, ecclesiastical or priestly compulsion, creedal compulsion, or parental compulsion. Religious freedom on its positive side is God appealing to the soul through truth and calling forth the soul's intelligent and obedient response. It is the soul's approach to God through faith and prayer and fellowship and obtaining grace to help in time of need.

Christ and the Will

Now it is the peculiar and special work of Christ to set free the individual will in such manner that it unfolds in moral beauty in the personal character and coalesces socially with other wills in the beauty of a holy society.

The Anglo-Saxons made one chief contribution to the civilization of the world. This was the love of individual freedom. Guizot claims that this Anglo-Saxon sense of personality and love of freedom was found nowhere else.[1] He is right, doubtless, so far as the natural man is concerned. But it is exactly this gift which Christ bestows. The same love of freedom and sense of personality, the same self-assertion and love of adventure, the same response to the challenge of danger and of great undertaking in a line of exact analogy to the old Anglo-Saxon principle, all this appears in Christianity, but with a vast difference. Under Christ all is regenerated and spiritualized. Anglo-Saxon liberty was limited only by the conditions of the physical environment—

---

[1] Francois Guizot, *The History of Civilization*, 3 vols. (London: W. Clowes and Sons, George Bell and Sons, 1873). Guizot (1787–1874) was a French historian and politician who argued for constitutional monarchy.

mountains and seas, and the stubborn moods of nature—and only these imposed a check upon its career. Christian liberty is limited only by the spiritual environment. But the inner impulse to personal and social development under Christ is like an endless spring fixed in the machinery of man's faculties and uncoiling itself through the centuries in ever-increasing vigor and power. Anglo-Saxon freedom without the Christian fire to purge and sanctify it leads to the overman of Nietzsche and his followers, the colossus of pitiless and selfish power, who glories chiefly in the fact that he is destitute of love and the softer virtues. Christian freedom on the other hand produces the moral and spiritual giants of history who, to the kingly elements of power, have always added the priestly elements of love and service. Christ made us to be "kings and priests unto God" [Rev. 1:6].

Power Conjoined with Freedom

A sense of power conjoined with freedom is characteristic of the best Christians—of the men who choose Christ for themselves and make him their ideal. Nowhere do you find such spontaneity and grandeur, such untrammeled energy and buoyancy as in men who do this. Look at Paul. He abounds in images which suggest spontaneity and exuberant joy. See him yonder when, like a mighty swimmer, he rises above the billows of adversity and difficulty, and exclaims, "I can do all things through Christ." [Phil. 4:13]. Hear him as he spreads the wings of devotion, and in a splendid flight of mystic passion shouts "To me to live is Christ, and to die is gain" [Phil. 1:21]. Observe him as he is caught in the mighty grip of moral enthusiasm and self-conquest, exulting in the joy of battle: "Thanks be unto God, who always leadeth me in victory through Christ" [2 Cor. 2:14]. See him again as he is impelled onward, the embodiment of flaming love and quenchless hope, and deathless ambition, running the Christian race as one who treads the air, and exclaiming, "Forgetting the things that are behind, I press on toward the mark" [Phil. 3:14].

The moral career of Paul reminds one of the flight of some mighty eagle long confined in a cage and then released; at first he is uncertain of his new feeling of freedom, but at length, becoming conscious of it the heavy eyelids open, he looks about him, his drooping wings he gathers for flight and then, with a scream of joy, he soars away to the clouds. His eagle soul has found its object in God's free air. Jesus Christ is the atmosphere of the soul. And this is the secret of Christ's authority over men. Through him they find themselves. It is a paradox, but it is forever true. Men are the slaves of Christ because he makes them kings—masters of their own destiny. He imparts to them spiritual autonomy and thus roots his throne in the deep foundations of the soul. Such free moral career, therefore, should not be hampered by infant baptism. Leave the soul to unfold under Christian nurture. Let the beams of Christ fall directly upon the will, the conscience, and the intelligence of the child, and as a rose responds to sunlight, it will unfold beneath his rays.

Evil of Infant Baptism

What, we may inquire now, in the light of this principle, is the evil of infant baptism? It is manifold. One side of the matter we have already expounded. Here we note another. Its cardinal evil is that the religious choice of the child is forestalled by the parent. The religious destiny of the offspring is thus assumed by another without warrant from Scripture and without any rational justification from other sources. To baptize a child in infancy is to treat it not as a free moral personality, but as a thing. Many writers of power and insight who hold no brief for the Baptists, but who discern the tendencies of things, have commented upon the baleful effects of clerical and parental interference with the human will. Guizot discussing this general principle says:

> For with what do they pretend to interfere? With the reason and conscience and future destiny of man—that is to say with that which is the closest locked up; with that which is most strictly individual; with that which is most free. We can imagine how up to a certain point, a man, whatever ill may result from it, may give up the direction of his temporal affairs to an outward authority. We can conceive a notion of that philosopher who, when one told him that his house was on fire said, 'Go tell my wife; I never meddle with household affairs.' But when our conscience, our thoughts, our intellectual existence are at stake—to give up the government of one's very soul to the authority of a stranger, is indeed a moral suicide; is indeed a thousand times worse than bodily servitude—than to become a mere appurtenance of the soil.[2]

---

[2] Mullins cites Guizot, *History of Civilization*, 1:127.

The same writer defining the function of religion in another place remarks:

> But while it is with human liberty that all religions have to contend, while they aspire to reform the will of man, they have no means by which they can act upon him—they have no moral power over him, but through his will, his liberty. When they make use of exterior means, when they resort to force, to seduction—in short make use of means opposed to the free consent of man, they treat him as we treat water, wind, or any power entirely physical: they fail in their object; they attain not their end; they do not reach, they cannot govern the will. Before religions can really accomplish their task, it is necessary that they should be accepted by the free will of man; it is necessary that man should submit, but it must be willingly and freely, and that he still preserve his liberty in the midst of this submission.[3]

In these words Guizot has touched as with a point of a needle the crux of the whole question and sketched for us a great principle which is of the essence of Christianity. That which does not address the will or the intelligence, that ceremony or rite or form which does none of these things is alien to the genius of the gospel. It belongs to another order and another system entirely.

Take now the case of the child baptized in infancy. When it grows up it may become immoral, a bad boy or youth. This boy may, in order to evade the force of Christ's requirement, "Ye must be born again," plead his baptism in infancy. "I was regenerated then and do not need a new birth now," he urges. So also Christ's command to "repent and be baptized" falls on deaf ears because he connects the act of repentance with the act of baptism which his parents assure him occurred in infancy. Thus baptism becomes a wall of separation between his soul and Christ—an opaque body interposed between him and the Sun of Righteousness throwing him into the shadow of a spiritual eclipse.

The same result may ensue even when evidences of flagrant depravity do not appear in the life. The way to a real experience of Christ's saving power, of his moral and spiritual energy in the soul, may be quite as effectually barred

---

[3] Ibid., 139.

in this case also by a baptism which occurred in infancy. For the question of personal repentance and regeneration is regarded as a closed question.

Awakening and Duty

But suppose the boy has come into the life that is in Christ with all its mighty awakening and quickening. His soul is keenly alive to duty and he longs for opportunities of service. He opens his New Testament and reads that men first believed and were then baptized. "Repent and be baptized every one of you," he reads. "He that believeth and is baptized shall be saved" [Acts 2:30; Mk. 16:16].

The question of baptism then becomes intensely personal. He searches his memory in vain for any evidence that he ever obeyed this command. All he knows on the subject is hearsay. Every other Christian duty he is permitted to perform for himself. The Lord's Supper, enduring temptation, moral struggle, all church and spiritual privileges are his except one. In all these other things his attitude is one of obedience to Christ. But here is a great exception. It was predetermined in some strange way by others, when he was in no sense a conscious party to the arrangement, that he should never be permitted to adopt the attitude of obedience to Christ in baptism. Thus he finds himself unable to fit his infant baptism into the scheme of his life at all. All other elements and factors of it run together harmoniously. This factor of baptism is alien. It came in on some other principle, one which is irreconcilable with all else in his experience and in his relation to Christ and the church. If any one says to him he is free to be baptized again if he so elects, this does not clear up the case of the first baptism. For he sees that it is the great exception and can by no process of forcing be made to fit into the plan of an obedient life.

Doing Violence to the Will

The natural effect follows. He is shocked, amazed, surprised, and asks, Who tampered thus with my will? Who dared assume to perform an outward act of religious duty for me? It is thus clear that infant baptism violates the moral axiom. It does not leave the soul free. It introduces a confusing principle into the spiritual career of the child which proves injurious to thousands.

The father and the mother, the sponsor, and the clergy have no right to rob the child of its right to obey God for itself. Who does not recall the joy of obeying his Lord in baptism? Who has not known the truth of the words of the old song—

Oh, happy day that fixed my choice
On thee, my Saviour and my God.
Well may this glowing heart rejoice
And tell its raptures all abroad.[4]

Who does not remember that experience who has ever had it? Who does not look back to it as the brightest day in a lifetime? But infant baptism leaves no room for fixing the choice; there is no glowing heart, for it is the heart of the unknowing babe; there is no rapture to tell abroad, for in such a life baptism is simply a tradition told in later years, when the power of understanding has come. The wrong of infant baptism is the wrong of a human shadow flung between the soul and God. Then and there the Sun of Righteousness passes into eclipse, the meaning of Christianity is confused, and the danger is that the soul's life will henceforth be spent in the shadow.

It would be easy to fill many pages with quotations from men of all Protestant denominations who insist upon the principle I am here advocating, although they do not all consistently apply it practically. Two or three brief citations must suffice, however, as our space is limited. Dr. Newman Smyth in his *Christian Ethics* denies that men sustain the same relation to the church that in some countries men sustain to the State Church, as in ancient Rome. There all citizens were members of the State Church. The Christian church, he says, "does not offer its citizenship simply as a Christian birthright, but also as a duty to be assumed with a personal faith in its truth, and in a free self-surrender to its supreme law of life." He then insists upon Christ's requirements for church membership and denies the right of any to change them. Repentance and faith, he says, a voluntary acceptance of the Christian obligation are indispensable. "The universal intent of the church as a blessing belonging by heaven's decree to all men, should serve as a perpetual injunction upon human devices or forms which narrow or limit its divine design. When we look solely at what may be imposed as an indispensable condition of fellowship with Christ in the visible Church, we may not go one

---

[4] "Oh Happy Day" by Philip Doddridge (1702–1751).

step beyond the Lord's own requirements of discipleship." There is of course no possible way of reconciling the principle thus expounded with infant baptism, and Dr. Smyth does not succeed in doing so.[5]

Professor Van Dyke on Freedom

Professor Van Dyke also, in his *Gospel for an Age of Doubt*, expounds the same general principle of individual and personal responsibility to Christ. "But this receiving," he says, "we need to assert again and again, is not a passive thing. It is an action of the soul, the opening of a door within the heart, the welcoming of a heavenly master. God does not save men as a watchmaker who repairs and sets a watch, but as a king who recalls his servants to their duty, as a Father who makes new revelations of his love to draw the lost children back to himself." Dr. Van Dyke is right. The watchmaker deals with a thing, not with a person, and hence he may do to it what he wills. But not so in dealing with a human soul. Its own integrity as a distinct personality cannot be violated. Speaking of Buddha and Mahomet he declares that their chief fault lies in failure here. "They despise and slight personality. Christ accepts and emphasizes it. They aim to reduce and evaporate responsibility, Christ aims to deepen and increase it."[6]

It is abundantly clear from all the foregoing that in dealing with children religiously we are strictly limited by the nature of the child and by the nature of religion. The law is simple and easy to grasp. Freedom and responsibility go hand in hand. A rite, ceremony, or ordinance, which can be observed or performed only with the free consent of the recipient can never be administered without evil consequences in the absence of that free consent. If free consent is the correlative to the intelligent administration of the ordinance, according to the nature of the religion itself, then administration without free consent renders it null and void, and mischievous besides.

---

[5] Mullins cites Newman Smyth, *Christian Ethics* (New York: Scribner's Sons, 1896) 423, 427. Smyth (1843–1925) was an American Congregationalist theologian.

[6] Mullins cites Henry Van Dyke, *The Gospel for an Age of Doubt* (New York: Macmillan, 1926) 237–38. Van Dyke (1852–1933) was a Presbyterian.

Many Radical Presuppositions

There are many radical presuppositions and assumptions underlying the practice of infant baptism which reinforce the plea we are making for the right of the soul to measure responsibility by freedom.

Infant baptism assumes the insufficiency of the word and the Spirit in parental and Christian nurture by anticipating and forestalling the action of the word and Spirit before the child's intelligence admits of it. Infant baptism assumes that Christ demands from the soul what the soul cannot give. For there are thousands of infants left without baptism, and when the child of the Christian parent dies without it, it leaves a heartbreak which no church has a right to inflict by such teaching.

Logically carried out infant baptism excludes conversion from the possible experiences of the children of church members and tends toward a church without a converted membership. Unless counteracted in some way by more spiritual means, as is happily true in most of our evangelical Pedobaptist churches in America, the churches become increasingly alienated in life and character from the Christian ideals. On the continent in Europe, however, this condition of affairs has attracted the attention and called for the grave comment of men like Professor Harnack and others in the State churches there. As infant baptism cannot be reconciled with the essential principles of Christianity, as we know these principles from the New Testament, so also if resorted to as a means of explaining the origin of Christianity in New Testament times it would lead us into inextricable confusion, and reduce the whole process to an inconceivable absurdity.[7]

Again, infant baptism substitutes natural heredity for spiritual, in assuming that natural birth into a Christian family entitles *per se* to the rites and ordinances of religion. This introduces a dualistic principle into our anthropology, or doctrine of human nature, and leaves the general theological system unintelligible. Baptism of course may be administered to improper subjects under any view of it, but to confine it to those who are capable of making a credible profession of faith at least respects human freedom and supplies a scriptural and rational basis for it.

---

[7] Influential liberal theologian Adolf Harnack (1851–1930) wrote *What is Christianity?* (New York: G. P. Putnam's Sons, 1903).

Natural, Does Not Imply Spiritual, Heredity

This ceremony applied to infants also proceeds upon the assumption that the Church is like the State and that natural birth entitles to membership in it. It is too well known to require elaborate proof here that in this, as in other respects, Christ's Church is radically different from the State.

In view of the lack of direct or indirect scriptural warrant for infant baptism, its practice assumes that the church belongs to us and not to Christ, and that the terms of admission within its pale are in our own hands. If an inferential warrant for the practice is insisted upon, as is usually done, this opens the door of the church so wide that it will be impossible to protect it. For all kinds of inferences may be drawn from the facts of the New Testament which the facts neither authorize nor require. The constitution of the church is too vital and important a matter to be made subject to precarious deductions in the interest of traditional practices inherited from the Roman Catholic Church, which consistently and avowedly rejects Scripture as the sole authority and holds to the joint authority of tradition and the church along with that of Scripture.

Infant baptism is a curious instance in which extremes meet. It really interprets God's decree of salvation in a manner like that of the antinomians and hyper-Calvinists. The latter insist that man's action is not required by God's grace. Irresistible grace will sweep the elect into the kingdom without cooperation on their part. This, of course, simply ignores human freedom. Infant baptism also assumes that grace operates without the cooperation of the will of the child, but with a striking difference. In the one case it is insisted that we must not intermeddle with God's plans of persuading sinners to believe, while in the other it is urged that we must intermeddle and assist God's decree by bringing the infant to the baptismal font. But, properly understood, God's execution of his decree of election is the shining example of wise method in dealing with the spirits whom he has created and endowed with freedom. For whatever may be mysterious in that decree, whatever beyond human knowledge and surmise, one thing stands out clearly in every instance of its execution which is brought before us in the Scriptures. He always makes use of persuasion. He respects the will. Even the Father in heaven refuses to forget that men are persons and not things, and that our freedom is our inalienable gift from his gracious hands.

10

Christian Nurture

The close of the last chapter opens the way to a consideration of Christian nurture. We devote a brief chapter to the subject. In recent years there has been more or less discussion of the question whether we should expect the conversion of children or not. The position has been taken that Christian nurture should lead to the unconscious development of Christian character in the child. Dr. Horace Bushnell, in his book entitled *Christian Nurture*, has given striking expression to this view. Before offering our own view of the subject, it may be well to give a few extracts from Bushnell's discussion by way of introduction.[1]

In the first chapter of this book Dr. Bushnell says that we should hold the view "that the child is to grow up a Christian, and never know himself as being otherwise." He elaborates this thought at length. He says that the organic unity of the family requires this, and that Christian principles make it necessary. We are guilty of an excessive individualism, he thinks, and we need to return to this conception of the organic unity of the family. In "Christian Nurture" he says:

> The tendency of all our modern speculations is to an extreme individualism, and we carry our doctrine of free will so far as to make little or nothing of organic laws; not observing that character may be, to a great extent, only the free development of exercises previously wrought in us, or extended to us, when other wills had us within their sphere. All the Baptist theories of religion are based on this error. They assume, as a first truth, that no such thing is possible as an organic

---

[1] Horace Bushnell (1802–1876), a Congregationalist theologian, is best known for his work, *Christian Nurture* (1847). See the reprint, *Christian Nurture* (Grand Rapids: Baker Book House, 1979). In this chapter, Mullins quotes the book extensively without giving page citations.

connection of character, an assumption which is plainly refuted by what we see with our eyes and, as I shall by and by show, by the declarations of Scripture.[2]

Bushnell and the Baptist Position

Dr. Bushnell wholly misstates the Baptist attitude in the above passage. Baptists do not deny that there is an organic unity in the family, as we shall see. Of course, Dr. Bushnell applies his principle in a way which Baptists object to seriously. Infant baptism, he thinks, is a logical inference. He says: "It is my settled conviction that no man ever objected to infant baptism, who had not at the bottom of his objection false views of Christian education—who did not hold a notion of individualism, in regard to Christian character in childhood, which is justified, neither by observation nor by Scripture."

"It is the prevalence of false views, on this subject, which creates so great difficulty in sustaining infant baptism in our churches. If children are to grow up in sin, to be converted when they come to the age of maturity, if this is the only aim and expectation of family nurture, there really is no meaning or dignity whatever in the rite."[3]

If Dr. Bushnell had pushed his investigations further, we do not doubt he would have discovered that there are other reasons for the growing disrepute of infant baptism among the churches which practice it. He might have found that regard for the headship of Christ had to do with it.

Dr. Bushnell has a sermon entitled "The Ostrich Nurture," in which he holds up the excessive individualism of the day, as he regards it, to a measure of ridicule. Parents deal with their children as ostriches with their eggs—leave them to be hatched out by the forces of nature—leave them exposed to the elements. "As a curious illustration of the looseness and the unsettled feeling of the times, in regard to this great subject, it is just now beginning to be asserted by some that the true principle of training for children is exactly that of the ostrich, viz., no training at all; the best government, no government. All endeavors to fashion them by the parental standards, or to induct them into

---

[2] Ibid., 10, 29.
[3] Ibid., 53, for both quotations.

the belief of their parents, is alleged to be a real oppression put upon their natural liberty."[4]

It is quite possible that such a view of child nurture exists, but it is among the religiously indifferent. Dr. Bushnell's extreme statement of the case scarcely applies to any religious denomination today, if it ever did.

The Position of Bushnell

In discussing the organic unity of the family, Dr. Bushnell states his general position. He says:

> Perhaps I shall be understood with the greatest facility if I say that the family is such a body that a power over character is exerted therein, *which* cannot properly be called *influence*. We commonly use the term *influence* to denote a persuasive power, or a governmental power, exerted purposely, and with a conscious design to effect some result in the subject. In maintaining the organic unity of the family, I mean to assert, that a power is exerted by parents over children, not only when they teach, encourage, persuade, and govern, but without any purposed control whatever. The bond is so intimate that they do it unconsciously and undesignedly—they must do it...All such acts of control therefore must, in metaphysical propriety, and as far as the child is concerned, be classed under the general denomination of *organic* causes. And thus whatever power over character is exerted in families one side of consent, in the children, and even before they have come to the age of rational choice, must be taken as organic power, in the same way as if the effect accrued under the law of simple contagion.[5]

Thus we see Dr. Bushnell introduces the principle of natural heredity into Christian nurture and makes it a controlling factor. To show that this is true, he makes the following statement: "In all of which it seems to be dearly held that grace shall travel by the same conveyance with sin; that the organic unity, which I have spoken of chiefly as an instrument of corruption, is to be

---

[4] Ibid., 67.
[5] Ibid., 92–93.

occupied and sanctified by Christ, and become an instrument also of mercy and life." Again he says:

> Now the true conception is, that baptism is applied to the child, on the ground of its organic unity with the parents; imparting and pledging a grace to sanctify that unity, and make it good in the field of religion. By the supposition, however, the child still remains within the known laws of character in the house, to receive, under these, whatever good may reach him; not snatched away by an abrupt, fantastical, and therefore incredible grace. He is taken to be regenerate, not historically speaking, but presumptively, on the ground of his known connection with the parent character, and the divine or church life, which is the life of that character. Perhaps I shall be understood more easily if I say that the child is *potentially* regenerate, being regarded as existing in connection with powers and causes that contain the fact, before time and separate from time.[6]

Dr. Bushnell maintains that a child comes to his individuality gradually as, of course, we all do, and seeks to divide the period of infancy into two sections: that of impressions merely, the earliest period, and the age of tuitional influences or, as he divides it, "the age of existence in the will of the parent, and the age of will and personal choice in the child."

The above extracts indicate with sufficient clearness and fullness the general position of Dr. Bushnell. Let it be said at once that the Baptists have no quarrel with his contention as to early influences and unconscious impressions upon childhood. They offer no objection to the general position that the child's life is in very large measure bound up in the life of the family. Nor is there any objection in general to the idea that Christian nurture in the home should be so thorough that the child will become a Christian at a very early age. The serious objection which Baptists offer is to Bushnell's position that the organic unity of the family requires an identification of the family with the church. Men do not become members of the church on the same conditions as members of a family. Again, the position of Dr. Bushnell assumes that the law of heredity from Christ is the same as the law of heredity

---

[6] Ibid., 113, 116–17.

from Adam. Christ is the new head of the race, but men are related to him by faith, and not through natural propagation.

Principles of Christian Nurture

We come next to a positive statement of the principles of Christian nurture. And, first of all, we assert that Christian nurture should recognize the organic unity of the family. The family life is the omnipresent influence surrounding the child. The child is molded by it unconsciously. Before it becomes intelligent, while it remains as a potential individual only, it may receive impressions that are lasting. If you hold in the palm of your open hand a lump of moist clay without closing your fingers upon it, the clay will nevertheless bear the imprint of the lines in your hand when you lay it down. Thus is childhood impressed by its earliest environment for good or ill.

What inference must be drawn from this? That the ceremonies and rites of religion should be forced upon the unconscious child? Far from it. The proper inference is, let the family life carefully and jealously protect the child against premature action here. Do not stifle the child's religious life with burdens it cannot bear. Guard it from the perils of the organic unity of the family, as well as expose it to the blessings.

Church and Family Are Distinct

A second principle of Christian nurture is that the distinction between the church and the family must be kept intact. The church implies personal relations between actual individuals and Christ, not potential individuals thrust into fictitious relations with Christ as in infant baptism. We may assume that the child will become a Christian, but we dare not assume that he is a Christian prior to his own choice.

This leads to the third law of Christian nurture, viz., that it must respect human personality. Let there be a recognition of the fact that in its earlier stages the child is but a candidate for personality, and not a developed person, and let the nurture correspond to the stage of development. The Baptist view of Christian nurture accords with modern pedagogy in its best conclusions. As we shall see in a later chapter, the best pedagogy ever respects personality, seeks to call forth the latent powers of the soul, and jealously guards the nature of the child from premature forcing.

Now, baptism belongs to the stage of intelligence and personality, to the stage of tuitional influences, and not to the stage of unconscious impressions.

139

There is no way to understand New Testament baptism save as the personal choice of the individual. To apply it therefore to the child in the earliest stage of unconscious impressions is premature, like requiring a child to read the *Anabasis* before it has mastered the Greek alphabet. Infant baptism is like requiring the mastery of algebraic symbols before the boy has learned the multiplication table. Infant baptism, in other words, is based on unsound pedagogy. Dr. Bushnell's general view on this point is directly against sound principles of pedagogy. He has much to say regarding potential regeneration in infant baptism, presumptive individuality in applying this ordinance to non-intelligent babes. In so doing, however, he advocates that which is contradictory and unreasonable. A babe is a presumptive walker, but it is dressed in long clothes and its feet left bare usually in the earliest months, both of which would impede it in the attempt to accomplish great things in locomotion. The babe in the mother's arms is a presumptive citizen, a potential voter, but the State never puts the ballot in the hand of babes. Now, in a real sense baptism is the ballot of the kingdom of God. It is the outward act which the citizen of that kingdom first performs to proclaim his citizenship therein. Therefore Christian nurture must respect personality.

Natural and Spiritual Heredity

A fourth point to be emphasized in Christian nurture is the distinction between natural and spiritual heredity. Natural heredity connects us with Adam through the physical bond. Spiritual heredity connects us with Christ through the mediation of teachers and preachers. Now, there is a revealed method by which the soul becomes personally related to Christ and a partaker of the spiritual heredity. This includes the attitude of faith, of repentance, the recognition of God as Father and Christ as Savior. Much is said in favor of the child's becoming unconsciously a Christian. But the child should become consciously a Christian also. Doubtless there are those who are genuine Christians who do not remember the time and place of their conversion, but unless they carry consciously the elements of the relationship necessary to the Christian life, they are sadly deprived. It is urged that children should not have a sense of sin. It is true that we should not require of them the same kind of conviction for sin that the hardened sinner has, but if the child grows up destitute of the sense of ill desert and demerit, its moral character is defective. This consciousness of sin is the mainspring of growth. It is proper to every man, every woman, and every child at the proper age. In its absence the tendency becomes marked towards self-complacency.

We should not impose our molds upon children. There are four of these molds to be avoided. One is experimental. We should not insist that the child have an experience identical in detail with the adult. Another is the intellectual mold. We should not insist that the child be able to give the same exhaustive account of his Christian life as the older person. The elements will be there, but frequently the child is unable to state them completely. Again, we should avoid imposing a theological mold upon the child, or rather, substituting a theological mold for vital faith. It is not difficult for a bright child to learn the catechism, but knowing the catechism is not knowing Christ. And finally, we should not impose the ceremonial mold. Baptism is entirely out of place for a child before it has reached the age of understanding. Otherwise, it becomes a mere mold into which we seek to force the child's nature. Apply all these means of nurture as the child is able to receive them. But there must be response on the part of the child, not compulsion.

Elements of Christian Life the Same

When all is said, however, it remains true that the elements of the Christian life are the same in the child as in the adult. There is variation, of course. In some cases one aspect of the spiritual experience is emphasized, and in others other aspects. The elements are the same. A child may become a Christian so early as scarcely to know the grosser forms of sin. Nevertheless, the sense of demerit and shortcoming is a necessary element in a rounded spiritual character. The difference, therefore, between the conversion of a child and an adult is one of degree, not of kind. One seed may be planted in good soil, with the right environment and be subject to wise cultivation until it bursts and roots itself firmly and springs upward to fruitage. Another seed may fall in scanty soil upon a stone, be subject to the elements, and yet swell until it bursts, striking its root downward, rending the stone and drawing nourishment from the soil below, while it springs upward also and bears fruit. Now, the life process in the seed is the same in both cases, only in the latter case the process was more violent. Such is the difference between the conversion of children and men. It is a difference easily recognized and important.

A child may be said to be converted when there is recognized the presence in the child of a permanent Christian motive and struggle. Observe that the motive is to be Christian, and it is to be abiding. We are to look not so much for attainment as for struggle. These two elements—the Christian motive and the Christian struggle—when they appear as permanent in the child's life, are sure indications that Christ has come into that life.

The Old and New Covenants

We must recognize in the next place in our Christian nurture, the distinction between the old and the new covenant. Writers who advocate infant baptism uniformly go back to the Mosaic system and plead the solidarity of Israel and the theocracy. They forget the vital distinctions between the church and theocracy. The commonwealth of Israel was localized; the church is a universal institution. Israel was maintained by positive laws and outward ceremonies; the church through spiritual laws. Israel was preserved through the organic physical bond and family ties, the church through the spiritual. One needs only to recall the strong language of Jesus concerning the individual in relation to family and friends to recognize how far Christianity is from Judaism. A man's foes shall be they of his own household. The Christian must forsake father and mother, sister and brother, if need be, in order to follow Christ. Much is made also by those who advocate infant baptism of the fact that in the first chapter of Acts the promise is announced to the hearers and to their children. The point is made that infants are included in the promise under the gospel because children are named. Doubtless the reference is to descendants rather than to little children, though of course children are included in so far as they are able to accept and partake of the blessings of the gospel.

But these advocates forget the sharp contrast which is made between the old and the new covenant in the eighth chapter of Hebrews. In the eleventh verse of that chapter the statement is made that "they shall not teach every man his neighbor, and every man his brother, saying, Know the Lord: for all shall know me, from the least to the greatest." Here we have a distinct statement that there are no exceptions in the kingdom of God under the new covenant. The new covenant does not include those who know the Lord and those who are unconscious infants and cannot know him. And this simply makes clear the fact that the kingdom of God, as revealed by Christ, is not a kingdom of heredity or a kingdom of magic, but a kingdom of truth. With gladness Baptists obey Christ's words, "Suffer the little children to come unto me" [Mk. 10:14] but they decline to bring them to him by force while unconscious infants by applying religious ceremonies without meaning save on the theory of magical efficacy. The new covenant does not require this. The new covenant is unlike the old in many ways, and they are not to be confounded.

The Child Environment

We name, as a further condition of Christian nurture that there should be created an environment of the child which will predispose it to Christ and the church. Environment counts for more in childhood than at any other period. There is no more vital element in the production of character in the earliest stages. A recent writer on the education of children has emphasized this in a striking way in connection with Shakespeare. He shows how Shakespeare's imagery, as it appears in his poetic writings, was derived largely from the environment of his childhood. Take this verse:

When daisies pied and violets blue,
And lady smocks, all silver whit,
And cuckoo buds of yellow hue,
Do paint the meadows with delight.[7]

In this verse there are, of course, many very pretty floral images. Now if the traveler examines closely the meadows about Stratford where Shakespeare was a boy, he will find these flowers growing today. Shakespeare had poetic genius, but his genius required material to work upon, just as a fire requires fuel to maintain it. The environment of childhood helped to make the poet Shakespeare. If we surround our children with the fadeless flowers of spiritual truth; if the home life is sweet and Christly; if patience and gentleness and love, combined with firmness and discipline and high purpose, are the traits of character discerned by the child in the parent, there is strong probability that they will be reproduced in him.

---

[7] These are the first four lines of William Shakespeare's poem "Spring and Water."

That is a striking picture in the Gospel of Luke where Jesus as a boy of twelve, upon the occasion of his first visit to the temple, is held spellbound amid its scenes [Lk. 2:42–51]. For the first time the great and wondrous significance of the Jewish system fell upon the sensitive soul of Jesus. All of it had a symbolic reference to his own person and mission. Doubtless there was an awakening in his soul, a calling forth thus of the powers that were in him, and a quickening into a new sense of his mission and destiny. Environment lifted him to a new stage in his career under God's blessing. Even so should it be with childhood ever—expose the soul of the child to the truth, surround it with every incentive to holy living, permit it to respond to grace in the home circle.

A Final Suggestion

A final suggestion for Christian nurture is that all the elements of Christian character be brought into the conscious experience of the child at the earliest possible moment. Let religion take its proper form of personal experience. Art is the response of man's soul to beauty. Science is his response to truth. Religion is the response of the soul of man to God and righteousness. Let not the ordinances of religion be applied before the capacity for response is present, but let truth and piety become the enveloping atmosphere of the child's life—its spiritual universe, so to speak—until it responds thereto. As physical nature calls forth the interest and the effort of the child, as the beautiful sky above attracts his steadfast gaze, as the stars that stud it at night kindle his imagination, as trees and mountains and rivers, as pebbles and brooks and flowers, call forth his nature and stir it into new energy, so let the truths of Christianity, the fact of God's fatherhood and Christ's saviorhood, of beautiful Christian character, and of eternal life, stand out as the objects of his spiritual world, warming him into life, and under God's blessing leading him out into the Christian profession. When the mind is sufficiently advanced to grasp the significance of the church, the ordinances, the doctrines, let these be interpreted, and let there flow into his soul the tide of joy and peace which comes from a recognition of the meaning of these things. But in all this let vital individual faith in Christ be recognized as the basic fact.

Unquestionably childhood is the strategic point in Christian culture, and in all our religious bodies increasing attention should be given to this great theme. A modern poet has symbolized the beauty of the task of training the child. Browning has a little poem in which he describes a picture. The picture attracts the attention of the beholder because an angel is seen close to a tomb engaged intently in some task which at first does not appear. Overhead the heavens are opened, and angelic hands beckon the angel upward. On the horizon earthly enterprises loom large and beckon the angel to them, but he remains unheeding, busily engaged in some great task. As the beholder looks closely he discovers by the side of the angel a little child, kneeling, with folded hands and closed eyes and uplifted face. There is no higher task for angels or men than to teach a little child to pray.[8]

---

[8] See Robert Browning's poem "The Guardian Angel."

11

The Religio-Civic Axiom:
A Free Church in a Free State

Relations between Church and State

The religio-civic axiom which states the American principle of the relations between Church and State is so well understood and is accepted by the people of the United States so generally and so heartily that it is unnecessary to spend time in pointing out at length what the axiom implies. Mr. Bryce in his *American Commonwealth* remarks: "It is accepted as an axiom by all Americans that the civil power ought to be not only neutral and impartial as between entirely different forms of faith, but ought to leave these matters entirely on one side, regarding them no more than they regard the artistic or literary pursuits of the citizens."[1] In short the entire contents of the axiom is summed up in the statement that the State has no ecclesiastical and the Church no civic function. Mr. Bryce also says: "Of all the differences between the Old World and the New this is perhaps the most salient. Half the wars of Europe, half the internal troubles that have vexed European States, from the Monophysite controversies in the Roman empire of the fifth century down to the Kulturkampf in the German empire of the nineteenth, have arisen from theological differences or from the rival claims of Church and State."[2] In this connection also I give a statement from Buckle. He says in his *History of Civilization*:

> During almost a hundred and fifty years, Europe was afflicted by religious wars, religious massacres, and religious persecutions; not one of which would have arisen if the great truth had been recognized that

---

[1] Mullins cites James Bryce, *The American Commonwealth*, 2 vols. (New York: Macmillan, 1900) 2:572–73.

[2] Ibid., 570.

the State has no concern with the opinions of men, and no right to interfere even in the slightest degree with the form of worship which they may choose to adopt. This principle was, however, formerly unknown or at all events unheeded; and it was not until the middle of the seventeenth century that the great religious contests were brought to a final close and the different countries settled down to their public creeds.[3]

Such quotations might be indefinitely multiplied, but it is needless. Neither of the writers quoted is an American, and yet each states the principle in a manner which is in complete unison with our way of regarding the matter. For many centuries the struggle between Church and State was an unequal one. By a sort of spiritual instinct the church tugged at her chains with various movements of protest against the English and European establishments. It was like the struggle between the eagle and the serpent. The church, as the eagle in the contest, was sometimes dragged down into the dust by the foe. Again, with the serpent's sinewy coils about her body she would rise heavily into the air only to be dragged downward again. At length the eagle, with beak and talons dripping with the blood of her slain foe, mounts upward and builds her nest on a lofty crag forever beyond the serpent's reach. This was when Roger Williams founded the commonwealth of Rhode Island. A new era in man's spiritual history began then.

The leadership of the Baptists of Rhode Island and Virginia in introducing the doctrine of complete separation of Church and State has already been pointed out in a previous chapter. Indeed two great conceptions were formally promulgated by the Baptists of the seventeenth century in their creeds and confessions, which in a striking manner show that they were far in advance of Christendom in general in their views as to the essential nature of Christianity. One of these is the doctrine of worldwide missions, which is absent from the Westminster and other creeds of the period. It is a well-known fact that Christendom at large was apparently dead to this great obligation until William Carey aroused it. Yet in their "Confession of Faith," issued by churches in and around London in 1660, the Baptists of England

---

[3] Mullins cites Henry T. Buckle, *History of Civilization in England,* 3 vols. (New York: Henry Frowde, 1904) 1:190.

promulgated the doctrine and obligation of worldwide missions as we shall see in a later chapter.

Another Great Baptist Principle

But we are here more directly interested in the other great Baptist principle in which they antedated others. Their view of soul freedom and separation of Church and State they promulgated in their earliest known creeds and their practice has never parted company with their doctrine. We find the following in the "London Confession," published in 1644. After declaring the duty of obedience to magistrates and all legally constituted authorities in all things lawful the Confession in the forty-ninth article says: "But in case we find not the magistrate to favor us herein, yet we dare not suspend our practice because we believe we ought to go on in obedience to Christ, in professing the faith which is declared in the holy Scriptures and this our confession of faith a part of them; and that we are to witness to the truth of the Old and New Testament unto the death if necessity require, in the midst of trials and afflictions, as his saints of old have done," etc. In the next article it is declared that it is lawful for a Christian to be a magistrate and to take oaths. Under the forty-eighth article the following language occurs: "As we cannot do anything contrary to our understandings and consciences, so neither can we forbear the doing of that which our understandings and consciences bind us to do; and if the magistrate should require us to do otherwise, we are to yield our persons in a passive way to their power, as the saints of old have done."[4]

Of like tenor with the above are all the Baptist creeds. There has never been a time in their history, so far as that history is known to us, when they wavered in their doctrine of a free Church in a free State. Nowhere in the American colonies before the Revolution, save in Rhode Island and among Virginia Baptists and in a few great minds such as Madison and others like him, had this novel and far-reaching conception taken root. Men in general regarded the separation of Church and State as a doctrine of anarchy and chaos, and honestly believed that its practical application would quench the sun of religion in the heaven of man's spiritual hopes.

---

[4] Mullins cites Edward Bean Underhill, *Confessions of Faith and other Public Documents Illustrative of the History of the Baptist Churches of England in the Seventeenth Century* (London: Hanserd Knollys Society, 1854) 45–46.

It is a singular fact, to be noted in this connection, that many writers of great intelligence in other respects even today fail to grasp clearly the distinction between religious toleration and religious freedom. Dr. Bacon in his *History of American Christianity* falls into the common error of referring to the Maryland colony under the Calverts as an example of religious liberty; whereas all who are familiar with the distinction know that in Maryland not religious liberty in the modern sense and in the ancient Baptist sense, but only toleration was enjoyed.[5] We find the same error in an address so recent as that of one of the speakers at the Congress of Arts and Science in St. Louis. Americans of today would no more rest content under a system of mere religious toleration than they were willing to endure taxation without representation under George the Third.

English Wrestling with the Problem

It is instructive to observe how the English people have wrestled with the problem of the relations of Church and State. Of course the Nonconformist bodies have solved the problem for themselves on its theoretical side, although in recent years they have been called upon to wage a noble war of passive resistance against an oppressive education act. The English Nonconformists in this matter are in line with their best traditions as descendants of the freedom loving Anglo-Saxons.

Many English writers who favor an established church have sought to justify it on various grounds. A glance at these theories will prepare us to consider briefly the theoretical grounds for our American principle.

The principle known as Erastianism has for a long time exerted a powerful influence over English thinking on the subject. This view asserts that the Church as such has no governing power. A part of the function of the State is to govern the Church.

Hooker maintained that in any country, Church and State are to be regarded not as two societies but as one.[6] This one organization viewed on its temporal side is the commonwealth, on its ecclesiastical side it is the church. Warburton took the position that while the Church and State were originally separate and independent they entered into an alliance and formed a union by

---

[5] Leonard W. Bacon, *A History of American Christianity* (London: James Clarke and Co., 1899). Bacon (1830–1907) was a Congregationalist historian.

[6] See n. 6 in chap. 8.

contract, with conditions on each side.[7] Coleridge distinguished between the national and the visible church of Christ. The national church is the general community with officers who are partly civil and partly ecclesiastical, while the visible church is a spiritual kingdom not of this world, self-governing and self-supporting. Gladstone advocated a view of the State like that proclaimed by Milton that the State is a "gigantic moral person." Gladstone asserted that as a moral person the State is bound to act in the name of Christ for God's glory, and that the promotion of religion is the chief end in government. Macaulay replied to Gladstone that the State has no such inherent or inalienable function. Government is primarily for the protection of life and property, urged Macaulay, and it is no more bound to promote religion directly than a life insurance company is so bound. But Macaulay held that the State may use religion for its own ends, especially education. Chalmers, in Scotland, maintained that the State should foster some one denomination on the ground of the truth held, if possible, and if not on this, then on some other ground. For only thus could Christianity exert its proper influence over men. The idea seemed ingrained in the English mind.

Canon Fremantle in his work *The World as the Subject of Redemption* maintains the theory of Christian Nationalism. In contrast with the limited view of the church as concerned chiefly with worship and dogma Fremantle says: "The church will be here presented as the social State in which the Spirit of Christ reigns; as embracing the general life and society of man, and identifying itself with these as much as possible; as having for its object to imbue all human relations with the spirit of Christ's self-renouncing love, and thus to change the world into a kingdom of God."[8] The means for the realization of this program of Christianity is to be found in Christian Nationalism. The statement of Fremantle's view of the relations between Church and State is as follows: "The principle of the royal supremacy means that the Christian community as a whole, represented by its sovereign, is to be supreme over all its parts."[9] The Church is regarded as a subordinate part of the State and as necessarily falling under its jurisdiction. Fremantle's general

---

[7] William Warburton (1698–1799) was an English prelate and theologian.

[8] Mullins cites William Henry Fremantle, *The World as the Subject of Redemption* (London: Rivingtons, 1885) 1, 7, 8. Fremantle (1831–1916) was a canon of Canterbury Cathedral and a fellow/tutor of Balliol College, Oxford.

[9] Ibid., 214.

theory is a singular attempt to unite an antiquated conception of the relations of Church and State with a very modern view as to the aims of the Church. It is like cutting off the head of the Bartholdi Statue of Liberty in New York harbor and attaching it to the trunk of the Egyptian sphinx.

Four Leading Considerations

Now it is clear to the student of English theory on the subject of the relations between Church and State that four leading considerations have affected English thinkers in their persistent efforts to justify an establishment of religion under government. The first is tradition and the conservative tendency of the human mind. The English church *was* established, therefore it ought to be established. Fortunately in America we had no such longstanding institution under national patronage to fetter our thinking when we organized the present government. The second consideration was moral. Englishmen felt that government is for moral ends. They were little influenced by Rousseau's social contract theory of government.[10] If the government is for moral ends it is closely akin to religion in its function and purpose. Religion indeed is the best instrument for the realization and accomplishment of moral ends. Hence Church and State should be one, with the church subordinate as a part of the larger whole.

The third consideration was the objection to a dualistic conception of human society. A free Church in a free State seemed to Englishmen like two nations trying to occupy the same territory at the same time. Fremantle's view seems to have grown out of some such considerations as the above along with a fourth, viz.; that Christ's kingdom is destined to embrace all life. Thus from the political side and from the religious it seemed incongruous and absurd for two sovereignties to attempt to exist side by side on the same ground and among the same people.

The American theory of Church and State which the prophetic soul of Roger Williams discerned clearly in the early seventeenth century, which the English Baptists also grasped and put into formal statement a little later in the same century, which Virginia Baptists championed against the established church in the eighteenth century, and which through their influence came to

---

[10] The influential Enlightenment philosopher Jean-Jacques Rousseau (1712–1778) published *The Social Contract* in 1762. He attacked the idea of the divine right of kings and advocated that the sovereign power in government was the people.

full expression in the first amendment to the Constitution of the United States, is in all respects opposed to the English and European theory. We thus make a real contribution to the world's civilization.

Americans do not deny that the ends for which government exists are moral, but they do deny that those ends are religious. Mr. Bryce is scarcely correct in the statement that our view regards the general government simply as a great business organization created by the people for certain specified purposes which do not include matters of the church or religion. While Americans have spent little time in theorizing about the nature of the State I think it is a fair inference from the Declaration of Independence that in the main they regard our Constitution as grounded in essential moral principles, and that ultimately government is the expression of moral relations which necessarily exist in human society and created [sic] by God.[11]

It does not follow, however, that because an institution is the expression of moral relations in one sphere that it is meant to promote moral ends in all spheres. Church and State might in a perfect society coalesce into one; but meantime their functions must be kept separate. Specialization is the law of their harmonious and healthful operation as society is today. In his reply to Gladstone on Church and State Macaulay put the case graphically. Said he:

> It is of much more importance that the knowledge of religious truth should be widely diffused than that the art of sculpture should flourish among us. Yet it by no means follows that the Royal Academy ought to unite with its present functions those of the Society for promoting Christian knowledge, to distribute theological tracts, to send forth missionaries, turn out Nollekens for being a Catholic, Bacon for being a Methodist, and Flaxman for being a Swedenborgian. For the effect of such folly would be that we should have the worst possible academy of arts, and the worst possible Society for the Promotion of Christian Knowledge.[12]

The same principle applies to the relations of Church and State.

---

[11] Mullins cites Newman Smyth, *Christian Ethics* (New York: Charles Scribner's Sons, 1892) 263ff.

[12] Mullins does not cite a source for the Macaulay quotation. Joseph Nollekens (1737–1823) and John Flaxman (1755–1826) were British sculptors.

E. Y. Mullins

Functions of Church and State Distinct

The functions of Church and State are quite distinct. The American view is based on fundamental facts of human society and of the gospel. The Church is a voluntary organization, the State compels obedience. One organization is temporal, the other spiritual. Their views as to penal offenses may be quite different, that being wrong and punishable in the Church which the State cannot afford to notice. The direct allegiance in the Church is to God, in the State it is to law and government. One is for the protection of life and property, the other for the promotion of spiritual life. An established religion, moreover, subverts the principle of equal rights and equal privileges to all which is a part of our organic law. Both on its political and on its religious side the doctrine of the separation of Church and State holds good. Civil liberty and soul liberty alike forbid their union. As Dr. Newman Smyth remarks: "History has permanently closed these two ways—the way of bringing Christ before the judgment seat of Caesar to be crucified, and the way of putting Christ on Caesar's throne to rule the kingdoms of this world."[13]

Now it is important to keep in mind the meaning of the phrase "a free Church in a free State," if we are to avoid confusion in thought at certain points in our practical application of the principle. If at any point, such as the legal holding of property, the functions of the church carry it over into the civil realm, then we must construe such function as properly pertaining to the church and *vice versa*. But this does not destroy the freedom of either Church or State. The Church is compatible with the State, but entirely independent of it. That is to say, it is free. It is a spiritual commonwealth. The citizenship of its members is in heaven, as Paul declares, although at the same time they are citizens of an earthly State. There will, of course, remain a borderland where it will not always be clear how to discriminate and apply the principle correctly.

Important Illustrations of Statement Made

We may note before closing this chapter two or three illustrations of the statement made. One is the appropriation of public money for sectarian schools. This is a flagrant violation of the principle and is a long step toward the establishment of one or more denominations in governmental support.

---

[13] Smyth, *Christian Ethics*, 284.

Direct gifts of money to religious bodies by the general government is of the essence of union of Church and State. It is not surprising, therefore, that it was when a Baptist, General Morgan, was Commissioner of Indian Affairs that this government, under his leadership, abandoned the practice of appropriating money for sectarian schools.[14]

As to the Bible in the public schools also there been much difference of opinion among Americans. Baptists very generally and consistently oppose the public reading of the Bible in the schools, because they respect the consciences of all others. The underlying question is a difficult one. The State, as it is based on the franchise, and as the franchise implies intelligence, quite properly provides through its educational system for making its citizens intelligent. Can it be said also that the State, as it is based on the franchise, and the franchise implies moral character, quite properly provides through moral teaching in the public schools for making its citizens moral? Religious teaching as distinguished from moral teaching is of course excluded. The answer to the question must be in the affirmative within certain limits. Moral teaching is not objectionable even to atheists. A moral textbook sufficiently elementary and simple, containing extracts from other works containing wholesome moral teaching, might be employed to advantage without violating any man's conscience.

The exemption of church property from taxation is another point which has been much contested. All religious bodies alike have enjoyed the privilege. It has been defended on various grounds as not involving the union of Church and State. The church enhances the value of all other property, adds to the desirability of any community as a place of residence, builds up our civilization in many ways, and is the most efficient of all police forces. It thus gives a *quid pro quo* to the State and more than earns its exemption from taxation. The governor of Montana a few years ago in a message to the legislature made a special request that all church property be exempt from taxation as the best means of advancing the welfare of the entire territory and speeding it on its way to complete civilization.

But others contest the point. They maintain that to exempt churches from taxation is to subsidize religion and to subsidize religion is to subvert

---

[14] Mullins is evidently referring to Thomas J. Morgan who served as commissioner from 1889 to1893.

our doctrine of a free Church in a free State. They urge also that to tax church property would have a wholesome effect in preventing extravagance in church architecture and in other ways would react favorably upon religion.

Now unquestionably a theoretical justification can be made out for either view, for exemption as well as taxation. It runs thus: To impose a tax is to assert sovereignty; but the State is not sovereign over the Church whose allegiance is to God alone. Moreover, to concede the right to tax involves a concession of the right to confiscate upon proper occasion. Thus the right to tax on the part of the State destroys the freedom of the Church, so that it is no longer a free Church in a free State.

A Question of Interpretation

After all, however, the question is one of the interpretation of a principle. If the sovereign State and the sovereign Church agree that a particular practice capable of theoretical justification in opposite directions is not a violation of a general principle of government and of religion then that interpretation must stand. Experience alone will demonstrate the wisdom or unwisdom of the interpretation. Time alone can give the final answer to many questions. Up to the present it cannot be said that time has demonstrated the unwisdom of exempting religious property from taxation. To impose a tax on such property would be a deadly blow to education as well as to religion.

12

The Social Axiom:
Love Your Neighbor as Yourself

Two truths have emerged into crystal clearness in the thinking of men under the influence of Christian civilization in modern times. One is the worth of the individual. The old Greek and Roman civilizations as well as those farther east never recognized this truth. Christ taught it and made it current. Since he lived it has been slowly becoming a part of the spiritual wealth of mankind. The other truth is supplementary to the above. It is that man is a social being. Monasticism in a way emphasized the worth of the individual but it did not value properly the social side of man's nature.

A Social Theology

In recent years there has arisen what is called a "social theology." Its aim is to supply a counterpoise to the excessive individualism of much of the prevailing theology. To be saved as an individual, to be "in the ark of safety" provided by the gospel, to escape from death and hell, has often been the sum of Christian teaching. By way of reaction men are demanding a sociological gospel. Some are asserting that individualism is a false teaching and that the gospel aims primarily at social results. Frequently this takes the form of an assertion that a change in environment is all that is necessary to effect a change in character. The happy are the good. The way to make men good is to make them happy. The way to make them happy is to make them comfortable. Good houses to live in, good food to eat, and good clothes to wear are the sum total of the equipment required to regenerate society. The apostles of this and similar doctrines rail much at the churches for failure to insist upon this view.

The social sins of the day are many and grievous it must be confessed. They are well known and need not be dealt with here at length. We are in sore need of better divorce laws. There is perhaps no evil which strikes so directly at the vitals of any civilization as that which corrupts the family and home life.

This condition is a marked characteristic of decadent nations in nearly every instance. The prevalence of graft in business and in politics is only too well known in America today. Students of our social and political life from the outside, like Mr. Bryce and others, seem most of all struck with the absorption of our people in money-getting. The money-getter is the American hero. Failure and success in life are estimated on the basis of the question whether a man is a money-getter or not. Commercial success is too often measured by the amount of money made regardless of the methods. The money-getting quality is indispensable in the pastor and the college president. Novel-writing and book-writing generally are largely with a view to profits. Political parties are called to the judgment seat of financial prosperity and are voted in or out according as they are able to wave the magic wand which sets the silver floods flowing.

The abuses connected with child labor in our factories have also attracted much attention and should receive careful thought. Another form of social service which presents peculiar difficulties is to be seen in the modern problem of charity and poor relief. Much thinking and planning yet remains to be done on this subject before a solution is in sight. Many of our reformers are telling us that the most fundamental and trying of all our evils is the competitive system, and that relief at this point would bring relief at all points. Closely connected with the money-getting passion of Americans is the great question of the stewardship of money. This, of course, in a peculiar manner affects professing Christians. The vast missionary and educational enterprises of the Christian denominations present an opportunity and enforce an obligation for social service unparalleled in the history of the world. We might extend this enumeration indefinitely. What has been said is sufficient to indicate the urgency of the need and the vastness of the opportunity.

A Question as to Duty

The question is what is the duty of a free Church in a free State where these conditions prevail? It must be replied that a mere sociological Christianity must fail since it ignores the basal law of Christianity. To regenerate the individual is the sole condition of permanent moral progress in the social sphere. It is curious to note the superficial view men have held as to human progress. Mr. Buckle in his history of civilization declares that morals have had little or nothing to do with human progress because morality is static or fixed; while intellect which is dynamic and progressive has carried on the process.[1] Christian morality may be "static" in the sense in which all ultimate things are static. The summit of Mount Blanc is "static," the constellations in a sense are "static," and so is the Christian moral ideal. For this very reason, however, along with its elevation above the ordinary attainment of men, and its ideal quality, it has been the "flying goal" of the race for two thousand years. This ideal assumes a moral character in harmony with it, and that character is created by the regeneration of the individual. Therefore Christianity cannot abandon its doctrine of "regenerated individualism" without committing suicide. It is by means of regenerated individuals associated together as churches that Christianity becomes a leaven to transform the social order. This is primary and fundamental.

Now it is on this foundation that the moral edifice rises in individual and in social life. Regeneration contains in itself the seeds of all righteousness. No moral interest lies outside the sphere of the church of Christ. Doubtless much of the failure of the church to leaven the social relations of men has grown out of the failure to recognize this truth. The duty of the pulpit and the church, therefore, may be stated in several ways. First of all there is need that this truth be grasped; the new birth means the regeneration of the entire life. Salvation is not a fragment. A Christian has been saved, he is being saved, and he will be saved. The great word salvation so understood becomes a far greater conception than that of a deliverance from death and hell simply and exclusively.

The Church ought to exert a powerful influence upon the State. The Church cannot take the State but it does take the citizens of the State into itself. It cannot undertake commercial enterprises with wisdom or safety but it does have the moral and spiritual guidance of business men. One of the most serious difficulties to be overcome is the artificial grouping of men with moral ideals to correspond. Politicians have become a professional class with us. Business men in like manner in important respects think and act on certain accepted lines and ideals, and church members also tend to become segregated from other interests. Sound moral ideas should penetrate all groups.

---

[1] Henry T. Buckle, *History of Civilization in England* (New York: Henry Frowde, 1904).

E. Y. Mullins

New Ethical Questions

Many ethical questions have arisen in our civilization which are entirely new. One man regards the trust as the sum of all evils and another maintains that it is the inevitable goal of commercial evolution. This illustrates, along with many other things, how our civilization since the industrial revolution is, in a real sense of the word, yet in the making. Christian thinkers have before them the great task of thinking these ethical problems through. We have indeed what is called the "new political economy." Professor Ely has said that the new political economy is simply the attempt to apply to society at large the principles of Christ's parable of the talents.[2]

Christian men cannot hold themselves aloof from public questions and public service if they are to embody the principles of Christianity in their practical conduct. Roughly speaking Christians may be classified as monastics, mystics, moralists, and missionaries. The monastic life is not in good repute, although the disposition to shrink from public service is in its essence the old monkish refusal to "look into the swarthiest face of things" and discharge unpleasant duty. The mystic loves communion with God and so far is in line with all great souls of the past. But "if a man is imperfect who is apart from the divine, so is a man imperfect who is apart from the human." The moralist is mistaken only when he attempts to obtain the fruit without the roots or is content with personal and indifferent to social morality. Some one has brought out the point by an incident in the experience of Alice. Alice in Wonderland saw a cat with a grin on its face. The cat gradually faded away until only the grin remained. This, however, was in the Wonderland of Alice, not in the real world. You may have a face without a grin, but not a grin without a face. You cannot produce morality apart from its spiritual cause. The missionary is mastered by the moral and evangelistic impulse. He is an aggressive advocate of a saving gospel and of all morality and social righteousness. It is of the essence of Christianity to send a man out after his fellows. The Christian who understands the meaning of his religion, therefore, will be a force for civic,

---

[2] Richard Ely was a major player in the development of modern political economic theory. He supported the public ownership of utilities and supported the formation of labor unions. An Episcopal layperson and a leader of the American Institute of Christian Sociology, Ely contributed to the early stages of the social gospel movement with his *Social Aspects of Christianity* (New York : T. Y. Crowell & Company, 1889).

commercial, social, and all other forms of righteousness. Thus Christianity in America will become the religion of the State, although not a State religion.

The True Imitation of Christ

The true imitation of Christ consists not in asking "What would Jesus do?" merely, but in asking "What would Jesus have us do?"[3] Christ cannot be copied. He is less a model for us than an archetype. We may imitate but not copy him. To copy Christ would be to attempt to cure the blind by anointing his eyes with clay mixed with our own spittle [John 9:1–12]. To imitate him is to devise measures legal and otherwise to relieve and to prevent blindness. To copy Christ is to attempt to feed the hungry thousands by a miraculous multiplication of loaves and fishes [Mk. 6:30–44]. To imitate Christ is to labor for equitable social conditions, just laws, and equal privileges for men that they may earn their own bread. To imitate Christ is not to take sides with labor against capital or with capital against labor in the contest for rights, but rather to teach capital and labor to perform their respective duties. Christ did not deal directly with human rights, though no teacher ever did so much to establish them. He dealt with human duties knowing that this was the point needing emphasis. Christ was not concerned so much with property as he was with persons. He valued men more than houses or lands. Our statute books exhibit their distance from him in nothing more than in their overweening regard for property along with slight consideration of life and person. Hundreds of people may be roasted in a theater fire or crushed to death in a collapsed building and the men guilty of the faulty and illegal construction go scot free on a legal technicality. But let injury to property take place and men are swept out of themselves by moral indignation.

We are disloyal to Christ so long as we regard the political or commercial world as a foreign country to the Christian. To think of it as under the curse of God is virtually to deliver it over to the dominion of Satan. Such a view, and it is by no means uncommon, involves as its underlying philosophy the old Persian and Manichaean dualism of two contending forces equally powerful, one good and the other evil.

---

[3] A popular evangelical phrase at the beginning of the twenty-first century, "What would Jesus do?" was coined by Charles Sheldon in his social gospel novel, *In His Steps* (1897).

Christ cannot be claimed as the special patron of any particular reform movement. The Socialists and Communists try to claim him, and so do the individualists, and the anarchists, and revolutionaries of all kinds. But he is greater than they all. His cause absorbs all the truth in each of them. These little systems have their day and then they cease to be. They grow to maturity and flourish like the trees of a forest and then, dying, fall piecemeal to fertilize the soil below. He is the sun which warms the soil in which lie slumbering the seeds of his kingdom and causes them to germinate and grow up to supply spiritual bread for mankind.

Congregational Church Polity Best

The separation of Church and State is the condition of the highest efficiency of the church in fitting men for social service. To be untrammeled by fetters which bind it to the intrigues and politics and to the varying fortunes of the State leaves the church free to render the State the highest possible service. Thus it may create spiritual character in men and women who in turn guide the destiny of the social order. The church is the dynamo whose task it is to charge all departments of life with righteousness.

To fulfill this task the best form of church polity is congregational. Local self-government is best adapted to produce the self-reliance and manhood needed in all the walks of life. Moreover it enables the church to escape from the snare of becoming a Church State, which is quite possible even when the theory of a State Church is repudiated. Roman Catholicism is a Church State. That is to say it is a highly organized and centralized piece of ecclesiastical machinery which absorbs a vast amount of energy, time, and money in government alone. The spiritual is always in danger of being swallowed up in the institutional. The work of making men righteous tends to become merged in the task of making them fit into their places in the ecclesiastical system. Indeed righteousness tends more and more to become formal and institutional instead of vital and real. The same remarks apply in a measure to all episcopal or centralized systems of church government. They are Church States, although in America not State Churches. To this extent they become rivals of the civil State and of the forces which make for righteousness in society at large, in that they absorb energy which should flow directly into these other channels.

The best service which Christianity can render to society is to produce righteousness in individual character and at the same time set the man free as an agent of righteousness in society at large. To regenerate him and sanctify him and then put a heavy tax upon his time and energy in the administration of the political life of the church is to call him away from his proper duties as a member of society. In short, other things being equal, the simpler the ecclesiastical machinery the better. The more completely the church's function is specialized in the direction of producing righteousness the more efficient does it become. The less complex the machinery of the church the greater the opportunity for her sons to cast their lives and influence into the complex and manifold affairs of the State, and into all great movements for the moral and spiritual improvement of society.

13

Baptists and General Organization: Developing after Our Kind

We have now concluded our general exposition of the axioms of religion. It is in order next to apply them in several directions. One of the first of these is suggested by the conclusion of our last chapter. Baptists oppose the Church State as well as the State Church, the undue centralization of administration and authority as tending to absorb energy in illegitimate ways, as well as the union of Church and State. What then is the true theory of general organization for religious purposes? For no one will contest the proposition that cooperation for religious purposes on the part of individuals and churches and societies is highly desirable and fully in accord with the nature of Christianity, and not opposed to the teachings of the New Testament.

Voluntary Principle Must Control

Now it will be entirely clear to the reader who has followed us thus far that the voluntary principle must control in all Baptist general organization, if we are to work out our destiny on logical lines and in accordance with providential indications. Our view of general organization grows directly out of our fundamental assumption of the competency of the soul in religion under God, and three of the axioms, the religious, the ecclesiastical, and the moral. Direct access to God, equality of privilege in the church, and individual responsibility are the core of the Baptist view. We may expand these general conceptions into the following statements. The voluntary principle must control in missionary and other general organizations because—

1. Religious authority is direct and not indirect. We have shown in a previous chapter that in human governments it is necessary to localize authority, from the nature of the case, and that in religion, on the contrary, from the nature of the case, the authority cannot be localized.

2. There are no legislative or judicial functions left for general bodies to assume. The Scriptures are the rule of faith and practice, and discipline is remanded to the local church.

3. The functions, therefore, of general organizations are strictly limited. They have no ends to serve save those of eliciting, combining, and directing the missionary, educational, or other forms of energy among the churches and smaller societies, for the advancement of the kingdom of God on earth. In short, they are simply means of cooperation on an entirely voluntary basis.

4. Most of the advantages of the centralized church governments can be attained thus without their abuses and shortcomings, and without the sacrifice of the Christian ideal at any point. There may be, and as a matter of fact is, a thoroughly graded series of missionary organizations under Baptist polity. There is not a dead uniformity in the constitution of these bodies and the members are at liberty to modify these constitutions at pleasure. But the exigencies of the work and needs of the churches may be provided for at any time by suitable organizations.

5. In consequence of the fact that Baptists exclude the principle of authority and rely upon the principle of voluntary cooperation, the course of general organization has been with them an evolution according to changing conditions and in order to meet new problems of the enlarging work. There is flexibility and adaptability, therefore, along with expansive capacity rather than a rigid machine which may become a burden as well as generate power.

6. The representative principle in the strict sense is excluded by our general position. If representation is real it binds, and this is excluded by the religious and ecclesiastical axioms. It shifts general organization at once from a Baptist to a Presbyterian basis. The Baptist principle is that a church, or individual, or society, cooperates with a general body whose objects and aims it approves, not delegating authority in any sense, or binding itself beyond its expressed purpose, and always reserving the right of dissent or withdrawal at pleasure. The evils of delegated authority may be illustrated thus: Suppose seventy-five or eighty years ago when some of our smaller general bodies were being formed, a church committed to worldwide evangelization had delegated its authority to the general body and bound itself to its decisions, and upon the assembling of the latter the anti-missionary forces had been in the majority and voted the missionary enterprise down. This would of course raise the question of conscience and the missionary church and individual would have

to face the question whether to obey God or man. Indeed, in Baptist history, more than once anti-missionary forces have been in the majority in district Associations and elsewhere. Chaos would have ensued under a system of delegated authority. Chaos did not ensue because the voluntary principle allowed each party to go its own way and organize for its own purposes answerable to God alone.

An Inevitable Result

The result is inevitable. Compulsory obedience to human authority in religion, where authority is necessarily direct and spiritual, always leads to collision and strife. The human authority to be of worth in religion must be assumed to be infallible and representative of God himself, or it ceases to be authority. Papal infallibility is the inevitable logic of all forms of religious authority. Thus there is an inherent contradiction in the idea of a centralized church government. If God in Christ is the ultimate authority in religion, if the right of private interpretation of Scripture is an inalienable right of believers, if the Spirit of God illumines the mind of the individual, then to centralize church polity is to put a premium upon schism and strife on the one hand, or it is to deaden conscience and reduce Christianity to formalism on the other. For the awakened conscience will not tolerate legislation at the hands of men, and the occasions for collision will be as numerous as there are questions of conscience. Christian history abundantly justifies all these statements. Baptists have been a remarkably united people in spite of their freedom and individualism. There have been divisions of sentiment on various questions doctrinal or otherwise, but gradually the separated parts gravitate together again under the quiet influence of personal conviction and spiritual and intellectual growth.

Plea For Centralized Church Polity

Occasionally a plea is made among us for a more centralized church polity. Looking at the apparent advantages of episcopacy and neglecting to consider its disadvantages, and forgetting that under all centralized systems there is a longing on the part of many for a more democratic polity, and that as a matter of fact there is an irresistible gravitation toward democracy in them all, some Baptist writer or speaker expresses a desire for a system where authority shall take the place of democracy. This tendency is relatively so slight among us that the present writer does not anticipate that it will become a serious question. At the same time it may be well to glance briefly at the assumptions underlying the plea and at the results which would follow should we give serious heed to it.

For one thing it assumes that the voluntary principle is a failure in religion. It proceeds upon the hypothesis that humanity cannot be made spiritual enough to be trusted to cooperate for spiritual ends. It rejects the idea that a regenerated and spiritual church membership can ever be made fit for self-government in the general affairs of the kingdom of God. The demand for a centralized polity among Baptists also assumes that the principle of the doctrine of the competency of the soul in religion under God, and the axioms of religion which assert the equality of men before God and with each other, have only a theoretical and not a practical value; and indeed that in this life working ideals are not practicable even in religion. This demand also involves the view that the one religious body which has consistently stood for a church membership based upon spiritual character alone, reinforced in its efforts by all the resources of modern education and culture, in the form of public education as well as through its own institutions of learning, has not the power to create a coherent system of administration to secure certain practical ends, without invoking the antiquated theory that religious authority is indirect instead of direct. In short, this demand for a centralized authoritative system assumes that liberty and unity are irreconcilable ideas. It banishes liberty and equality in the name of unity, and assumes that while all the rest of the world in political theory, in art, in science, and in education, is gravitating irresistibly toward the doctrine of the competency of the soul under God, toward democracy and freedom, the one religious body which has made its history glorious through its advocacy of that doctrine, must now abandon it.

Not Weary in Well-Doing

Let Baptists be not weary in well-doing. Our inability to enlist all our people in all our work at all times is discouraging to a superficial view. If our ecclesiastical machinery could be so adjusted and oiled as to run without a jar it would doubtless save trouble and please the esthetic faculty. But there is a profound reason why such adjustment can only come slowly: we are dealing with persons and not with things—with human wills, not with wood and iron. When you step into a great power plant you admire its smooth running. The ponderous machinery answers to a human ideal as the planets in their orbits answer to the will of God. But this is because a human will has impressed itself upon material things. When the ideal has been perfected in the mind of the constructor the rest is simply a question of mechanical execution of details. But the process is far more complex in an orchestra. The players on the various instruments conquer each his individual harmony and his place in the general effect by slow and painstaking effort under the direction of the leader. It requires much time and much patience and persistent practice after a high degree of proficiency has been reached to maintain a high standard of musical perfection.

Now it is the ideal of the orchestra and not that of the machine which must control in religion. Not one human will stamping itself upon other human wills by authority, but Christ's will leading his people to the unity and harmony which will reproduce his own moral ideal. If art and science and education belong to the kingdom of the free spirit of man, so does religion under God. If science cannot be developed by authority, if art can only attain excellence through the free play of genius, if education in its fundamental ideals must conform to the organic laws of the soul, so must religion unfold under the light and guidance of God's Spirit, and not through the repressive influences of human authority.

When God had finished his creation of living things he commanded each to reproduce "after his kind." Baptists may well give heed to that injunction today. Our strength lies in our freedom and democracy. Herein lies our appeal to the universal heart of the race. We cannot mix episcopacy or presbyterianism with our democracy without an immense weakening of our hold upon humanity, loss of self-respect, and lowering of spiritual tone. We must develop "after our kind." If the way seems long and steep and if we grow weary from time to time, it is because the goal is high and spiritual—even the city that hath foundations whose builder and maker is God.

14

Baptists and Christian Union

The Question of Christian Union

No question which has engaged the thought of religious men during the past generation has been more complex or difficult than that of Christian union. The matter was brought to a practical issue in 1888 when the Church of England issued the famous Lambeth articles—a platform of union containing four planks. These articles were a slightly modified statement of the platform promulgated just before by the Protestant Episcopal Church of the United States. The Lambeth articles are as follows:

(A) The Holy Scriptures of the Old and New Testaments, as containing all things necessary to salvation, and as being the rule and ultimate standard of faith.

(B) The Apostles' Creed as the Baptismal Symbol, and the Nicene Creed as the sufficient statement of the Christian faith.

(C) The Two Sacraments ordained by Christ Himself—Baptism and the Supper of the Lord—ministered with unfailing use of Christ's words of Institution, and of the elements ordained by Him.

(D) The Historic Episcopate, locally adapted in the methods of its administration to the varying needs of the nations and peoples called of God into the Unity of His Church.[1]

These articles were discussed in pulpit and press to a greater or less extent in all parts of modern Christendom. But no serious movement toward organic

---

[1] This is sometimes called the 1888 Quadrilateral Statement of the Anglican Church. Lambeth Conferences, meetings of Anglican bishops, have been held since 1867. Although Mullins refers to the 1888 document, the term "Lambeth Articles" is also used for nine doctrinal statements approved by Archbishop of Canterbury John Whitgift in 1595.

union followed. Attention was thus called to the subject afresh, however, and there has been a tendency toward union among some of the groups of religious bodies most closely related in doctrine and polity. There seems at present to be little sentiment in favor of practical efforts toward organic union of all the Christian denominations. The agitation has served to bring into bold relief the obstacles, which are many and formidable. The principle of federation, however, has been invoked and a federation of most of the larger bodies has been effected. This federation ignores the ecclesiastical issues entirely and seeks to unite all forces of righteousness in the various denominations on a common platform of civic, social, and moral reform.

Christian Union in the Deeper Sense

The subject of Christian union in the deeper sense abides, however, and will doubtless abide until Christ's prayer for the unity of his people is fully answered. At least three points seem to have been gained by the discussion of the subject hitherto, and through the efforts toward practical Christian union. The first is that premature union is fraught with much peril as illustrated in the efforts of the Presbyterians to reunite with their Cumberland brethren. The second is that Christian union cannot be made to order, but must come as a result of growth. The third is that there is a very deep and widespread conviction in the Christian world that somehow union will come in due time, that the present divided state of Christendom is not the ideal state, and that God is at work among his people with this end in view.

The best service can be rendered to the cause of Christian union by a discussion not so much of programs of union as of the principles of union. Real and radical Christian union, or to employ a word which is open to more or less objection, "organic" Christian union, as distinguished from the spirit of unity and cooperation, can never come as a permanent and abiding condition until it comes in obedience to the organic laws of Christianity. The most serious defects in the programs of union have been that they have viewed Christianity as institution and organization first, and only secondarily as spiritual law. The process must be reversed.

A Serious Objection

The most serious objection to the Lambeth articles is that they include the historic episcopate. This approaches the matter on the institutional side and sets up one form of church polity as essential. There would be no objection to this method of procedure, provided the historic episcopate could be shown to rest upon fundamental spiritual laws, primal Christian convictions, or New Testament requirements. In short, no plea for an institutional basis of Christian union can stand which does not show that the proposed institution is the outgrowth of the essential nature of Christianity itself. The unity of every living organism in the vegetable world, of every plant or flower, is the result of the cooperation of the elements of the atmosphere, the soil, and the sunshine under the action of an inner life principle. That principle rejects every alien element and assimilates all that is needful. The institutions of Christianity must conform to its inner nature. The polity will answer to the life, and conserve those fundamental relations of the soul of man to God which constitute the core and essence of the New Testament revelation.

We may approach the question as to the proper basis of Christian union in two ways. We may assume on the one hand that all church polities are equally valid, and on the other that some one is entitled to the claim to the exclusion of others.

Consider briefly the first view. It asserts that the New Testament is indeterminate as to church organization. That Christianity being a life principle is subject to growth and development; that variety and not uniformity is the law of growth; and that the various Christian denominations as they exist today are simply examples of the freedom of the Spirit in the religious struggles of the race. This view must recognize as equally legitimate the democracy of the congregational bodies and the autocracy of the Roman Catholic Church, as well as all the polities which lie between. Under this view a Baptist would feel bound to maintain his doctrine of the church, as would also the Presbyterian and others, on the ground that each is necessary to the expression of the variety and fullness of the life in Christ.

It would become apparent at once, however, that "organic" union would be impossible. For the polities are incompatible with each other. Any authoritative source of unity which should embrace all the denominations would at once annul such polities as deny authority in this sense. Episcopacy in any form would nullify democracy, and any real democracy would cancel the episcopal principle. Federation would thus remain as the only mode of Christian union. The principle of federation is essentially the democratic principle. It recognizes the autonomy of each denomination, and declines to interfere with the ecclesiastical integrity of any religious body.

E. Y. Mullins

The Principle of Federation

Now as a matter of fact Baptists achieve all their results in general organization on the principle of federation—that is to say, on the voluntary principle. Only they carry that principle to the local congregation and to the individual. It applies to all missionary and benevolent organizations whatever. When they cooperate for common ends they organize without any centralized authority. Those who join and those who withdraw from the organization do so at will. Not the principle of legal solidarity but that of voluntary unity is their principle.

It is obvious, now, that if the principle of federation alone is to be invoked to secure Christian union it can never achieve the result unless it is applied in a far more thoroughgoing manner than at present. For, while it may mitigate the evils of a divided Christendom at certain points it cannot abolish them. It may stimulate the system with a moral tonic but cannot eradicate the disease. For denominational rivalries will continue to exist. Doctrinal controversies will survive in one form or another. The waste of labor and money through the duplication of effort, so often complained of in our day, will continue.

Our conclusion from the foregoing discussion, therefore, is that the theory that all the existing church polities are equally warranted by the New Testament or by the essential nature of Christianity, is false. It does not and cannot yield an answer to Christ's prayer that his people may all be one. Federation of incongruous and contradictory systems is the best it can do.

A Single Principle to Be Found

We are forced, then, to the view that somewhere there must be found a single principle broad and flexible and energetic enough to answer the ecclesiastical needs of the gospel. Where shall it be found? The reply is that it must be found in the congregational or Roman Catholic polity. The reason for the assertion is that these two alone are self-consistent. Those which lie between are dualistic, they seek to combine authority and democracy in a way which in time will surely fail. As intelligence and autonomy increase in these churches the authority will lose its hold; or if authority tightens its grip it will be because capacity for self-government wanes.

Consider how embarrassing the case for Christian union becomes when it is discussed by the non-Roman and non-congregational bodies. We will suppose a Presbyterian is arguing the case with an Episcopalian. The logic of the Presbyterian is that representative church government is better than episcopal because it brings it nearer to the people. But this is Baptist logic stopping half-way. If it is good to bring the government of the church one step toward the people surely in due time it will be good to carry it all the way. The Episcopalian, on his side, urges episcopacy because centralized government is better than the non-centralized. But the Presbyterian at once replies that if the principle be sound Romanism is the logical outcome. In the one case, therefore, we have incipient congregationalism and in the other incipient Romanism. The reader does not need to be told, of course, where the sympathies of the writer lie as between these two polities. He is fully persuaded that the congregational form of church polity is the predestined goal of development for all Christendom. It is not so much as a result of argument that men will be convinced and flock into the Baptist fold, or that any ready-made scheme of Christian union will win the universal approval. It is rather that by a sort of spiritual gravitation men will reach it; by a deeper apprehension of the New Testament they will come to it.

A Twofold Method

Having examined the two theories on which the subject of Christian unity may be approached we may now examine briefly the twofold method which has been applied in the past. One of these is the method of addition, the other the method of subtraction.

First we consider the method of addition. Some standard is set up which is regarded as the combination of all the necessary elements in the ideal and others are asked to add to what they already have and thus attain to Christian union. This is the method of the Lambeth proposals as cited earlier in the chapter. The historic episcopate is to be incorporated as an addition to all the other polities which seek union on the Lambeth platform. But this platform of union failed. It approached the matter in an unhistoric way. Change in church polity comes of growth, not by mechanical accretion. Besides its method is psychologically defective. Men do not find common standing ground by the imposition of something new by one of the parties to the agreement upon the other. They seek out the things on which there is some measure of agreement already.

This brings us to the second method, viz., the method of subtraction. This puts on one side the things which give offense, as far as possible, and seeks a common point of view. This is the usual mode of procedure in attempts at union of any kind. It is that which controls in the federation of the churches. There is not agreement in polity, but there is in certain doctrinal views and moral ends. Hence the latter alone are brought into the question.

Now in applying the principle of subtraction in order to a common standing ground for union, Baptists have stood apparently at a great disadvantage although in reality their position is a very strong one. They have reduced the elements of church organization to the lowest possible terms, and hence, when urged to surrender this or that they see no way of doing so without striking a blow at their ecclesiastical integrity. Their church polity is the simple undeveloped polity of the New Testament. They have the minimum of church government, congregationalism; the minimum of office bearers, pastors or elders and deacons; the minimum of ordinances, baptism and the Lord's Supper; the minimum of doctrinal tests for membership, not subscription to a creed but vital faith in Christ and the spirit of obedience to his commands as evidenced in the first instance by submission to baptism in the name of Father, Son, and Holy Spirit.

It is evident from the preceding that if the method of addition were the correct one in attaining Christian union Baptists would be in a position to add all the elements of episcopacy, and sacerdotalism, the Methodistic principle, and the principle of authoritative representation, a series of graded courts and legislatures. But, as previously remarked, the enforced introduction of new planks into platforms of union is never the correct method, but rather the finding of a common standing ground, or the method of subtraction. Now in the quest for this common standing ground Baptists occupy a peculiarly advantageous position. For not one of the elements of their polity as enumerated above is without recognition throughout the evangelical world. Immersion is not the preferred mode of baptism, of course, in some denominations, but it is universally recognized as a valid mode, while sprinkling and pouring are not thus universally accepted. If we were to subtract anything from our congregationalism in the matter of church government proper we would be without any church organization whatever. Moreover, congregationalism is quite generally accepted as one legitimate form of church order. Baptists have, in short, carried the process of subtraction to the limit, or rather they have eschewed the tendency to incorporate new features into the simple New Testament polity which renders subtraction necessary.

Baptists and Organic Union

It is at this point that we find an explanation of the fact that Baptists have not been particularly active as a rule in efforts toward organic Christian union. They are not indeed without profound interest in the matter. But being unable to surrender any element of their simple church order without fatally weakening it, and being unwilling to urge others to violate their consciences, they have awaited the leading of Providence rather than sought to reorganize Christianity.

There is, however, a still deeper reason for their attitude. The movement toward Christian union has, in their view, too often conceived Christianity primarily as an ecclesiasticism, whereas it is essentially a life involving certain relations to God through Christ. To secure a unity of Christendom under the aegis of the Church of England with its doctrine of the historic episcopate, or in any other external way would not necessarily add to the real spirituality or efficiency of the church.

The plea of Baptists, therefore, is not a plea for "organic" union as the chief goal of endeavor at present, however desirable and important Christian union is in itself. Their plea is rather for the spiritual rights of mankind: the competency of the soul in religion under God, the equality of all men in direct dealing with God, the equal rights of believers in the church, the principle of responsibility as growing out of the freedom of the soul. The axioms of religion lie at the heart of New Testament Christianity. If the evangelical bodies which have added to their systems those elements which contravene the axioms and subvert the spiritual rights of the race, will discard them, Christian union will come of itself. We do not mean that all denominations will then come at once into the Baptist fold so far as external organizations are concerned. For the voluntary principle would leave them to organize as they might see fit. But it would secure unity of doctrine and polity. It would enable the entire evangelical world to present a united front against sacerdotalism and sacramentalism which violates the religious axiom, and against episcopacy which deprives the spiritual of their rights and privileges in the church, and against infant baptism which is out of harmony with the moral axiom. It would give to American Christianity the tremendous advantage of a simple, consistent, New Testament church order in missionary endeavor in heathen lands.

The axioms of religion, as expounded in previous chapters, enter vitally into the primal instincts of all men who have been under the guiding hand of Christ and who have been nurtured in New Testament teaching. No effort or device for ecclesiastical or "organic" union can ever permanently succeed which ignores those instincts. We must learn to think God's thoughts after him as revealed in Christ if we are to find the clue to unity. The deeper currents of thought and life in the Christian world, the fundamental relations of the soul to God, must find embodiment in the final church order.[2]

Modern Life and Democracy

Now it is evident to the careful observer that the deeper tides of modern life are all setting toward democracy in Church and State. By an inevitable gravitation the world is being carried that way. The universe about us is a symbol of the spiritual order. It is a universe because it is one, a coherent system of interrelated parts. "He hangeth the stars upon nothing," and yet they keep to their courses and swing in their orbits.[3] In the early stages of our solar system, doubtless much was chaotic and disorderly, as in modern Christendom. Conflicting tendencies, aberrations, comets, and nebulae, were features of that early universe. But had there existed then an astronomer with insight and vision to discern the secret of the movements of that confused and chaotic world, he would have perceived the action of the one universal law of gravitation, bringing into being a cosmos instead of chaos. Even so in the modern spiritual world the deepest law of total movement is that which is embodied in competency of the soul in religion under God, equality of men in direct approach to God and believers in the church. This is the universal

---

[2] Southern Baptists voiced their opposition to organic church union in J. M. Frost, ed., *Christian Union Relative to Baptist Churches* (Nashville: Sunday School Board of the SBC, 1915). Mullins contributed chapters on "Baptism and Church Union," 61–64; "Christian Union and Infant Baptism," 65–68; "The Spiritual Meaning of Baptism," 79–89; and "The Baptist Position as to Restricted Communion," 90–98.

[3] Job 26:7 says He "hangeth the earth upon nothing."

law of spiritual gravitation. If our moral and spiritual life is to become a "universe," a cosmos—an orderly and coherent kingdom—it will be through the action of this universal law of spiritual gravitation.

15

Institutional and Anti-Institutional Christianity

A Churchless Christianity

There are two tendencies in our day which make for a churchless Christianity. Strange to say one of these is within while the other is without the church itself. We will note the latter first. Weary of the controversies over ritual and doctrine, of heresy trials and strife among the religious denominations, many men of fine moral character, especially in college and university life, eschew all church relations and insist upon the sufficiency of the individual in the culture of the spiritual life. These men see and appreciate the value of Christianity as a means of moral culture and seek thus to distil its essence from the outward forms and observances with which it has become involved.

Professor Harnack in his *Essence of Christianity* has fostered this tendency in his effort to reduce Christianity to two or three essential elements. God's fatherhood and human brotherhood are the core of Christianity—the glowing heart within. All the rest is shell and needless wrapping. Scores of others cherish similar views. Ecclesiastical Christianity with these men is in bad repute. The sole need is individual culture, a life "under the eye and in the strength of God."[1] The revolt is in part against dogma as well as against church organization. For doctrinal formulae of some kind are held by all the churches. These men admire Christianity for its moral and esthetic value, but draw the line at creeds and church order.

The second type of opinion which runs counter to the integrity of organized church life is found within the pale of the church itself, and usually

---

[1] Adolf Harnack, *What is Christianity?* (New York: Putnam's Sons, 1903) 8. Harnack, a leading German historian and theologian, asserted that Christian doctrine had been adversely molded by Greek thought. He consequently stressed the ethical nature of Christianity and found historic doctrine a hindrance to the authentic religion of Jesus.

among those religious bodies which have the least of church organization. Be it said, however, that in America this tendency inside the churches is so slight that as yet it has attracted little attention. In England and Australia it is more pronounced. It does not take the form of opposition to church organization in so many words. It rather promulgates a view of the ordinances and the relation of the believer to these, which if consistently carried out would destroy the church. In England it takes the form of what is known as the theory of "open membership." It holds that baptism, while commanded by Christ and binding upon all believers is not a condition of church membership. Men should be received into the church solely because they sustain a personal relation to Christ—that is, faith in him as Redeemer and Lord. Their obedience to his command to be baptized is a private matter on which the church cannot sit in judgment, and as the spiritual is always above the formal, the vital above the ceremonial, the question of baptism must be waived in all cases where the believing applicant for church membership so desires. Naturally and necessarily therefore obedience to Christ in observing the Lord's Supper would in no way enter into the question of church membership. This too is private and personal.

Thus the church is reduced to a society of the spiritual, held together through a common faith in Christ, but entirely destitute of ceremonials of any kind, and without any external badges to distinguish it from other organizations. Those who hold this view urge it on the ground that nowhere in the Scriptures is baptism specifically declared to be a prerequisite to church membership and that, while both are required by Christ, disobedience to one does not necessarily carry with it disobedience to the other. This tends to dissolve the church entirely as we shall soon see. The practical energies of Christianity cannot be fruitfully guided without some external means of giving them distinctiveness and character.

An Important Fact Overlooked

Now the brethren who adhere to this opinion overlook a very important fact. They do not take into account that the *assumptions* of Scripture are the most binding and fundamental of its contents. The thing everywhere taken for granted, and coming to light in an incidental manner only, or assumed in everything else is most likely to belong to the group of things never doubted and always understood by readers or hearers. A piece of music is pitched in a certain key, and while that particular note may not be sounded with frequency, it nevertheless dominates the whole performance. It is there as a sort of musical tether to control the range of sweet sounds.

There is no express command by Christ to organize churches, but only a declaration of his own purpose to build his church. In like manner baptism is not declared formally to be a condition of church membership, but only as a duty universally binding upon penitent believers. Yet the apostles organized churches wherever they preached, and without fail believers who became members were baptized. So that, just as the New Testament Scriptures everywhere assume the unity and omnipresence and omniscience of God without explicitly and formally announcing these truths but only in the most incidental way, so also the duty to organize churches and the requirement of baptism along with it, are everywhere assumed. In short, the "open membership" plea so far as it is based on the absence of all express command of Scripture regarding baptism and church membership would on the same general ground abolish the church itself.

Baptism Precedes Church Membership

That the writers of the New Testament do everywhere assume that baptism precedes church membership is easily made clear by a glance at a few passages. The Commission in Matthew 28:19 commands that disciples be made and that these be baptized.[2] Certainly discipleship and baptism are thus bound up together in a real relation, the latter being the fitting and required expression of the disciple's attitude of obedience to Christ. As discipleship, by consent of the advocates of "open membership," is necessary to church membership, so also baptism, the appropriate act of the disciple would thus

---

[2] Mullins included this footnote: That part of the Commission which represents baptism as being administered in the name of the Father, Son, and Holy Spirit has been called in question by some recent critics on the ground where the rule is baptism in the name of Christ. Eusebius, who has a habit of abbreviating his quotations, gives the Commission without connecting baptism with the Trinity, but only with the name of Christ. The textual evidence, however, is overwhelmingly in favor of the genuineness of the words. All the Greek manuscripts and extant versions give them. The reader will observe that this critical question is only indirectly involved in the above argument. The position maintained stands regardless of the critical point at issue. Critical objection to the Commission as a whole rests on a foundation too slender to require discussion here.

naturally precede church membership. In Galatians 3:27 we read, "For as many of you as were baptized into Christ did put on Christ." In Colossians 2:12, where the apostle is addressing Christians in their collective capacity as a church, he says of them, "Having been buried with him in baptism, wherein ye were also raised with him through faith in the working of God, who raised him from the dead." So also in I Corinthians 12:13: "For in one Spirit were we all baptized into one body, whether Jews or Greeks, whether bond or free; and were all made to drink of one Spirit." In verse twenty-eight of the same chapter he distinctly indicates that he is addressing the church and giving instructions for its guidance. Such passages might be multiplied. They do not contain a distinct declaration in a formal and explicit way that every believer must be baptized before uniting with the church. But underlying them all is this assumption. It was understood by all and disputed by none. And the things thus assumed enter into the warp and woof of New Testament experience, thought, and life. The process by which a crystal is formed in nature is determined by fixed laws. Its angles and faces come into being in a stated way. He would be a poor naturalist who should state the formula for the formation of crystals and ignore a part of the process uniformly present. The same principle applies to the formation of churches.

To deny the necessity of baptism as a condition of church membership because not explicitly commanded requires that we also deny faith and repentance and regeneration as conditions. For nowhere are these explicitly commanded as conditions. They are everywhere assumed. In fact the "open membership" plea which rejects baptism as a condition of church membership is a two-edged sword. It cuts both ways. It dissolves the church as the social expression of the life of the kingdom of God into an individual and subjective principle which leaves each man free to do as he wills. It plays directly into the hands of the men described at the opening of this chapter who repudiate the church entirely and hold that the individual is sufficient unto himself in spiritual culture.

A False Assumption

The advocates of "open membership" not only overlook a pervading assumption of the New Testament. They introduce a false one of their own, viz., that baptism as a required condition of church membership interferes in some way with Christian liberty. It is conceded by them that baptism is a binding obligation and that church membership also is commanded. The making of one a condition of the other is what they deny and assert to be subversive of our liberty in Christ. But if so then to require any positive or ceremonial act of obedience subverts our liberty. If I should adjudge baptism worthless for my spiritual culture and church membership also valueless, as so many do, why am I adjudged disobedient if I refuse both? My liberty in Christ would be thus assailed. But it is replied these are commanded by Christ, and we must obey them. Are they? Where is there an express command that all believers unite with the church? Moreover to require baptism as a condition of church membership involves no infraction of the law of liberty in Christ not wrapped up also in the two commands to be baptized and to become church members when these are taken separately. Let us not be deceived. Christian liberty is not in peril, nor even called in question here. Liberty easily runs into license. If the Scriptures join baptism and church membership together uniformly it savors of license to attempt to separate them.

Faith in Christ is urged by the advocates of "open membership" as the sole condition of union with the church, although they concede that for this they have no express statement of Scripture. But there are various degrees and grades of faith. To accept Christ as a great teacher does not imply necessarily that vital and saving faith is present. There are various degrees of historic and intellectual faith in Christ, and to make faith alone the condition of membership would be to leave the whole conception of faith misty and vague. Baptism safeguards this point in a remarkable manner in that it fixes the contents of faith. It has no meaning save as an act of personal obedience to Christ in which the essentials of vital and saving faith are symbolized. The frozen particles which enter into the formation of a snowflake are in themselves colorless and transparent like water or ordinary ice. The beauty of the snowflake comes as the result of the sunlight falling upon the frozen particles, imparting a heavenly whiteness which transfigures them. It is the truth symbolized which imparts its meaning and its beauty to baptism. From it is flashed back the saving message of the gospel. The ordinance keeps faith pure. It interprets religious experience to the obedient soul. It keeps faith directed toward its proper object and in its true channel. Otherwise faith widens like some mountain stream as it descends toward the plain, leaving its proper channel, spreading in sluggish flow over a wide region, and finally disappears in the sand.

Another Plea Urged

Another plea is urged in favor of "open membership" to the effect that to require baptism as a condition of church membership is to impose a condition for entrance into the church not required for entrance into the kingdom of God. This has a plausible look only. There are two possible replies. Some might urge that baptism is the ceremonial door into the kingdom, and the teaching in John 3:5 is cited in proof. This would place entrance into church and kingdom on precisely the same basis on the ceremonial side. The New Testament does not contemplate the presence in the kingdom of any who are unbaptized as the normal condition. The New Testament instances, as of the dying thief [Lk. 23:43], are obviously exceptional and not normal cases. This would of course leave the question of spiritual qualifications for entrance into the kingdom unaffected. It would simply assert that the same ceremonial observance is placed at the entrance of both church and kingdom.

The passage in John is not entirely clear, however, and it cannot be asserted that the above answer has explicit New Testament warrant, although it will appeal to some minds strongly. There remains, however, another reply. Church and kingdom are not identical as we have sought to show in a preceding chapter. The church has officers, the kingdom has not. The church is local, the kingdom is a comprehensive movement and power on earth. The church reproduces the spiritual elements of the kingdom, but as it has a specific task and a definite organization it is not at all proper to reduce them to the same terms as to organization and external form.

The plea for "open membership" has taken yet another form. Let Baptists accept sprinkling as baptism. Let us insist on this mode or some mode, but let us accept anything as baptism which passes current in the Christian world. It is claimed that if we should adopt this position we would gain many members whom we cannot now receive, people who have been sprinkled and who belong properly in other denominations. Also, it would give a new sense of unity to the Christian world and bring Baptists into line with other bodies, and thus we would cease to be sectarian. Again, it would bring the note of reality into our life and take the emphasis from the formal and ceremonial. Best of all it would assist Baptists where their power is waning and where they appear to be leading a forlorn hope. In short it would lift us to a higher spiritual plane and enable us to realize our destiny.[3]

This plea, however, will scarcely carry conviction to the Baptist family. Without doubt we would gain a member here and there whom we do not now receive; but there would be no urgent reason for them to join us if, as is alleged, we are to seek a common basis of church life with other denominations. The plea for "open membership" in the full sense—that is for church membership without baptism in any form, is a stronger one than this. For sprinkling as baptism destroys the meaning of the ordinance from the Baptist point of view. In the other case immersion is urged as the Scriptural form of baptism and insisted upon as a duty, but is not required as a condition of church membership.

The chief argument which is urged for accepting sprinkling, for extending our definition of baptism, is its effect in increasing our spiritual power and in imparting greater efficiency. This is a total misconception of the relation of spiritual causes to spiritual effects. It really assumes that baptism and questions regarding baptism are fundamental among spiritual causes and forces. We might modify our views of baptism and the Lord's Supper and church polity every decade with a view to increased spiritual power. But it would be without effect. The causes lie deeper. The announcement that all Baptist churches had decided to accept sprinkled persons as members would doubtless create a momentary excitement in the Christian world, but it would of itself bring no revival of religion. It would not increase one whit the force of our general appeal to men to accept Christ, but would rather weaken it. Where Baptist churches are inefficient they would remain inefficient. It is a very inadequate diagnosis of spiritual conditions which imagines that a surrender of a clearly taught scriptural form of baptism in the interest of expediency and catholicity would rejuvenate the churches which have yielded to the secular and materialistic forces of the age to the serious injury of their spiritual life. It would be like trying to restore the falling timbers of a great building to their places by means of mucilage, or to bail out the water from a foundering ship with a teacup.

---

[3] In a footnote, Mullins said to see Rev. E. F. Snell of West Newton MA, "Shall We Go Forward?," "a plea addressed to American Baptists for a larger conception of their mission."

Ceremonies have their proper place in religion as we shall see in a moment. They are of exceeding value in so far as they accurately express life and truth and for the specific ends with reference to which they were given. They do not produce life. The proposal to modify baptism or other of the externals of Christianity in the interest of convenience or expediency merely implies two radically defective suppositions. The first is that in externals in ordinances and polity the church should modify its practice whenever expediency calls for it. To abolish entirely not only baptism but the Lord's Supper if necessary would be in direct line with the view. The externals of religion have rested on some kind of conviction, some sense of fitness and right hitherto, in all the Christian bodies. The proposal we are considering removes the element of moral conviction entirely from our regard for the ordinances. The second implied presupposition in the proposal is that external forms which symbolize and express life merely can be converted into spiritual causes which produce life. The assumption is that by manipulating ordinances we can create spiritual changes and rejuvenate the church. Lurking in this view are contradictory conceptions of the ordinances themselves: one that they are sacraments with life-giving power, the other that as they may be modified at will they have no binding power upon conscience at all. Among Baptists, who are anti-sacramental, the latter tendency would prevail in the end if encouraged generally, and what little of ecclesiastical order we have would soon be dissolved entirely.

Another Matter of Vital Importance

This leads to another matter of vital importance. Those who plead for "open membership" in our churches and those who cleave to the view that the church is needless, overlook alike a great teaching of history. They really raise the far-reaching question whether Christianity was or was not designed by its founder to be an institutional religion. They plant themselves on the platform that Christianity is anti-institutional. The "open membership" plea does this as well as the other view we are considering; because for Baptists to exclude the two simple ordinances from the essentials of church organization is to leave nothing, for them at least, from which an outward church organization can receive distinctive character. A flag is a slight thing, a mere badge or symbol. Yet a nation without a flag would be at tremendous disadvantage in peace and war. The flag kindles the spirit of loyalty and enthusiasm in time of peace. In war an army without a flag would be in great measure helpless, a navy would be exposed to attack from friend and foe alike. A voluntary assemblage of people claiming to be spiritual but with no outward badge or conditions of membership would soon lose its identity as a church and take its place with other human organizations maintained for moral purposes in a greater or less degree akin to those of the church. Infants might be received and enrolled, as in the "cradle roll" of Sunday school. Inquirers and searchers after truth would like to enter the circle and environment of the spiritual, for obvious reasons, and with nothing to test or sift, with no external means of determining the real character of the applicant there is no reason to suppose that the church would not lose its character entirely.

The fact is that no great historic force in the religious or political life of the race has ever impressed the world profoundly or changed it radically without taking on institutional form. Christianity is not exempt from the law. The Quakers ignore the ordinances. They are simply the assembly of the spiritual. But Christ has grown dim in their Confessions of Faith and his is a waning figure in their experience. Unitarians also abjure the ordinances, but where have they shown power to grapple with the great practical and missionary movements for the spiritual regeneration of the race? No great religious body since the New Testament was written has ever attempted with any sort of success an anti-institutional form of Christianity. Great truths and ideals must have institutional embodiment if they are to become great historic forces.

Vital Elements Symbolized

Now baptism and the Lord's Supper together symbolize all the vital elements in Christianity. Baptism accents the individual and the Supper the social aspect of the gospel. The life and creed of the church are reflected in them. The "open membership" plea tears asunder this parallel between the life and the symbols of life. To remove the ceremonial barrier between the church and the world would mean in time the removal also of the spiritual barrier. The spiritual principles and ideals would become corrupted. The necessary proportion and symmetry of statement and emphasis would be lost, whole truths would become half-truths, vital and saving faith would become intellectual and historic faith, the church as a redemptive and militant spiritual force would become a social club with moral and esthetic ideals.

185

Church Not Mechanically Constructed

The New Testament church arose as the result of a vital process. It was not mechanically constructed by Jesus through formal commands or through a statute book of legislative enactments after the manner of the tabernacle in the Old Testament. The Spirit guided the early Christians. There were elements both formal and vital out of which the church was constructed. Baptism and the Supper and external organization were the formal, regenerated life and social worship and effort were the vital. These elements were taken up one by one as the church advanced, by a sort of vital integration, like the cells of an organism. None of them are expressly prescribed as timber out of which to build the church. All are assumed. What we have in the New Testament therefore is a constructive spiritual process going on under our eyes. It is redeemed and regenerated life, under the guidance of God's Spirit, readjusting itself according to its own renewed nature, saved men expressing the saving impulse in a practical way. The result is the church and its ordinances. Or, to put the same truth in slightly different language, it was the kingdom of God acting under a twofold impulse, that of redemptive love and that of self-preservation. The church is the device, so to speak, for the realization of both these ideals of the kingdom. The kingdom is like the current of electricity in the telegraph wire. The church is like the instrument in the office where the current is localized, where the kingdom utters itself. The kingdom is like the sunlight traveling ninety million miles to this earth to brighten and to bless. The church answers to the flowers and fruits which the sunlight creates lest its long journey be made in vain. Lest the rays of the sun be utterly wasted nature must respond in concrete visible forms. Lest the energy of the kingdom come to naught churches must gather it up and reproduce it. The institutional idea of course, like every other, can be carried too far. Ordinances and forms may be multiplied and transformed into instruments of spiritual tyranny until a great hierarchy is created and Christianity loses its distinctive power as a spiritual religion. This is one extreme.

Another Extreme

The other extreme is to discard all institutional forms. This leaves the community of believers, so to speak, gasping in a vacuum. They are thus left powerless to define their aims and purposes on the stage of history. They have no visible outline as an organized power and hence cannot challenge the attention of men. The Abbè Loisy says, "History knows of no instance of a religion without a cult, and consequently Christian ritual should cause no surprise. But one easily conceives that if the essence of Christianity is such as Harnack has defined, such a pure Christianity excludes all external forms of worship. That would be a peculiar religion designed for a legion of angels, of which every individual constitutes a separate species, and not of men destined to live together on earth."[4] To this we may add a statement from Sabatier, who is of course not in harmony with the Abbè Loisy on many questions, but who clearly recognizes the peril of mere individualism in religion and the rejection of all church life. He says: "The Protestant Christian who isolates himself, believing that he can draw all religious truth from the Bible for his individual inspiration, lives and thinks in unreality. His intellectual obstinacy springs from ignorance and keeps him in it. We have need one of another, quite as much from the point of view of the moral life as of material existence…Only in this social solidarity can the Christian life blossom out, and find at once health and security. An unsocial Christianity is a stunted and sterile Christianity."[5] De Tocqueville has given a clear statement of the general principle:

> I firmly believe in the necessity of forms, which fix the human mind in the contemplation of abstract truths, and stimulate its ardor in the pursuit of them, while they invigorate its powers of retaining them steadfastly. Nor do I suppose that it is possible to maintain a religion without external observances; but on the other hand, I am persuaded that, in the ages upon which we are entering it would be peculiarly dangerous to multiply them beyond measure; and that they ought rather to be limited to as much as is absolutely necessary to perpetuate

---

[4] Mullins cites Abbè Loisy, *L'Evangile et l'eglise* (Paris: A. Picard et Fils, 1902) 121. For a reprint, see *The Gospel and the Church* (Buffalo NY: Prometheus Books, 1988.) Alfred Firmin Loisy (1857–1940) was a French Catholic who supported modern methods of biblical criticism. Increased tension over his writings (the Roman Catholic Church had condemned modernism in 1907) led to his excommunication in 1908. Loisy's *L'Evangile et l'eglise* was written as a challenge to Harnack's *Wesen des Christentums (1900)*.

[5] Mullins cites Auguste Sabatier, *Religions of Authority and the Religion of the Spirit* (New York: McClure, Phillips & Co., 1904) 340–41. Sabatier (1839–1901) was a French Protestant liberal theologian.

the doctrine itself, which is the substance of religion of which the ritual is only the form. A religion which should become more minute, more peremptory, and more surcharged with small observances at a time in which men are becoming more equal, would soon find itself reduced to a band of fanatical zealots in the midst of an infidel people.[6]

Discussion Summed Up

We may now sum up the substance of the preceding discussion thus: the advocates of the "open membership" idea in Baptist churches virtually rob Christianity of its only distinctive institutional features. Thus, they join forces with the moral culturists who renounce the church entirely. This position is directly at variance with the New Testament which exhibits the kingdom of God expressing itself for purposes of conquest in the form of the church with its ordinances. It is at variance with practical wisdom which inevitably contrives instruments for the execution of distinct ends. It is opposed to the consensus of Christendom which has for two thousand years recognized and insisted upon the necessary relations between the ordinances and the church. It violates the philosophy of history which recognizes the necessary connection between triumphant ideas and institutions which embody them.

Finally, we remark that while all the above is true, while institutions and ceremonies within limits are necessary to give distinctness and historic impressiveness to any set of religious ideas destined to play a large part in the world's life, we must nevertheless carefully distinguish between the causes and the outward expressions of religious life. We must seek to adjust the ceremonies and forms to the essential nature of the life and to its characteristic ideas, because this is the only stable adjustment which is possible. Congruity is the fundamental law of the relations between life and form. It is the law in nature as well as in poetry, in sculpture, in music, and all other art. In religion the law holds good. Ideas, spiritual forces, follow the law of congruity in the creation of ceremonies and in organization. That is to say, the form expresses, embodies, or symbolizes the life; otherwise it has no function, serves no end. The New Testament obeys this law of congruity. So should we. We must not, on the other hand, commit the blunder of confounding ceremonial and

---

[6] Mullins cites Alexis de Tocqueville, *Democracy in America*, 2 vols., trans. Henry Reeve (New York: The Colonial Press, 1899) 2:26.

symbolic expressions of life with the life-giving forces which lie in the background of all forms and ceremonies. When we would rejuvenate our Christianity and bring the tides of spiritual life back again we must seek the eternal sources of life in the spiritual sphere.

16

The Contribution of the Baptists
to American Civilization[1]

I read some years ago a book by Sir Walter Besant, entitled *Building the Empire*, in which he sketches the development of the British empire. I was startled to observe that he excludes Ireland and India from the British empire and includes Australia, Canada, and the United States. But when I came to understand his point of view I was disposed to concede that in some sense of the word in his inclusion of the United States and his rejection of the other countries he was correct. He meant that British ideas of liberty had come to fruitage in the United States.[2] In this sense of the word we may regard American civilization as a Baptist empire, for at the basis of this government lies a great group of Baptist ideals.

Civilization and Society

Civilization is the movement of human society under the influence of general ideas. As an avalanche is a movement of a mountain side under the action of gravity, or as the tides are the movement of the sea under the attractive power of the moon, so civilization is the movement of the social organism under the sway of great general conceptions. In the Dark Ages the chaos was due to the conflict of general ideas. Theocracy in the form of a papacy, aristocracy in the feudal system, democracy in the free cities, and monarchy in the rise of the centralized governments of Europe in turn tried their hand at guiding human destiny. All failed because no one principle or consistent set of principles gained the ascendancy. Hence the dream of

---

[1] Mullins's footnote: An address delivered at the Baptist Convention of North America, held at Jamestown, VA, May, 1907.

[2] Sir Walter Besant, *The Rise of the Empire* (London: Horace Marshall and Son, 1897). Besant does say that there has not been "real emigration" of the English to France, Scotland or Wales (22). But, he does claim English extension to India (75–81).

medieval Europe was unlike that of Joseph in the biblical story in which one sheaf of social ideals arose in the midst and the other sheaves stood around and did obeisance to it; it was rather a wild delirium of conflicting ideals in which the sleeper was dimly conscious of a coming day of better things, but had no clear conception of what it was to be. That day was ushered in by Martin Luther.

The historian Hase says that since the Reformation the movement of civilization has turned on the conflict between the Catholic and the Protestant principles; that is, the conflict between human authority and human freedom.[3] A glance at history confirms this. The thirty years' war in Europe, the struggle of the Dutch Republic, the English Revolution under Cromwell, the American Revolution, the tragedy of the French Revolution, and the conflict in modern Italy, as well as the current revolution in Russia, are all echoes of the deep cry of man for freedom, the rise of the sense of the inherent worth and the inalienable rights of man against tyranny. De Tocqueville has remarked that this same principle is the fundamental issue in all American politics which finds expression in two tendencies—first, the tendency to extend and secondly, the tendency to limit the power of the people.

A fundamental law of all civilization is that political and religious life travels on parallel roads. They never diverge greatly in direction, so far as the great organizing principles are concerned. Religion is the ultimate fact of man, and civilization is the dim reproduction of religion. Now my thesis at present is that the Baptists have furnished the sheaf of religious ideals around which the others have gathered and have done obeisance; that those ideals have imparted their peculiar glory to our temporal and political organization; that they have fallen from heaven on the hard forms of earthly power and glorified them, like a sunbeam dancing on the helmet of Achilles, or like the sunlight gilding and glorifying the darkened face of the moon until the latter shone with a power capable of guiding the benighted traveler to his destination. I do not of course claim that Baptists have a monopoly of these ideals, that in no sense have others advocated any of them. It is a question rather of degrees, and what I maintain is that no other religious body has adequately set them forth,

---

[3] Karl August von Hase, (1800–1890) German Protestant church historian. His best known work was *Kirchengeschichte, Lehrbuch zunächst für akademische Vorlesungen* (Leipzig: Weidmann, 1834;1900).

and that the Baptists have done so. The contribution of Baptists to American civilization may be stated under a fivefold classification.

Baptists Interpreters of the Reformation

Baptists have been the only adequate interpreters of the Reformation. The advocates of any great movement in religion or politics may usually be divided into two classes—the practical men, the men of compromises and expedients on the one hand, and the idealists on the other, the men who in their practice carry out the logic of the movement to the utmost limit, tolerating no compromises and scorning every tendency to temporize, and ready always to lay down their lives. Such were the Anabaptists of the Reformation, the idealists who alone stood for all that the great movement signified. In the abandon of their devotion they did many extravagant things. When the Scriptures said, "Except ye be converted and become as little children ye cannot enter the kingdom of heaven" [Matt. 18:3], they proceeded to make mud pies and to ride stick horses. When the Scriptures said, "What ye hear in the ear in the inner chambers proclaim from the housetops" [Matt. 10:27], they mounted the roofs of the houses and preached to the passers-by. This was folly indeed, but also remarkable courage.

Now Luther and Calvin and Zwingli suffered the Reformation ideal to pass into eclipse in large measure. In their adherence to the union of Church and State they repudiated the modern religio-civic axiom, "A free Church in a free State." In their retention of infant baptism they violated the religious axiom that all souls have an equal right to direct access to God, and in principle repudiated their own doctrine of justification by faith and the right of private judgment in religion. Thus they introduced Romanism into Protestantism and perpetuated a double principle of religion, a double conception of salvation, a confusing and disastrous attempt to mingle the gold of the Reformation with the clay of medieval Christianity. The churches which retain infant baptism and Protestant countries which have religious establishments have never been able to cast off this burden.

The Anabaptists in Germany and the Netherlands and their spiritual successors, the Baptists of England, from the beginning grasped the inner logic of the Reformation, and were from two to three hundred years in advance of others. That they did grasp the inner logic of the Reformation is seen in many ways: in their assertion of the freedom of the individual and the autonomy of the local church under Christ for one thing. The Baptists declared for separation of Church and State in their earliest confessions. The Presbyterians a few years ago demanded a revision of their doctrinal standards because there was no sufficiently explicit teaching in them on the work of the Holy Spirit, or on worldwide missions. In the Baptist creeds of the early seventeenth century there are formal articles on both.

The denominations generally, except Baptists, have been much perplexed over the salvation of infants dying in infancy, until recent years. Our Confession of 1660 contains a distinct article declaring that all infants dying in infancy are saved. I quote Article 10:

> That all children dying in infancy, having not actually transgressed against the law of God in their own persons, are only subject to the first death, which comes upon them by the first Adam, from whence they shall be all raised by the second Adam, and not that any one of them (dying in that estate) shall suffer for Adam's sin eternal punishment in hell (which is the second death), for of such is the kingdom of heaven, I Corinthians 15:22; Matthew 19:14; not daring to conclude with that uncharitable opinion of others, who though they pleaded much for the bringing of children into the visible church here on earth by baptism, yet nevertheless, by their doctrine that Christ died but for some, shut a great part of them out of the kingdom of heaven forever.[4]

---

[4] Edward Bean Underhill, *Confessions of Faith and other Public Documents Illustrative of the History of the Baptist Churches of England in the Seventeenth Century* (London: Hanserd Knollys Society, 1854) 112. In a footnote, Mullins wrote: On missions note Article 34, Confession of 1656, of several churches of Christ in the County of Somerset, England, which says (Underhill, 96): "That as it is an ordinance of Christ, so it is the duty of his church in his authority to send forth such brethren as are fitly gifted and qualified through the Spirit of Christ, to preach the gospel to the world." This article also quotes Acts 13:1–2 on the separation of Saul and Barnabas to the mission work, and Acts 11:22, 8:14. Note also Article 4, Confession of 1660. On the Holy Spirit, Articles 18, 19, and 20, Confession of 1656, give an elaborate account of the work of the Holy Spirit, in all about four pages. Also Article 7, Confession of 1660. Also Article 12, Confession of 1660, (Underhill, 113, 127).

More on this point is contained in Article 44, Confession of 1678.[5]

And so in other respects Baptists have embodied in their life the consistent working out of the great principles and ideals of the Reformation.

Spiritual Interpretation of Christianity

Baptists have furnished to American civilization the most spiritual interpretation of Christianity the world has seen.

This interpretation is seen in the following: We hold to believers' baptism because it prevents fictitious naturalization in the kingdom of God; we reject the principle of vicarious faith involved in infant baptism because it is incompatible with the doctrine of justification by faith, and because added to that doctrine it introduces a spiritual bimetallism into the kingdom of God, or a gold and silver standard of spiritual values, with a very bad grade of silver at that. We hold to a regenerated church membership because thus only can the church become a spiritual organism progressing by growth under God's Spirit, instead of a human mechanism progressing by accretion under man's manipulation. We reject the sacramental conception of the Lord's Supper because the "real presence" of Christ is not a fact in the realm of matter but a fact in the realm of mind. We adhere to baptism by immersion alone because the thing signified is everything in external forms, and sprinkling or pouring destroys the thing signified in baptism. We hold to democratic polity and local self-government because we prefer to listen to God's voice as it speaks to us by his Spirit rather than to an echo of it in presbytery and synod, or an echo of an echo of it in a bench of bishops or an infallible pope. We prefer a polity which can always be made compact enough in general organization for spiritual work, but never compact enough for tyranny. We prefer a polity which is flexible enough in general organization for growth and adaptation to changing conditions to one which is forever tied hand and foot by corporate unity and legal solidarity. We believe that a polity which can organize itself for general work without disturbing anybody's peace, and can, when its usefulness is ended, dissolve itself without a denominational cataclysm, is better than one that can do neither.

Under Baptist polity you cannot organize the churches for any but good ends. You can organize them for missions and education, but not to try heretics or to impose creeds or to pass general laws. The Baptist polity has its

---

[5] Underhill, *Confessions of Faith*, 163.

shortcomings, doubtless, but it has unmatched advantages. It localizes disease in the particular church and generalizes health through larger organization. All these things we derive from the New Testament which we accept as the only rule of faith and practice.

Thus we make to American civilization our unique contribution, viz., an interpretation of Christianity in the highest degree spiritual, with the fewest of the carnal elements present. Thus we hold up to civilization in doctrine and polity the burnished mirror of New Testament Christianity, in which it may study its own image to advantage and discover the spiritual basis of American institutions.

Baptists and Denominational Unity

Baptists have exhibited to American civilization the most striking example of denominational unity.

There are three forms of power which enter into denominational unity. These are the capacity for integration, elimination, and propagation. By integration I mean harmonious coherence of parts. Baptists have shown marked power of unity in this respect. In the years preceding the Civil War the various religious denominations in the United States, including the Baptists, were split asunder by the divisive issues connected with slavery. Of all those bodies the only one which has had the genius to overcome the resultant barriers and become reunited is the Baptist, and the American Baptist Convention is the living expression of Baptist leadership in the genius for denominational unity. The Methodists and Presbyterians have no corresponding organizations, and while Baptists will continue to do their mission work in Northern and Southern organizations for expediency's sake and efficiency's sake, they will nevertheless henceforth exhibit in American life this organization which proclaims that our church polity never rules common sense and religion out of court in the adjustment or the readjustment of ecclesiastical relations. There is indeed an older organization than this which signalizes the Baptist genius for integration—the Baptist Young People's Union of America.

Doctrinally our genius for integration has also been marked. There have always been extremists among us, and mischief makers, but somehow the rule in railroad accidents has been reversed so that the trains on the curve of steadfast loyalty to Christ have escaped disaster, while those on the tangent have come to grief. We have two kinds of radicals among us today—the high church radicals who want to bind us hand and foot with the multiplication of minute tests of fellowship, on the one hand, and the broad church radicals on the other, who are without doctrinal moorings of any kind. The high church radicals would give us a creed like the tight fitting shoes and trousers and dress coat of a dude which forbid the free action of the limbs in any direction. The broad church radicals would give us a creed like the flowing robe of the Oriental, exactly adapted to the life of indolence and self-indulgence, but not for strenuous endeavor. The great mass of Baptists, however, will insist on a creed like the garments, not of a dude nor yet of the voluptuary, but like the habiliments of the athlete, which gird the body and protect it at every vital point but which leave it free for conquest.

A Baptist Specialty

We have also shown capacity for elimination. This I may say is the Baptist specialty. There is no ecclesiastical machinery in which a church can become entangled and borne onward after life is extinct. Where are the hardshells? Someone has compared their former numbers and prosperity to a great plantation with fine crops and fences and other improvements. Today there is nothing left of them but a solitary gatepost to which the curious traveler may hitch his horse while he surveys the scene of desolation. Where are the Two-Seed-in-the-Spirit-Predestinarian-Baptists? I hear there is a church or two of them left in Ohio.[6]

Not the least of the advantages of the Baptist polity is its facilities for burying the dead. The interment usually takes place with little ceremony and often with no flowers at all, but the operation is none the less effective for all that. The chief point is to get the corpse under ground.

In the matter of propagation also there has been unity. We have adhered rigidly in our general work to the legitimate objects, missions and education. We have never been torn asunder by a controversy over creed revision or creed construction. We have never been rent in twain by the trial of a heretic in any ecclesiastical court. There have been heretics and heresies, of course, but they have not been dealt with by the denomination as a whole. There have been

---

[6] Mullins is referencing strict Calvinistic groups. Hardshells was a reference to Primitive Baptists. Daniel Parker (1781-1844) is considered the founder of the "Two-Seed-in-the-Spirit Predestinarian Baptists.

false cries of heresy also, but usually the agitators have become wiser and better men, or else they have been left as the voice of one crying in a wilderness and with diminished following and influence.

Baptists and Liberty

Baptists gave to American civilization the complete idea of liberty.

Mankind has pursued liberty over mountain and across valley, by land and by sea, through fire and through flood, since the first man caught a glimpse of liberty's white robes leading on to glory. The love of liberty is now a volcanic fire which breaks out into revolution and consumes and destroys the ancient fabrics of government, and now it is a tide of life which rolls across the face of nations, causing them to burst into the beauty and fragrance of a new springtime. The spirit of liberty in its quest for the goal of its desire has sounded all the notes in the gamut of human experience, from the minor notes of abject despair to the ringing paean of victory over every foe. But liberty is a relative term. Some men employ it who do not know its essential meaning, because they have never looked into the face of the ideal itself. An ox under the yoke and groaning beneath the heavy burden has liberty—to switch his tail; and so has the Russian peasant today. A bird in its cage has liberty— to hop from the lower to the higher perch and back again; and if birds have piety doubtless some of them are duly grateful. But neither the one nor the other understands what freedom is. Cardinal Gibbons has said: "A man enjoys religious liberty when he possesses the free right of worshiping God according to the dictates of a right conscience and of practicing a form of religion most in accordance with his duties to God."[7] Dr. John Pollard comments on this as follows: "In Cardinal Gibbons' definition of religious liberty is snugly wrapped up every religious persecution that ever raged in the world. In that definition is hidden away every fetter that ever galled the hands and feet of God's saints, every scourge that ever tore their flesh, and every rack that ever pulled their joints asunder. In that definition, as in a heap of ashes, lie sleeping embers enough to girdle the globe with martyr flames. I am

---

[7] James Cardinal Gibbons (1834–1921) was Archbishop of Baltimore from 1877 to 1921 and was the most influential American Catholic of his era. In 1876 he wrote the popular defense of Catholicism, *The Faith of Our Fathers: A Plain Exposition and Vindication of the Church Founded by our Lord Jesus Christ.* Gibbons was known for his support of American democracy.

unwilling to charge that when Cardinal Gibbons framed this definition he saw all these horrors hidden away in it; but they are there, nevertheless."[8]

Our Anglo-Saxon forefathers knew no limit to personal liberty, except natural barriers like mountains, rivers, and oceans. But they knew little of ordered freedom under law. Our English ancestors who wrested Magna Charta from the hands of tyranny drank a deep draught from the exhilarating cup of constitutional freedom, but there were higher ranges of spiritual liberty unknown to them. Our New England ancestors drank deeply of the enchanted cup when they came for conscience' sake to these inhospitable shores and "the sounding aisle of the dint woods rang with the anthems of the free." But they failed to grasp the idea that religious liberty requires not only that we enjoy, but that we grant liberty to others. As Josh Billings or some one else remarked, "The Puritans came over to worship God according to the dictates of their own consciences and to keep other people from worshiping him according to the'r'n."[9]

Roger Williams and Religious Freedom

Now the coming of liberty to the world has been delayed so long because men did not know where to look for the fountainhead of liberty, or what is the rationale of liberty, the root from which all forms of it spring, until the Baptists taught it to the world. Religious freedom is the nursing mother of all freedom. Without it all other forms of it wither and die. The Baptists grasped the conception of liberty in its full-orbed glory from the beginning. This doctrine and those related to it shine in the early Baptist Confessions of Faith among contemporaneous creeds like a constellation in the clear sky seen through a rift in the darkness of the surrounding clouds. It found its sublimest embodiment when Roger Williams took it in his hand as a precious seed and planted it in the soil of eastern New England, saying in the words of God's true prophet, "Out of this seed shall arise the most glorious

---

[8] John Pollard (1836–1905) was a professor of English at Baptist-related Richmond College from 1886 to 1901. John Garland Pollard (1871–1937) was an active Virginia Baptist layman and eventually served as governor of Virginia.

[9] Josh Billings (1818–1885) (pseudonym for Henry Wheeler Shaw) was a popular nineteenth-century writer of humor.

commonwealth known to human history."[10] The same principle found heroic champions in our Virginia Baptists fathers, who gave neither sleep to their eyes nor slumber to their eyelids until the opposite idea was not only wiped off the statute book of Virginia, but the principle itself incorporated in the first amendment to the American Constitution.

Whitelaw Reid says the greatest fact of modern history was the rise of the American nation.[11] He is mistaken. The greatest fact of modern history was the discovery of the idea of liberty, and that discovery was made by the Baptists. The discovery of this idea is the spiritual analogue to the discovery of the New World by Columbus and its emancipation by Washington. I would like to see a heroic group in marble setting forth the facts. I would have a perfect image of liberty carved from the purest marble. I would have Columbus, the intrepid navigator and discoverer of the New World placing the pedestal in position, and George Washington, the dauntless soldier, lifting the statue into place, and Roger Williams robing the image in the garments of righteousness and placing the chaplet of divine approval upon its brow. And if the sculptor of that image of liberty should look for her original photograph in modern times, he would have to search until he found it written in the earliest Confessions of Faith of the Baptists and embodied in their church life and political creed. There is no other literature during or before the seventeenth century which portrays the perfect image.

It was no accident that a Baptist wrote our national anthem. The Baptist heart was the native place of liberty, and when S. F. Smith wrote

My Country! 'tis of thee, Sweet land of liberty,
Of thee I sing;
Land where my fathers died! Land of the pilgrim's pride!
From every mountain side
Let freedom ring!

---

[10] Mullins's footnote: The purpose and limits of this work do not admit of discussion of the relative merits of Roger Williams and John Clarke in the founding of Rhode Island. The author appreciates the work of Clarke and in a historical discussion would emphasize it. But here and elsewhere in the book it is important only to call attention to Roger Williams as the great pioneer of religious liberty.

[11] Whitelaw Reid (1837–1912) was the editor of the *New York Tribune* and served as an American Ambassador to France and Britain.

it was but the natural union of faith in God on the part of the Baptist preacher joined to patriotism in an American citizen. It was but the deep spring of religious liberty bubbling up and over into thrilling song through the lips of a loyal citizen of this greatest country on earth.

Spiritual Analogues

Baptists have furnished the spiritual analogues of our entire political system. They supply the moral and spiritual assumptions on which is reared our political fabric. Now there are two principles which sum up the political theory of the American commonwealth, and these are reducible to one, viz., the competency of the citizens to work out their political destiny. This applies to the individual, and is well expressed by De Tocqueville, as follows:

> In the United States the sovereignty of the people is not an isolated doctrine, bearing no relation to the prevailing manners and ideas of the people; it may on the contrary be regarded as the last link of a chain of opinions which binds the whole Anglo-American world. That Providence has given to every human being the degree of reason necessary to direct himself in the affairs which interest him exclusively; such is the grand maxim on which civil and political society rests in the United States. The father of a family applies it to his children; the master to his servants; the township to its officers; the province to its townships; the State to the provinces; the union to the States; and when extended to the nation it becomes the doctrine of the sovereignty of the people.[12]

This is the political side of the fundamental Baptist conception of the competency of the soul in religion under God.

This principle of the competency of the citizen applies to the body of the people acting collectively, as well as to the individual. The town meeting is the cornerstone of our entire system. So the philosophic observers from a distance as well as our own best writers hold. Our fundamental conception is not representative government, but direct government by the people.

---

[12] Mullins doesn't cite what edition or page of de Tocqueville he was quoting. For this quotation, see Alexis de Tocqueville, *Democracy in America*, 2 vols., trans. Henry Reeve (New York: D. Appleton and Co., 1904) 2:459.

Representative government is an expedient made necessary simply by increase of numbers and geographical extent. Pure democracy resorts to representation only when it is compelled to, and reverts to pure democracy whenever possible. Now local church government held by the Baptists is the religious and Christian analogue of the town meeting. It is not too much, perhaps, to say with due allowance for the figure of speech, that a local Baptist church is the town meeting of the kingdom of God, and the town meeting is the political church of the temporal commonwealth.

Presbyterians seek to justify their system often on the plea that it conforms to the American system of representative government in having a graded system of courts and legislatures. But they forget a fundamental fact, viz., that in the kingdom of God the authority cannot be localized, while in the State it must be localized as soon as it assumes more than the dimensions of the town meeting. The authority of the State has to be localized and distributed because it is a human authority. In the kingdom of God it cannot be localized in a series of courts or legislatures because the authority is divine and omnipresent. Christ alone is King in Zion. So that pure democracy in the church is the only true analogue to representative government in the State, because the latter is simply an expedient for registering the will of the people. Representative government is necessary in the State when the State becomes large enough to require distribution of authority; it is never necessary in the church because the authority of Christ never can be localized or distributed.

A New Testament Church and the American Government

Look into a New Testament church and then at the American government, and insight discovers that the latter is the projection of the shadow of the former. One might in a certain sense say that the primary election which determined whether or not there should be an American government was held two thousand years ago on the shores of the Mediterranean when the little Baptist democracies assembled to worship.

I go further. Beginning with the religious competency of the soul under God as the distinctive significance of the Baptists in history, and passing to the civic competency of the citizen, we complete the analogy by showing that the six Baptist axioms of religion are the analogues of our political axioms. The theological axiom, "A holy and loving God has a right to be sovereign," has its counterpart in the recognition of God's sovereignty by this government in

201

granting to the church the rights of an *imperium in imperio*; that is, in giving independence to the church. In so doing the State recognizes an authority higher than itself.

The religious axiom, "All souls have an equal right to direct access to God," finds its political counterpart in the American axiom, "All men are created free and equal."

The ecclesiastical axiom that "All believers are entitled to equal privileges in the church," finds its political counterpart in the American axiom that ours is a government "of the people, for the people, and by the people."

The moral axiom that "To be responsible, man must be free," finds its counterpart in the franchise and in all our American practice in legal and criminal procedure.

The religio-civic axiom, "A free Church in a free State," has become naturalized in our speech until it is as much political as religious.

The social axiom, "Love your neighbor as yourself," has its political counterpart in our political axiom, "Equal rights to all and special privileges to none."

In short, the Baptist axioms of religion are like a stalactite descending from heaven to earth, formed by deposits from the water of life flowing out of the throne of God down to mankind, while our American political society is the stalagmite with its base upon the earth rising to meet the stalactite and formed by deposits from the same life giving stream. When the two shall meet, then heaven and earth will be joined together and the kingdom of God will have come among men. This is the process which runs through the ages.

Baptist Bed-Rock Ideals

In conclusion be it said that the intelligent Baptist can yield to none in his patriotism, for his religious ideals are the bed-rock of the political fabric. Indulge me in a little fancy as we contemplate "old Glory," the name we have learned most to love to describe our flag. The stripes of continuous color across the flag tell of a homogeneous American life, and being equal in width they tell of justice and equality; and the red, white, and blue in the color scheme tell of American variety and of unity in variety; and the cluster of stars in the flag, each star separate from the other stars, tells of the principles of autonomy and individualism which underlie our whole system; and they are stars to show that those principles of freedom were born in heaven, and that freedom and individualism are the freedom of an ordered universe, and not of chaos.

We are approaching the Baptist age of the world, because we are approaching the age of the triumph of democracy. I seem to see dimly the outlines of that coming age.

> A solemn murmur in the soul tells of an age to be,
> As travelers hear the ocean roll
> Before they view the sea.[13]

Like a vine growing in the darkness of some deep cavern, and slowly stretching itself toward the dim light shining in through the distant mouth of the cavern, so has humanity slowly crept along toward freedom. The mighty hordes of the Asiatic and the European world, weary and sad, yet courageous and resolute, are hasting forward with unresting feet toward the gates of destiny. Toward those gates these hundreds of years the Baptists have been pointing, and today in the foremost files of time they lead the way. As humanity enters they will shout with the full knowledge that God in Christ has led all the way:

> Lift up your heads, O ye gates;
> And be ye lifted up, ye everlasting doors;
> And the King of glory shall come in.
> Who is the King of glory?
> Jehovah strong and mighty,
> Jehovah mighty in battle.
> Lift up your heads, O ye gates;
> Yea, lift them up, ye everlasting doors;
> And the King of glory shall come in.
> Who is the King of glory?
> Jehovah of hosts, he is the King of glory.[14]

---

[13] See Daniel Hoffman Martin, *Concerning Them which Are Asleep* (Chicago: The Winona Publishing Co., 1904) 14.

[14] Psalm 24.

And the goal of human progress shall be realized in an eternal society wherein absolute democracy is joined to absolute monarchy, God the Father being the monarch and his people a vast family of free children.

17

Baptists and World Progress

The preceding chapter indicates the contribution of Baptists to American civilization. This raises another question: Do the axioms of religion, as we have expounded them, contain in themselves sufficient virtue to guide the destinies of the race? Do we find in them the *principia*, or first principles of advancing civilization? Let us seek an answer to these questions.

Guizot's Idea of Christianity

Guizot in his well-known history asserts that the idea of civilization contains the following elements: the idea of order and social well-being, the idea of progress, the development of man as an individual, and the growth of society as a whole. In his definition he fails to give proper recognition to the fact that the core of all real progress is moral. He succeeds better in doing this in his discussion than in his definition. Guizot's definition regards society somewhat externally.[1] It would be perhaps more fruitful to define it from within, to note it as a process in the spirit of man and society rather than in its outward appearance. As life is more interesting than forms, and as potencies are more significant than attainments, so also is the inner law of civilization more valuable for study than its manifestations at any particular point in history. The flame is greater than the fagot. The genius of Raphael transcends the Sistine Madonna. The imagination of Michelangelo is a more splendid thing than even his marble image of Moses.

The star of the world's progressive civilization rose in the West centuries ago. The eyes of Europe rather than those of Asia were first permitted to gaze upon it. In India and China and other Oriental lands arrested development has held the peoples back for thousands of years. That civilization is well symbolized in the bound foot of the Chinese girl. Trammeled in its youth by

---

[1] Francis Guizot, *The History of Civilization* (London: George Bell and Sons, 1890).

some repressive principle it became club-footed at the outset and went mincing on its way. It could climb the long low slopes of the mountain of progress, but such feet could not scale the loftier heights. So it sat down after a short while on a low tableland and folded its hands. It has been sitting thus thousands of years. Western civilization itself did not assume definite form and outline until after the Reformation. Its destiny was fixed, however, when the Apostle Paul crossed the Hellespont into Greece. Prior to the Reformation the conflict of ideals left the issue in the balances. After Luther the Western world was launched upon a new career. The prow of the ship points steadily to its goal and the shining shores appear, though perhaps as yet but dimly in the distance.

The Significance of Personality

The key to this movement of civilization is to be found in the idea and in the significance of personality. The value of the soul of man, the rights and privileges of the individual, the capacity of man for growth and happiness, for the attainment of moral and spiritual character, for fellowship with other men and above all with God—these are some of the rich contents of the great word, human personality. The reader recognizes at once the echo in the above of the teaching of Jesus and of Paul as to the worth of the human soul, of the value of man as man. This is the pivot of modern civilization. The whole movement turns upon it. The revolt against tyranny and oppression in every form is but the expression of it. In the political, industrial, and religious spheres every contest in which men are engaged today turns upon this idea. Two objects are sought for the individual man and for society, viz., that man may be free and self-legislative. He seeks constitutional freedom and moral progress. Liberty, equality, fraternity, are the great words which set forth the ideal as it pertains to society as a whole. The ideal of all forms of social life, as men are coming more and more to see, is that it is moral fellowship of persons. Business life should be so regarded as well as civic and political. These are associations of men and women for mutual helpfulness and growth. Science, art, philosophy, philanthropy, and religion are the higher regions in which the principle has play.

Now in what follows we propose to show that the axioms of religion as previously expounded, taken with the general truth of the competency of the soul in religion under God, contain the essential elements of modern civilization and are fitted to guide it to the highest and best issues. We will view them first as a moral and religious force, and secondly as an intellectual, and thirdly as a social and political force. In all these spheres it will appear that the axioms of religion are the mainspring of civilization. Our sketch must needs be brief. Ground covered in previous chapters must here be assumed. An outline of the salient points of the argument will present it sufficiently, we trust, to make good our plea.

First we consider the axioms as a religious and moral force in the world's progress.

Evangelism and the Soul's Competency

Evangelism, in the complete New Testament meaning of the word, is a striking illustration of the axiom and of the doctrine of the competency of the soul in religion under God. Evangelism is the proclamation to the soul of man that God has provided a trysting place, so to speak, for God and man in Christ. In Christ they meet, and face to face settle their controversy. The incarnation is God's self-revelation as a person, the atonement is his provision for human sin. Evangelism is the approach of the divine to the human person. The high respect which God pays to human personality is seen in the fact that his transaction with every sinner in Christ is on the basis of that sinner's private and personal needs and conditions. Dr. H. C. Mabie, in his suggestive book on *Method in Soul Winning*, touches the heart of true evangelism when he says the chief business of the soul-winner is to "put the sinner on the clue."[2] The clue is always found in the sinner's own private experience, and Christ always meets him within the sphere of that experience. Where many paths converge upon a given point in a forest it is usually because a spring of water is to be found where they meet. The gospel is the fountain of life constructed with a path running to every man's dwelling. To put a man on the clue is to turn his feet into the path at his own door. Out of his subjective experience and sense of need he finds Christ. Evangelism connects the thirsty man with the fountain, puts him on the private path that leads to life.

Now the bearing of this fact on infant baptism will be obvious to those who have read our preceding chapters on the religious and moral axioms.

---

[2] Henry C. Mabie, *Method in Soul Winning* (New York: Fleming H. Revell Company, 1906) 7–8. Mabie was the corresponding secretary of the American Baptist Missionary Union in Boston.

Infant baptism forestalls evangelism. Churches which practice it in a thoroughgoing manner and on a large scale have no place in their systems for New Testament evangelism. The Lutheran Church in Germany is an example. The reason is clear. Spiritual thirst is impossible to the infant and water applied to its body is a vain substitute. Evangelism assumes the competency of the soul under God's grace. It assumes also the religious and moral axioms while infant baptism assumes none of these truths.

Later in this chapter we shall see how profoundly New Testament evangelism, as sketched above, harmonizes with the best modern educational theory and the fundamental principles of psychology. Meantime we cite evangelism as an illustration of the axioms of religion as a moral and religious force in modern civilization. Evangelism is the method of God for setting the soul free. He regenerates the spirit of man and thus transforms it into a regenerator of human society. Through evangelism, therefore, God grapples directly with man's deepest problem, emancipation from the power of sin.

Evangelism and Modern Civilization

Evangelism is, therefore, a central force in all modern civilization, because the freedom which religion gives is the only inclusive freedom. Individual freedom, freedom of thought, freedom of conscience, freedom of action, industrial freedom, civil liberty, these are all imperishable treasures of the human spirit, achieved as working principles, if not ideally attained as yet, at the cost of much blood and of age-long struggle. Yet ultimately they all rest on religious freedom. The free fellowship of man with God, implied in the doctrine of the competency of the soul in religion, and in the religious axiom the right of men to direct access to God, is the ultimate basis of freedom. All forms of liberty are alike in the respect they pay to human personality; but they differ in the degree of their inclusiveness, like a series of concentric rings. The outside ring which alone can include all the rest is the soul's free intercourse with God. The ultimate authority for man is God. For God we were made. When adjusted to God through Christ we find liberty, and all other adjustments follow in due time. Democracy and its attendant blessings in the State in modern times have gone hand in hand not with sacramental and sacerdotal Christianity, but with the Christianity of free grace and the direct relation of the soul to God. The Dutch Republic, Scotland, England, America, not Russia, Spain, and Portugal, have made great progress toward government by the people. The regeneration of individuals through evangelism issues in church democracy, which we will now consider as a religious force in civilization.

Three Important Witnesses

We have in previous chapters indicated the value of democracy in the church as the only possible expression of the ecclesiastical axiom. But in order to make clear the general proposition that democracy in the church is fitted to guide civilization at all stages, if properly applied, we propose now to call to the stand three witnesses widely separated in some respects from each other. They bear testimony to the value of a democratic church with reference to widely separated aspects of Christian effort and progress.

The first will be Mr. Loring Brace who has written powerfully in defense of the Christian faith in his well-known work *Gesta Christi*. Says Mr. Brace:

> The union of the Christian Church with the State under Constantine we regard as one of the great blunders of the historical church, which has drawn after it a long train of evils, whose effects are even yet experienced. Could Christianity have been permitted to grow, as it did under the apostles, in little voluntary associations of believers, unconnected with the civil power and with a simple organization, we should not have had, indeed, the grand spectacle of an apparently converted imperial court, and an official hierarchy, and a church supported by armies and governed by warriors, courtiers, and vast populations suddenly made into nominal Christians—but we should have been saved a paganized peasantry, a corrupt priesthood, a hierarchy full of greed and ambition, ages of blood and religious warfare, and a church which persecuted both science and differing opinions. The Christian faith would have grown up where it belongs—in quiet, humble places—and have reformed manners and morals before it took hold of legislation. Christ's principles would have been a spiritual power in the world, not a form or an institution, and would thus have finally permeated society. So far from regarding the spread of the Christian religion in the Roman world as a sign of its divine origin and evidence of its triumph, we consider it as almost a

fatal occurrence, and as having impeded the spread of Christ's real truth ever since.[3]

Those who regard the medieval Church of Rome as the great providential agency for preserving civilization from chaos will of course reject Mr. Brace's view. But if they will recall the character of the New Testament church, as made up of the regenerate alone, and not of those baptized in infancy; and if they will recall the tremendous spiritual energy of the early church as shown in its speedy conquest of the empire in spite of fearful persecutions, the force of the language of Mr. Brace will be felt.

Professor Harnack's Testimony

Let us next take Professor Adolf Harnack as a witness. In an essay published a few years ago entitled "Thoughts on Protestantism," he arraigns the established churches of Europe in a severe manner, and points out the perils which confront them. He is of course not a member of a congregational or Baptist church, but throughout his essay he insists on principles which lie at the heart of church democracy, and the axioms of religion supply the fundamental conceptions of his general plea for more spiritual and more biblical Christianity than that found in the State Churches. The great peril to which he calls especial attention is "*the progressive Catholicizing of Protestant churches.*" He means by this that these State Churches are more and more becoming centralized and secularized, that sacerdotalism is creeping in, that tradition is acquiring, in increasing measure, a binding force. Men are forgetting the real nature of the church as a congregation of believers, a spiritual body owing the first allegiance to Christ and guided by the Spirit.

Professor Harnack, in proving the existence of a Catholicizing tendency says:

> The first thing to notice relates to the very conception of a church. What we in Germany call the evangelical conception of a church has almost vanished; and if any one in practical life ventures to remind people of it he is cried down as an impractical dreamer. The majority of our influential clerical newspapers, with which must also be

---

[3] Mullins cites Loring C. Brace, *Gesta Christi* (New York: Hodder and Stoughton, 1882) 51–52.

reckoned one or two political journals, go to work with ideas which are quite Catholic. One of these church newspapers I have been reading regularly now for several years and in all its countless references to the church I cannot remember ever to have come across a single passage in which full justice is done to the seventh article of the Augsburg Confession...Hardly any distinction is drawn between the Church of the Faith and the National Church; and all the decisions and regulations of the National Church, so far as they are agreeable to the greater number, are placed under the protection of the sacred authority.[4]

We insert at this point the seventh article of the Augsburg Confession referred to by Professor Harnack. The reader will be interested to observe its contrast with the modern developed and centralized hierarchies. The article is as follows:

Also they teach that one holy church is to continue forever. But the church is the congregation of saints, in which the gospel is rightly taught and the sacraments rightly administered. And unto the true unity of the church it is sufficient to agree concerning the doctrine of the gospel and the administration of the sacraments. Nor is it necessary that human traditions, rites, or ceremonies instituted by men should be alike everywhere, as St. Paul saith: 'There is one faith, one baptism, one God and Father of all.'[5]

Again Harnack says: "Added to this Catholic conception of the church, which identifies the Church of the Faith with the Church of History, we evangelicals are also gradually experiencing everything that naturally goes with it—fanaticism, the despotic tendency, impatience, a mania for persecution, clerical uniform, and clerical police."[6] He remarks in closing this division of his discussion that "a clear insight into the conditions of Protestant life is on the

---

[4] Mullins cites Adolf Harnack, *Thoughts on The Present Position of Protestantism* (London: Adam & Charles Black, 1899) 32–33.
[5] Mullins cites Philip Schaff, *Creeds of Christendom,* 3 vols. (New York: Harper and Brothers, 1877) 3:11–12.
[6] Harnack, *Protestantism,* 35.

point of disappearing" and that unless something is done it will disappear entirely. He quotes a description of the Roman Catholic Church in France by an intelligent French Catholic in which France is described as the most "orthodox country in the world because in matters of religion the most indifferent." Catholicism is declared to be full of myths, superstitions, and absurdities; and on the other hand, full of profound ideas, significant ritual, and flourishing symbolism. Church authority, not investigation settles all questions. No one is expected to understand or believe the system. There are no doubts because there is no thought. The believer may be in the church but also the unbeliever, for he is undisturbed so long as he conforms to the outward requirements. Professor Harnack then adds: "The image of Catholicism which is here portrayed is the image that threatens us." Again, "If the development insensibly advances, and we simply capitulate to it a second Catholicism will be formed out of the consolidation of Protestantism; but it will be poorer and of less religious intensity than the first."[7]

What remedy does Professor Harnack propose? This: that fresh emphasis be given to two vital truths of original Christianity. The first is that "in the end religion is only a steadfast temper of the soul, rooted in childlike trust in God." The second truth is "That this childlike trust is inseparably bound up with the plain simple rule that the moral life, in all its solemnity and earnestness, is the correlative of religion, and that without it religion becomes idolatry and a deception of the soul."[8] In his protest against the institutionalism which he cannot resist successfully Harnack urges in particular the need of "independent personalities." He says "Truly it is not uniform institutions that our age demands, but personalities of the most various type —wide awake, rounded, free."[9]

Thus Harnack on the European churches. It is a severe indictment. It points clearly to one of our chief contentions in preceding chapters, viz., that democracy in the church above all polities, and indeed alone among the various polities, safeguards the spiritual rights of the soul. Man loses his spiritual birthright in due time when he commits his religious interests to human authorities and centralized institutions, when he adopts the indirect

---

[7] Ibid., 51.
[8] Ibid., 55.
[9] Ibid., 63.

instead of the direct method of dealing with God. The axioms of religion would solve the religious problems of Europe if consistently applied. Free thought in France is fundamentally anti-clerical rather than anti-Christian. If the Christian religion could be set before the eyes of unbelief in European countries in its original, simple, universal elements, thousands of men and women thirsting for the truth would hail it as famished pilgrims crossing a desert hail the oasis with crystal fountain and spreading trees. A significant fact is that in the State Churches in both Germany and England there is a distinct inner movement toward a deeper spirituality. In England the Keswick movement offers a haven for the dissatisfied and spiritually hungry.[10] On the Continent and in England this spiritual movement from within is regarded by the constituted authorities as an alien element and disturbing force. Thus the freedom of the spirit ever struggles for existence in bodies where the practice of infant baptism obscures or nullifies conversion, and where centralized power suppresses democracy.

Foreign Missions and the Churches

The progress of foreign missions is a matter of vital moment to the churches of Jesus Christ. President C. C. Hall in his recent work, *The Universal Elements of the Christian Religion*, has discussed the question of church organization and of foreign missions in a suggestive and fruitful way. He does not commit himself to the idea of democracy in the church in any formal way. But his entire plea looks in that direction.

Referring to the church troubles in Scotland due to "technicalities in a trust deed given sixty years ago," and to the pending struggle of the Noncon-formists of England against the Education Bill Dr. Hall says: "Assuredly the ongoing of truth is not to be holden by parliamentary decisions. God may have in his plan not the disestablishment of the Church of England only, but

---

[10] Keswick was the center of the Holiness movement in England in the late nineteenth century. Keswick Holiness emphasized sanctification as an enduement of power from the Holy Spirit. Sanctification, according to advocates, could be received instantly and empowered a believer for a "higher Christian life" of service.

that larger disestablishment of the whole sectarian principle which implies reorganization on simpler lines of service with faith and love."[11]

Denominationalism and Missions

Coming then to the discussion of denominationalism in relation to missions Dr. Hall declares that it is not expedient to attempt to perpetuate the various forms of modern Protestantism on the mission fields of the East. It is confusing and disastrous. He pleads rather for some simpler form of Christianity which contains only its universal elements as these lay in the mind of Christ. Such a form would allow scope for the unfolding of the spiritual life of China and Japan and India according to its own needs and conditions. It is wrong to compel the East to wear the highly developed ecclesiastical armor of the West.

President Hall says:

It is vain to make a calculation of the number of those for whom the denominational aspects of the church are already dim, as the outlines of a receding coast, and on the horizon line of whose hope is rising the image of a more glorious and homogeneous church, not having spot or wrinkle or any such thing; a church of the living God, the pillar and ground of the truth, built upon the foundation of the apostles and prophets, Jesus Christ himself being the chief Cornerstone.

Again, he says whatever form the new interpretation of the church may take, it

can crystallize around one axis only—the Cross of the Redeemer. Give that and all else is given. Give that and all are one in him. This crystallizing of unorganized sentiment into a reinterpretation of the church on non-sectarian lines would be, not a new ecclesiastical unity—not a new dogmatic unity—that were but to impose a new Catholicism, to revive the dream of an external seat of human authority, to give the stone of death for the bread of life. The next great reinterpretation of

---

[11] Mullins cites C. C. Hall, *The Universal Elements of the Christian Religion* (New York: Fleming Revell, 1905) 94. Charles Cuthbert Hall (1852–1908) was a Presbyterian minister and president of Union Theological Seminary (1987–1908).

the church must be through the centralizing power of the Eternal Truth lifted up and drawing men unto itself, with the vitalizing power of the Eternal Spirit giving liberty unto every man. Through such a church the Christianization of the world becomes possible, if not immediate. The witness of such a church would be an irresistible witness. The effect of such a church would be the advent and fruition of the kingdom of God.[12]

The writer has no desire, of course, to construe the language of another in a way which its author would repudiate. Nor does he wish to ascribe to President Hall views identical with his own as to the essential elements of Christianity. But the careful reader will discern very clearly in the preceding sentences of Dr. Hall the substance of the "Axioms of Religion" as set forth in this volume: The soul's direct relation to God's Spirit, the union of believers in the truth, the equality of men before God, the central position of the cross of Christ in human redemption, and the competency of the soul in religion under God.

Christian Union and the Voluntary Principle

It should be noted here that modern progress toward Christian union is shut up to the voluntary principle as the only pathway toward the goal. There is no way in which a law of unity can be imposed from without. It can therefore find expression only through an inward movement which is free and voluntary. Systems therefore, which are based on authority are prevented by virtue of that fact from supplying the principle of union, unless it be supposed that the free bodies will, with growing intelligence and spirituality, choose to assume a yoke of ecclesiastical authority. This is scarcely conceivable. Birds which have been confined in cages may, through force of habit, fly back into them after being released; but the birds which never knew anything but God's free atmosphere and overarching heavens will scarcely fold their wings and hop into a prison. Revolutions, religious as well as political, never go backwards. The planet in the solar system may be tilted more or less on its axis, and it may vary somewhat in its distance from the sun, but it never reverses the direction of its rotation. The swing of the spiritual movement is away from human authority in religion, not toward it.

---

[12] Ibid., 97–99.

The axioms of religion do not require external uniformity in the mechanical sense. "Organic" church union is not necessary to union in Christ. Every other body might become Baptist in doctrine and polity and, if it saw fit, remain distinct from the present Baptist denomination in organized effort. Baptist principles require the utmost freedom in these things. This point is emphasized here to show that the writer is not dealing with the subject of Christian union in a merely sectarian spirit, with a desire merely to have others "come over and join us." If bodies of Christians can find sufficient grounds for separate organizations for general missionary and benevolent purposes, Baptists have no word of objection, only let them restore to humanity their spiritual rights under God, as Christ and his apostles have revealed them to us.

The Axioms of Religion as a Religious Force

To sum up now this section of our discussion we assert that as a religious force in the progress of the race the axioms of religion are of incalculable value first, because all forms of human freedom are ultimately grounded in religious freedom. Evangelism or its equivalent in religious instruction is the usual method by which religious freedom in the deepest, truest sense is achieved for individual souls, and the method through which the emancipating power of religion becomes active and potent in human society; and evangelism is a concrete expression of the principles of the axioms at a particular point.

These statements admit other ways of bringing saving truth to the soul, as well as all forms of Christian nurture. Evangelism is simply the most convenient illustration of the principle. Secondly, the value of the axioms is further seen in that, according to Mr. Brace, their loss from early Christianity robbed the church of its power as a great social force; their loss from modern European Christianity, according to Harnack, imperils those spiritual rights of man against the loss of which he so vigorously protests; and their presence alone, according to President Hall, will impart the simplicity and homogeneity necessary in propagating Christianity in the Orient. Thirdly, the voluntary principle underlying the axioms at every point, in the nature of the case, is the chief dependence in efforts for Christian union.

Intellectual Force and Axioms of Religion

We next consider the axioms of religion as an intellectual force in world progress. Here it will be sufficient to note their relation to three intellectual movements, modern educational theory, modern science, and modern philosophy.

First, modern pedagogy and educational theory. A brief sketch of the progress of the principles of pedagogy through history will aid us in realizing the truth. Prof. Paul Monroe in his *Textbook in the History of Education* has given an excellent outline. A chief virtue in his manner of presentation lies in the fact that he relates educational method everywhere to the development of personality. [13]

Among the Chinese we find one of the most primitive forms of education. As Professor Monroe says, Chinese education is education by "recapitulation." The pupil simply memorizes the details of Chinese life and literature. Charles Lamb's humorous essay on the origin of roast pig suggests the method of Chinese education.[14] A Chinaman upon returning home found his house burned and his pig dead and roasted to a brown. By accident his son burnt his finger on the roasted pig and put it in his mouth for relief. Thus he discovered the savory qualities of roast pig. Henceforth when this article of food was desired the Chinese method was to shut up the pig in the dwelling and burn the latter to the ground. In other words, the Chinese pupil is a slavish copyist. Here, of course, is no play for personality. Originality is at a discount. Repression and suppression of individuality rule in all effort.

As contrasted with that of the Chinese, Greek education was "progressive adjustment," a vast advance upon the Chinese. Here personality and individuality come into view in some measure at least. The principle of growth is recognized. The adjustment sought was progressive, it was an adjustment to the world of practical life and the world of thought. Greek education aimed to make a man a free citizen. But it too came far short. It was aristocratic. Women and slaves were left out of the account. So also was the future life. The soul for its own sake, the worth of man as man they did not appreciate.

Roman education was similar to the Chinese in that it had chiefly the aim of equipping the boy for practical life. The Roman boy must also imitate, copy, gather up in himself what the past knew and especially what it did. The

---

[13] Paul Monroe, *A Text-Book in the History of Education* (New York: Macmillan, 1905). Monroe (1869–1947) was an educator born to a Baptist minister in Indiana. He was considered the leading historian of education in America during his era.

[14] Charles Lamb (1775–1884) was an English essayist.

models for imitation were higher than among the Chinese, but initiative was wanting here also. Individuality was suppressed.

In the Middle Ages and in modern times education was regarded chiefly as discipline. To drill the mind, give it bone and sinew, so to speak, and make it capable, this has been the aim. The preferences of the child, his aptitudes, and individual disposition or genius, were ignored. The practical value of the study, its immediate utility counted for nothing. The school was simply a gymnastic exercise.

Rousseau transferred the emphasis. Remove the trammels. Let nature have its course. Do not force traditions and old customs and ancient methods upon the child. Let its own nature unfold like a flower in the sun. Respect individuality. This was Rousseau's plea. It was one-sided, defective, inadequate. But it contained a profound insight.[15]

Rousseau was followed by Pestalozzi who simply gave form and added some positive elements to Rousseau's conception. The teacher can only assist the child to develop. Follow the free natural bent of the child. Ordinary schools are "stifling machines." Up to five years of age the child is free. Nature lies before him in entrancing beauty. His nature responds and unfolds. Then we clap him into a dungeon. Intellectually we murder him. Nay, nay, says Pestalozzi. Education is symbolized by a tree growing from a seed under the influence of rich soil and fertilizing waters. It is spontaneous, free, progressive, and after its kind.[16]

Pestalozzi, however, went only part of the way. He confined his view to impressions upon the senses, from external nature. The moral element was lacking. Herbart introduced it. Use sense perceptions as the basis for moral training, urged Herbart. Let the mind of the child obtain impressions from nature and from society. Then on the basis of these impressions and this knowledge seek to develop moral character. A chief point of Herbart's psychology is apperception—building at each stage on the material preexisting

---

[15] Jean-Jacques Rousseau (1712–1778) was an Enlightenment philosopher whose ideas greatly influenced the French Revolution. His views on education are found in *Emile: or, On Education* (1762).

[16] Johann Heinrich Pestalozzi (1746–1847) was a Swiss educational reformer. His educational method is found in the book, *How Gertrude Teaches Her Children* (1801).

E. Y. Mullins

in the mind. It is like the evangelist's work of putting the sinner "on the clue," as Doctor Mabie expressed it.[17]

The modern educational movement may in a true sense be said to culminate in Froebel. He gathers up the best elements in his predecessors and adds some of his own. Beyond others he recognizes the freedom and personality of the child. Particularly did he lay stress upon the fact that the mind of the child is creative and not merely receptive. Self-activity is its fundamental law. The mind is not a box into which you are to put all kinds of coins for safe keeping. It is a living, growing thing. Education is not information, it is self-realization. Froebel held that the ultimate fact and bond of all unity is God. He says: "All things have come from Divine Unity, from God, and have their origin in the Divine Unity in God alone." The child then, in its education, should learn of God. This is the one great comprehensive fact of all life. Nature everywhere, as a symbol, reveals God, and through it the child should learn of God.[18]

Culmination of the Educational Process

Here then the educational process culminates in the axioms of religion. The right of the child to its individuality in education, to direct access to God, its equality of privilege in the schoolroom with all other children, its freedom and responsibility, its self-activity, these are Froebel's fundamental principles. Their exact counterpart in ecclesiastical and religious life is what we have pleaded for in this work. It is not strange that Froebel himself was a deeply religious man. We see how, step by step, educational theory and method have made their way back to the great universals of Christianity, the first principles of religion. Thus, we see how one generation has added to the work of another. Each great thinker has carried the truth a step beyond his predecessor. Like a succession of great sculptors chiseling a beautiful statue out of marble, each has laid down the mallet and chisel with the work unfinished. Now that the truth of educational theory and practice begins to be seen as a whole, we may discern

---

[17] The German psychologist Johann Friedrich Herbart (1776–1841) has been called the father of scientific pedagogy.

[18] The German educator Friedrich Wilhelm August Froebel (1782–1852) is considered the father of kindergarten education. He founded a "pre-school" in 1837. He believed in the divine unity of nature and thus thought spiritual training was vital to education.

219

how the crude beginnings of the Chinese even are gathered up in the result. We see also the greatness of Jesus, the King among teachers, and how our best thoughts and maturest theories as to the priceless value of the soul, the unique meaning of personality, individuality, and freedom, are but dim reflections of the truth as embodied in and taught by him. We also see how potent are the axioms of religion as an intellectual force in the progress of the world.

There have been developments since Froebel, of course, but none that are radical or fundamental. The combination of the idea of discipline with that of interest is now being wrought out. It was clearly perceived that the figure of the flower unfolding in the sun was not sufficient of itself to express the process. Flowers do not become petulant and unruly. They do not disobey and play truant. Children, in short, have wills, and evil impulses lead them astray. Self-control and intellectual and moral mastery of self must be achieved by effort, by self-denial and discipline. Thus the two ideas are being fused into one in the best recent educational method. Our sketch does not require that we include later movements. Nor has it required that we discuss the philosophic theories of the men whom we have been reviewing. We have sought simply to indicate the relation of the development to our general point of view.

Relations to Science and Philosophy

We need add but few words upon the other two topics under our present head, the relation of the axioms of religion to science and philosophy. In a previous chapter intimations have been given. Moreover, the reader will perceive the truth on this point without difficulty. Science results from the direct and free approach of competent observers to the world about us. Philosophy is born of the free approach of human thought to the universe of abstract truth. The world of nature and the world of thought, these are the regions in which the men of science and the students of philosophy ply their callings. Both these forms of activity and the rights of both sets of observers are implicit in the right of all men to direct access to God.

The axioms of religion assume the following: 1. The correspondence and ultimate agreement between external truth and the powers of the human mind. 2. That man is capable of grasping the truth as to his relations to the universe. 3. That the ultimate object of man's thought and devotion on the one hand and the human mind on the other, act and react upon each other in such a way that they will finally come to mutual adjustment. Time will be required of course. The Christian assumption that God is seeking man as well as man seeking God is of far-reaching import for philosophy. The competency of the soul in religion under God is the guarantee of the competency of man as an investigator in God's universe. Science has not always been open-eyed to spiritual truth. Philosophy has sometimes groped in the darkness and floundered in the quagmire of materialism. But today men of science and of philosophy are gazing upward as never before. The light of the eternal is beginning to beam on them. Men have delved into nature, they have tunneled through the material world in the dark until they have suddenly broken through upon the vision of the pearly gates of the beautiful city of God. We are beginning to see that the city of nature which science is building is but the counterpart of the city of grace which revelation disclosed to John on the isle of Patmos. The city from below is rising to meet the city from above, the New Jerusalem which is coming down from God to this earth. The two cities will become one. The empire of truth has no mountain barriers, no oceans rolling impassably between the scattered parts. For we hasten to the time when there will be "no more sea" [Rev. 21:1]. "And there shall be no night there, For the Lord God giveth them light" [Rev. 22:5].

The Axioms as a Social Force

We next glance briefly at the axioms as a social and political force in world progress. We have shown that the axioms require democracy in the church. In a preceding chapter we have pointed out their relations to American civilization. In so doing we have rendered unnecessary an extended discussion of our present topic. A few general remarks will suffice.

What then is the probable direction of the social and political progress of mankind? The negative side of the reply can be given easily. Surely the world will not return to autocracy, or monarchy, as the ideal of human government. The blood shed at Marston Moor and at Naseby, that which drenched the earth at Saratoga and Yorktown will cry out forever against it.[19] Again, men will not return to aristocracy. They will not set up an oligarchy and give it plenary powers. Feudalism is dead. Theocracy again, in the sense of the Middle Ages,

---

[19] Marston Moor (1644) and Naseby (1645) were key battles in the English Civil War. Saratoga (1777) and Yorktown (1781) were key battles in the American Revolution.

is out of the question. God's reign through an autocratic head of the church may remain for a time as a form of human government. But the stars in their courses fight against it. Every movement toward liberty and enlightenment opposes it.

Democracy holds the future. Every barrier to the free expression of the will of the people, to the ultimate authority of the people in civil government must and will be broken down. The signs are multiplying all about us that even in America we are not satisfied with our approximation to democratic government. The adoption of the initiative and referendum by one State, and the growing interest in these expedients of governments, are one of the signs of the times. The tendency to the popular election of senators is another. This is already being accomplished indirectly in many States without a specific law on the subject. We cite these things not to approve or condemn but only as marking tendencies. The rising tide of moral sentiment against the corrupt government of cities is a significant evidence of the direction in which our life is tending. A look at Russia, and India, and Japan, and at European countries, confirms the view that democracy holds the future. It may come slowly. It may not always find the same formal expression, but it will come. The world is becoming conscious of itself. The prodigal in the far country is coming to himself. He will arise and return to his home and his inheritance. The prisoner in bonds is beginning to discern that the chains of tyranny which bind him are rusting in two. He will arise in his might and cast them off.

A New Force

A new force which is making itself powerfully felt in modern life is Socialism. Many assert that this form of propaganda holds the key to the future. What have the axioms of religion to say regarding Socialism? The reply is that the axioms are anti-socialistic but righteous. They stand for the voluntary readjustment of economic conditions in righteousness, not their compulsory adjustment. Socialism recognizes the terrible inequality of material conditions, the pitiless cruelty of the competitive system at many points. It says turn over the instruments of production to the State. Abolish competition. Provide for each man according to his needs. Exact from each according to his strength.

But individualism is a fact of human life and of Providence. Inequalities in human personality will always create inequalities of condition. The social-

E. Y. Mullins

istic scheme ignores this fact of Providence. It seeks to cure a recognized evil by ignoring a fact which is organic in human nature, and which belongs to the providential order. Socialism will modify the present social order at many points, but it cannot permanently reorganize society. God loves us too much to be content with anything but our best. Enforced equality is not the best achievement of man in government. Voluntary readjustment in equity and love is the best. Unregenerate majorities may thrust Socialism upon men for a time. It will not endure because it does not express finality in economics, morals, or religion. The socialistic propaganda borrows its glamour by contrast with present conditions which, in truth, are bad enough. But the best always comes slowly. Undue haste is often fatal in moral and spiritual movements.

Socialism and Axioms of Religion

The axioms of religion leave room for all that is worthwhile in Socialism. But they also recognize individualism. The axioms of religion, on the economic side, conform to the parable of the Talents. They, with Christ, take into account that one man has five talents, another two, another one [Matt. 25:14–30]. Socialism asserts that no man shall have five. If nature endows him with five times the ability of his neighbor, Socialism says he shall not have scope for its full exercise. Socialism not only protests against the overman of Nietzsche, the ruthless, pitiless giant spurning love and kindness as weak and effeminate qualities; it likewise has no patience with the " big brother" of Christianity. Socialism is in straits to dispose of Christ himself. Sindbad the sailor was shipwrecked on an island where there was a giant as tall as a palm tree, having only one eye in the center of his forehead, with lips that hung down to his chest, mouth deeper than that of a horse, and ears like those of an elephant. This giant picked up the shipwrecked sailors one by one and turned them around and inspected them, like partridges, and selected the fattest for supper. When his hunger returned he ate another sailor. Sindbad himself escaped only because he was mostly skin and bones.[20]

The vision of such a monster haunts the imagination of the socialist. But his fear, while not wholly groundless, may be offset by other facts. We place over against this gruesome image the radiant figure of Jesus Christ, taller than all the sons of men, and bearing with and in himself all the resources of God

---

[20] "The Seven Voyages of Sindbad the Sailor" is a story within the *Arabian Nights*.

to regenerate mankind. The type that is arising is the great man after Christ's image, great in thought, and in love; great to will, great to plan, great to execute. All the race is rising in stature with him. All will not, cannot be equal in mental, moral, or physical stature. But all have equal rights and privileges, all are equally responsible, all who obey God are hastening to the glorious image, and the glorious estate and the glorious liberty of the sons of God.

Axioms and Progressive Civilization

We conclude this long chapter and end our task by declaring that the axioms of religion derived from the gospel of Jesus Christ are fitted to lead the progressive civilization of the race for the following reasons: First, because as religious ideals they supply the profoundest basis for civilization. Secondly, as ideals preserved through the religious life of man in a Church which is separated from the State they can influence civilization from without and be exempt from the peril of becoming themselves involved in political movements and thus suffering corruption. Thirdly, because they embody the laws of man's intellectual progress. Fourthly, because they respect and conserve every fact of human nature and the providential order of the world; man's freedom and personality; his capacity in art; morals, government, and religion; his passion for growth and progress, his hunger and thirst for God. In the fifth and last place, because they conceive the universe as a kingdom of free spirits wherein under the tutelage and guidance of God man is to work out his destiny. This is the guarantee that that kingdom will in due time become a kingdom of perfect justice, of spotless righteousness, and enduring love.

Index

Index

Index

Scripture Index

Job
26:7, 175

Matthew
6:6-15, 50
8: 21, 91
10:7-8, 50
10:20, 50
10:27, 192
18:3, 192
10:34, 36, 37, 91
11:25-27, 50
13:11, 90
16:17, 89
16:19, 90
25:14-30, 223
28:19, 179

Mark
6:30-44, 160
10:14, 143
16:16, 130

Luke
2:42-51, 144
23:43, 182

John
3:3, 16, 50
3:5, 182
4:23-24, 56
9:1-12, 160
10: 17-18, 125
14:6, 89
17:17, 57

Acts
2:30, 130

1 Corinthians
2:4, 90
2:6-16, 50
12:12-31, 57
12:13, 28, 180

Galatians
3:27, 180

Philippians
1:21, 127
3:14, 127
4:13, 127

II Corinthians
2:14, 127
11:7-11, 57

Ephesians
4:16, 57

Colossians
2:6, 53
2:12, 180

Hebrews
8:10-11, 90

Revelation
1:6, 127
21:1, 221
22:5, 22